BRINGING HENRY HOME

WE ALWAYS DO WHAT IS BEST FOR KIDS, UNLESS…

CURTIS CZARNIAK

outskirts press

Outskirts Press, Inc.
http://www.outskirtspress.com

Paperback ISBN: 978-1-9772-1220-7
Hardback ISBN: 978-1-9772-5630-0

Library of Congress Control Number: 2022916571

Outskirts Press and the "OP" logo are trademarks belonging to Outskirts Press, Inc.

PRINTED IN THE UNITED STATES OF AMERICA

Table of Contents

Prologue

JULIO CAME TO my Algebra class just about every day. He really did not have a choice. He could not play hooky because he was a resident at the juvenile detention center where I taught. Julio was a bright, and angry, young man. Life had not dealt him a good hand.

I convinced my boss that Julio and two other 14/15-year-old students were good candidates for taking the New York State Regents Exam in Algebra, something no student had ever done before at the detention center. Some days the three boys came to class ready to work. Other days I had to use every motivational strategy I knew to keep them focused and on task. And on some days, nothing I could say or do made any difference with one or more of the boys. I would still try to work some magic to get them to focus, but on the days when they came to class angry or frustrated, my efforts earned me nothing more than a dirty look, a stubborn refusal to do anything, and/or a "fuck you Czarniak."

Over several months the boys slowly, ever so slowly, seemed to turn a corner. As June approached, I felt confident that my boys were going to do well on the exam. I checked with my boss on test day to make sure that the surveillance cameras in the testing area were working and recording. If anyone questioned my students' scores, I wanted to be able to prove that they received no assistance. I knew that no one expected much from them.

The boys took the exam without incident, and each passed. Not only did they pass, but they all demonstrated mastery with scores of 79, 81, and 82 (technically the 79 was not mastery, but ever so close – 80 was considered mastery). I was never more proud of a group of students. I felt positively victorious.

A year and a half later a name caught my eye as I was reading the morning newspaper. Julio, then 17, shot a 13-year-old boy in the head with a shotgun. He spent four years in prison, was paroled, and then became an Honor Roll student at a local community college. Three years later he was arrested again for involvement in a drive by shooting that killed an 11-month-old baby girl. He is currently awaiting trial.

In hindsight, my effort to prepare Julio and his two fellow detention center residents for the NYS Regents Exam in Algebra was a hollow exercise. My hope was that if the boys saw a connection between their hard work and a positive outcome on the exam it might somehow change something inside of them, something that might alter the course of their lives. I was deluding myself. I was guilty of the same mistake that the entire educational establishment was making. I was focused on the numbers, the test score results. And absent a larger context that focused on helping the boys to succeed both in school *and in life,* those test score results were meaningless. Meaningless to the boys. Meaningless to their families. Meaningful only to the number crunchers in Albany who could show that three more students had passed the New York State Regents Exam in Algebra.

There are times when I imagine Julio saying to me, "Hey Czarniak, screw the test scores. What about *me*?" In my imaginings Julio's voice is but one of thousands in a chorus of student voices. They would all be right to call me out because preparing students to pass state tests at the end of the year is not our job as educators. It is only <u>part</u> of our job. Our schools do not exist simply to stuff our children's brains with facts about Math, Science, English, and Social Studies. Our schools shape young people's lives and their future. *Our job as educators is to change students' lives for the better – to help them grow and develop (intellectually and otherwise) into successful, productive adults who will make positive contributions to society.*

Introduction

I AM OFTEN asked the following questions.

Why bother reimagining public education? Why reinvent the wheel when our public schools work just fine for most of our students? Why not just tweak our schools a little bit to make them better?

Individuals who question the need to reimagine our public schools are often those who most successfully navigated their way through school. Their feeling is, "I did alright. Our schools are fine. We should just leave them alone."

But our schools do not work "just fine" for all our students. Not now. Probably not ever.

As a teacher, I learned long ago that if you ask middle school or high school students to anonymously fill out a form on how well you are meeting the expectations of your job, you had best be prepared. They will be refreshingly, and brutally, honest in their responses. The students will <u>not</u> tell you what you <u>want</u> to hear about your teaching, but what you <u>need</u> to hear. The truth. The cold, hard, unvarnished truth.

In *Bringing Henry Home* I try to emulate my former students in this regard. I present you with the cold, hard truth about education as I see it after 35+ years working with adolescents and teachers in a variety of settings. Some of what I say about kids, teachers, principals, and the way we conduct public education may make you feel uncomfortable. You may, on occasion, even be offended by what I have to say. But I offer only muted apologies. A gentle, comfortable, controversy-free discussion of how to improve American public education is not going to help our students, our teachers, our schools, or our communities. There can be no sugar coating of facts. We all have some educational soul-searching to do.

Let me start by stating as plainly and simply as I can that our schools were never designed to do what is best for students and teachers. Our schools were not designed *"to change students' lives for the better – to help them grow and develop (intellectually and otherwise) into success-ful, productive adults who will make positive contributions to society."* These may seem like harsh statements, but the reality is that our schools were never thoughtfully designed at all. The way we conduct the busi-ness of educating our children in our schools simply evolved over time, from one room schoolhouses to the large elementary, middle, and high schools we have today.

During this decades long evolution people knew that something was not quite "right" about the way our schools functioned. Most of the unease felt about our schools centered around student academic performance. Too many students struggled to succeed academically. Too many students dropped out. Too many students never graduated or graduated with low skills. Achievement gaps between student de-mographic groups were pronounced, persistent, and deeply troubling. And, in the last few decades, poor test score performance bedeviled teachers, parents, administrators, school boards, politicians, state edu-cation departments, everyone.

Over the years the collective angst over academic achievement levels led to many educational reform efforts. Reformers of all stripes searched for the policies, programs, curricula, or procedural or structur-al changes that would "fix" education in our schools. Reform ideas and efforts came in many shapes and sizes, some local, some state-wide, some national in scope.

But despite all the attempts at school reform, student academic per-formance issues persist across the country to this day. After 50 years of reform, we are still failing our students and their teachers on many lev-els. Efforts to "tweak" our schools to make them better have generally not been successful for several reasons.

First, in our efforts to "reform" education we forgot the kids. We were too often focused solely on the numbers and not enough on the personal issues that students face that dramatically impact those num-bers. In our schools, students must deal with anxiety and depression at record levels (70% of students say that anxiety and depression are a ma-jor problem among their peers[1]). More than one in five students reports being bullied at school. Just under one in five (18.8%) students aged 14-18 reports seriously considering suicide. All these issues are intertwined and linked, and all of them impact student academic performance. And yet, historically, school reforms aimed at improving students' academic achievement largely ignored other student issues. I understand why reformers focus solely on academic outcomes. They are clean and easily measured. Addressing related student issues is messy and difficult.

Second, reforms were often based more on unproven philosophical, political, economic, or educational _beliefs_ than on facts. Education reformers tend to be passionate people with strong beliefs. Believing strongly that their ideas will make a significant difference on student achievement, reformers push hard to get their beliefs put into practice. Unfortunately, you would be hard pressed to find any belief-based educational reform that was first tested in schools and proven to be effective prior to its wide-ranging implementation. Facts and educational truths are often cast aside in the pursuit of belief-based reform.

Third, reforms often failed to produce the desired effects because they were put into place too quickly, without taking time to enlist the support of those individuals (teachers) who were charged with implementing the reforms. I understand this too. Reformers want and need to demonstrate results quickly, before the next election cycle, before an educational consulting group's contract is up for renewal, or before a district superintendent moves on to another district. To maximize speed, reforms were put in place in a top-down manner with little or no buy-in from the teachers on the front line who would be implementing the reforms. Getting the backing and cooperation of front-line workers is time consuming and difficult, but also essential for successful school reform. With school reform, speed kills.

And finally, reform efforts failed in the past because, for all the media hype that touted reforms as "creative" and "new," the way teachers and students conducted the business of teaching and learning ultimately did not change. And predictably, outcomes did not change significantly either.

We cannot afford to muddle along under the mistaken assumption that our schools are doing a good job for most students, that we can "get by" with some tweaking to try to improve test scores. Life is not a math test where you can feel pretty good about a grade of 80 or 85, a solid "B." Behind every educational statistic there are real live children. An 85% national high school graduation rate means that more than half a million of today's ninth graders will likely not graduate from high school. And every one of those ninth graders has a face, and a less than bright future.

When a 2019 survey done by the US Department of Education showed that 78% of students aged 12-18 reported that they were _not_ bullied at school during the school year it sounded great, a high "C" grade for our schools on bullying. But that means that over five million of the 23 million students in grades 7-12 in public school (22%) _were_ bullied at school.[2] And every one of those students has a face, and feelings.

A 2019 US Department of Health and Human Services/CDC survey showed that almost 81% of students aged 14-18 reported _not_ seriously considering suicide during 2019. Outstanding! Another solid "B" grade. But the survey actually reported the results in this manner: 18.8% of all high school students aged 14-18 _did_ report seriously considering suicide.[3] That translates into 2,820,000 students in grades 9-12 in our public schools who thought seriously about killing themselves. 15.7% reported making a suicide plan. And every one of those students has a face, and a family. Maybe your family.

We cling to a traditional educational paradigm, a way of conducting middle school and high school education, that simply does not work well for a large swath of students, academically, socially, or emotionally. I want no part of an educational paradigm that leaves so many children at risk.

If we hold fast to the way we have conducted public education for decades, our schools will continue to fail the thousands of students who drop out every year, or who fail to graduate, or who graduate with skills so low they are unprepared for college or the workplace. We will fail the bullies and those they bully in our schools. We will fail the record number of students who are stressed, lonely, depressed, or suicidal. We will fail the students in our schools who see themselves as losers and, in many ways, we will even fail the students who most adults perceive as the winners. And when our schools fail our students and teachers, they ultimately fail our communities. Our schools may not have been designed to do what is best for students and teachers. But our schools can do, and need to do, so much more to ensure that *all* our students and teachers thrive and succeed, in school and in life.

Before we, as a country, head down yet another dead-end road in public education reform, chasing the latest idea promoted by self-proclaimed "experts," we need to pause, take a deep breath, and consider the possibility that there might be a better way to approach our search for solutions to problems in public education.

In our search for solutions might we be better off to first consider the needs of the human beings most intimately involved in the teaching/learning process – students and teachers?

Might it be better to listen more closely to everyday teachers and less to educational "experts" who are far removed from what happens in classrooms day in and day out?

Might it be better to base any changes on a foundation of generally accepted educational *truths* and hard empirical data, not on strongly held philosophical (or political or economic) *beliefs*?

And might it be better to take a long view toward solving our educational problems, a view not tied to the next election cycle? Would it not be better to first pilot any changes to our educational system in a few school districts to gather data over several years. Then, if the changes produce positive results over time, offer them to states and individual school districts for large-scale, across the board, implementation.

I came to these conclusions after spending thirty-five years as an educator working in the trenches with young men and women and fellow teachers. I worked as a teacher (21 years), principal (7 ½ years), Dean of Students (1 year), community recreation coach (9 years), varsity coach (6 years), religious education instructor (12 years), youth center director (3 years), and tutor. I taught at the middle school, high school, and college level (ever so briefly). I was the principal of middle schools and junior-senior high schools (grades 7-12). I taught in, and led as a principal, both public and private schools. I spent time teaching at a Native

American school and at a juvenile detention center.

All this experience working with students and teachers may not qualify me as an education "expert" in anyone's eyes, and that is fine. You may be disappointed to learn that I am not a professor of education at a prestigious research university, nor a state commissioner of education, or even a consultant with a national educational think tank. But during my thirty-five years working in education I learned a great deal about teenagers and teachers, and what does and does not work for teachers and students in our classrooms and in our schools. Thirty-five years gave me the opportunity to separate out real-world educational truths from fantasy world educational beliefs.

In *Bringing Henry Home* these real-world educational truths form the foundation for reimagining American middle school and high school education. I present you with a new way to conduct middle and high school education, an educational paradigm that works better for students *and* teachers. This new paradigm does not change the primary mission of our schools to educate. Rather, it reimagines _how_ we can carry out that mission to better serve students and their teachers.

This book is divided into three parts. In Part One I lay out the foundation of the paradigm. You will meet Henry and see why it is so difficult for all of us to break away from using traditional educational paradigms that continue to fail our teachers, students, and principals, year after year. We will take a brief look in the rear-view mirror at recent reform efforts that brought us to where we are today. In Part One you will first encounter twenty-four fundamental truths of education that form the foundation of this new paradigm. And you will discover that there is more to the roles of teacher, principal, and student than you ever imagined.

Part Two contains a complete and detailed description of the paradigm. You will see how its philosophical underpinnings are incorporated into the culture of the classroom and how school structures (not the buildings, but rather things like class schedules, grade reporting, teaching assignments, etc.) and operations are modified to support both student and teacher growth and development. And, most importantly, you will see how relationships built on caring, collaboration, and professional interactions drive the paradigm forward.

Part Three describes, in step-by-step fashion, <u>how</u> this new paradigm can be implemented. Obstacles and sources of resistance that will be encountered on the road to implementation are identified, along with strategies that can be used to overcome or circumvent any obstacles or resistance.

As evidenced in the preceding paragraphs, repeatedly referring to a reimagined approach to middle and high school education as "the new paradigm" is awkward. A new educational paradigm needs a name. So, the new paradigm is called, quite simply, the Czarniak Paradigm, or the CP for short.

Some might see this choice of name as unbridled arrogance on my part. Choose to believe that if you wish, but the CP is named in honor of five Czarniak women, Sarah, Laura, Katarina, Catherine, and Jean.

My daughter Sarah bumped me out of my educational comfort zone and changed my life forever. She started me down a road that forced me to look at students and teachers in a different light. Much of what is found in *Bringing Henry Home* I first glimpsed in that light.

My daughters Laura and Katarina had the distinct pleasure, or misfortune, to have me not only as their dad, but also as their high school Biology teacher, AP Biology teacher, Confirmation instructor at church, community recreation coach, and their varsity softball coach. They had to live their entire lives with a man who could not stop teaching, although I am quite sure that over the years I learned as much or more from them as they ever learned from me.

My mother, Catherine (Kay), shaped me early on with her high expectations and provided me with the support and opportunities I needed to meet those high expectations. She instilled in me a faith, both in myself and in a higher power, which would carry me through the tough times, always with an eye toward a greater mission in life. Catherine helped me to see the truth in the expression that our lives are not valued or judged by what we get, but by what we give.

And Jean, my wife, without whom there would be no CP, plain and simple. In 35 plus years working with young adults Jean has been there at every turn, not just giving support, but as a partner and active participant. Together we grew to understand the needs and wants of young adults. Our Labor Days were usually "celebrated" with Jean helping me to set up my classroom before the start of school. For my bizarre ideas for middle school or high school science lessons she contributed her artistic skills, ones I seriously lacked. She co-taught religious education classes with me at church, kept the scorebook for our girls' softball teams, and worked with me on what seemed like a thousand fundraisers and special events. When I moved on to the role of principal, Jean was the "first lady" of my schools, always there when I needed her, and incredibly tolerant of the 70-hour work weeks when I was away from her. Jean was, and to this day still is, always there for me and for the kids.

So, if you cannot get past thinking that the name of this new paradigm is an ego trip for me, I am sorry. I can only quote a former 7th grade student of mine who used to play chess with me during lunch. Upon the capture of one of my pieces he would look me in the eye and say, "Too bad, so sad, get over it."

The name of the new paradigm is the Czarniak Paradigm. Going forward it is, simply, the CP.

It is my greatest hope that you (my readers) share my love and deep concern for the children in our schools. If you care deeply and passionately about children, you will understand – you will "get it" – when you read about the need for a new educational paradigm (the CP). If you _do_ care deeply and passionately about children and teachers, then please join me on this journey. Together we can reimagine and, perhaps a bit audaciously, design, construct, test, and implement an educational paradigm that works well for _all_ students and _all_ teachers. A paradigm that is built upon a foundation of facts and educational truths, not untested theories, ideas, or beliefs. A paradigm that proactively addresses the issues that face both students and teachers.

As you might imagine, designing, constructing, and implementing such a paradigm will be no easy task. There will be many sources of resistance and significant obstacles to overcome, not the least of which will be _ourselves_.

And now, I think it is time for you to meet Henry.

1. _Pew Research Center: Survey of U.S. Teens ages 13-17 conducted Sept. 17 to Nov. 25, 2018, "Most U.S. Teens See Anxiety and Depression as a Major Problem Among Their Peers."_
2. _U.S. Department of Education, National Center for Education Statistics. (2021) Report on Indicators of School Crime and Safety; (2020) Bullying at School and Electronic Bullying._
3. _US Department of Health and Human Services/Centers for Disease Control and Prevention, "Suicide Ideation and Behaviors Among High School Students – Youth Risk Behavior Survey, United States, 2019." MMWR/August 21, 2020/Volume 69/No. 1_

Part I
Laying the Foundation

CHAPTER 1

Bringing Henry Home.

"It was one thing to get yourself out of a stuck place, I real-ized. It was another thing entirely to try and get the place itself unstuck."

<u>Becoming</u>, by Michelle Obama

HENRY WAS A fixture in a small town where I taught for seven years. He was a harmless old man who lived about 4 miles outside of town. Throughout the year Henry spent his time wandering about the village at all hours of the day and night. He would hang out near the local IGA grocery store where people sometimes bought him his favorite foods, liverwurst and potato chips. He would sit in the shade and shelter of the front porch at Sarah's Place, the youth center that my wife and I ran in the center of town. Everyone in town knew Henry. Late in the day, when Henry had enough of hanging around town, he would start walking the long road home or someone would give him a ride. I had done so my-self late one afternoon after finishing up at Sarah's Place.

Henry was "limited," mentally disabled to some degree. He always seemed to wear the same clothes and didn't always smell that good. While I never witnessed it myself, Henry was rumored to be incontinent at times. He stuttered badly, but he could communicate his wants and needs. He was like a child in many ways, simple and uncomplicated.

Late one January night in 1994 my wife and I were wrapping up a "Friday Night Live" event for teens at Sarah's Place. Our daughters, Katie, age nine, and Laura, age eight, who always accompanied us to the center on Friday nights, also prepared to leave. As was the custom, Laura called out her preference to ride with me in my beat up 1979 Chevy pickup truck while Katie chose to ride with mom in our small, new Eagle Summit. It was near midnight when we turned out the lights and started toward the front door. As we exited the door and stepped out onto the front porch, there was Henry.

Henry stood there, shoulders hunched, wearing a thin coat and an old-fashioned brimmed hat with ear flaps (we called them "Elmer Fudd" hats as kids). It was a clear winter night, one of those nights where the temperature drops like a rock after sunset. I am guessing the temperature hovered somewhere between 10 and 20° when Henry looked me in the eye and stammered, "I'm, I'm, I'm, I'm cold, I wanna, wanna go home." I did not respond right away so he pleaded again, "I'm, I'm, I'm cold, I wanna go home."

I looked at Henry, and then at my daughters. I pictured Laura sitting next to Henry on the bench seat in the front of my old pickup (there was no back seat). I do not recall my exact thought process but I am sure it involved dirty clothes, smells, and incontinence. I said, "I'm sorry Henry, but I can't, not now." I got in my truck with Laura, my wife got in the car with Katie, and we drove off, leaving Henry standing out in the cold in front of Sarah's Place.

It was only about 4 miles from Sarah's Place to our home, not in the same direction as where Henry lived. I was no more than a mile out of town before I realized what I had done. When we pulled into our driveway, I told my wife that I was going back to town to bring Henry home. I left Laura with her mom and raced back to Sarah's Place. When I arrived not more than 10 or 12 minutes could have elapsed, but Henry was not there. The village was (and still is) tiny so it took me only a few minutes to ascertain that Henry was gone. I started driving in the direction of Henry's house, hoping to find him walking along the side of the road, but he was nowhere to be found. To this day I have no idea how Henry got home that night, or if he got home at all.

I still regret my actions that night after 25 years. Call it fear, cowardice, selfishness, or being dishonest with myself. I would not help Henry because I did not want him sitting next to my eight-year-old daughter in the front seat of my truck, a beat up, 15-year-old Chevy truck I bought for $1100. I did not give a damn about the truck. The truck had an inexpensive seat cover to hide tears in the original seats. It would have been no problem to wash it if Henry did have an accident. I just did not want Henry sitting next to my daughter.

As I drove home that night after looking for Henry the light bulb in my brain finally turned on. I realized what I should have done, and what you probably already figured out. All I had to do to comfortably get Henry home that night was to send Laura home in the car with her mom and sister. Then I would be in the truck alone and I could bring Henry home. Easy solution. A no-brainer. And yet, I could not figure it out in time to help Henry that night.

Over the years I came to realize and understand more clearly why I did not bring Henry home. I did not bring him home because I was locked into a certain way of doing things (a paradigm) that I just could not see my way out of at that moment. My wife and I always brought two vehicles to Sarah's Place on Friday nights. And every Friday, ritually, Laura rode home with me in the truck and Kate rode home with mom in the car. That was the way we did things. That was our paradigm, and in my mind, that was the way it always had to be.

So, you ask, where is he going with this? What does this have to do with education and helping children to grow and succeed?

In American public education we are also locked into paradigms, ways of doing things that drastically limit our ability to respond to the needs of students and the teachers who serve them. Truthfully, it is probably not accurate to say our schools are <u>locked</u> into paradigms, because saying "locked" makes it sound like there is a key we can use to quickly unlock them and be free to creatively address student and teacher centered problems with innovative and imaginative solutions. It is probably more correct to say that our schools are <u>cemented</u>, rock-solid stuck, in antiquated educational paradigms, and have been for more than 50 years. Breaking out of them will require lots of time and effort on our part to hammer our way out. There is no magic key. There is no simple fix.

In our schools many of our kids are metaphorically "out in the cold" and they want us, the responsible adults in their lives, to "bring them home." What does that mean? It means that our students want and need a whole lot more from us than just teaching them how to score well on standardized tests and getting them to meet arbitrary and shifting criteria for graduation. They want us to motivate and inspire them to succeed. They want us to share our passion and joy for learning with them and spark their creativity. They want us to guide them, advocate for them, and challenge them. They want us to make them feel that they are part of an educational family where they can meaningfully partici-pate in the educational process with their peers. At the same time, they want us to empower them and give them the freedom to make decisions on their own. Most of all, they want us to genuinely care about them – to love them – as individuals, as people, not just as data points on a test score report. They want us to give them hope and a legitimate op-portunity to realize their dreams. They want us to help them grow and develop into successful adults. But the reality is we do not do all these things for all our students. Instead, we leave many of our kids out in the cold because our feet (and brains) are solidly cemented into antiquated and unresponsive educational paradigms. We are stuck.

You can challenge me on this and ask, "Come on, how do you know that kids want and need all those things? Do they ever actually come out and ask for them?" And my reply is, "No. The kids rarely ever verbalize those needs and wants, certainly not in school settings." But those cries are there. If you spend countless hours in the presence of teens, you will "hear" them. But do not just take my word for it. Ask anyone who has spent a lifetime working with adolescents as I have. They will readily agree.

Many teachers in our schools are no less "out in the cold" than their students. Teachers desperately want all their students to succeed, but they are often shackled in their efforts by a lack of resources, by isolation that stifles collaboration and innovation, and by unsupportive teaching environments. They are too often constrained by structures and procedures over which they have little or no control. For our teachers to succeed with their students they need a whole lot more from us than a paycheck and the omnipresent threat of "teacher accountability."

When designing an educational paradigm that works for all our kids, we cannot forget that there is an inextricable link between student and teacher success. When teachers succeed, students succeed. And when students succeed, teachers succeed. If we want all students to be successful then yes, provide them with what they need. But at the same time, we must provide teachers with what *they* need to help their students be successful. When someone says, "We will do whatever it takes to ensure that all kids succeed" it should immediately translate in our minds to "We will do whatever it takes to ensure that all students <u>and teachers</u> succeed."

Paradigm is just a fancy word for how things usually are done. In education there are lots of different kinds of paradigms. Some are structural, like a high school day being broken down into instructional periods, each designated for instruction in a particular subject. Other school paradigms are operational, like the way attendance is taken during class periods or the way we report student progress back to students and parents. Still other paradigms are cultural. Cultural paradigms have to do with our beliefs and attitudes, the reasons <u>why</u> we do what we do.

Recalling that night in January of 1994 it is painful to remember being locked into the structural – operational paradigm of Laura always riding with me in the truck. It hurts to think that I could not free myself to bring Henry home. I feel stupid because the solution was so easy. But that is _not_ what burdens me and hurts the most about that night. What really hurts is the knowledge that I was also locked into a cultural paradigm in which I felt no direct and compelling responsibility for Henry's welfare. Henry saw me as someone who cared, someone who would not hesitate to take him home. But I was not that person on that night. I was willing to abandon him, to let him suffer alone in the frigid, January cold. Maybe there was an underlying thought that he would figure it out on his own, or that someone else would step up to help him. The bottom line is that at that moment in time Henry's safety and comfort were not a priority for me.

I like to believe that I am (and was on that night in 1994) a nice person, a kind and caring person, who will help people whenever I can. But operating within a cultural paradigm where you help someone "whenever you can" is a far cry from a paradigm of taking personal responsibility for the safety and welfare of others. My "whenever I can" paradigm invited a million reasons or excuses why I could not bring Henry home. It was too late and we were all tired. It was out of our way. He was too smelly. I didn't want him sitting next to Laura. He might urinate on the front seat.

What if my cultural paradigm at the time was one of personal responsibility for Henry? If I had operated within the cultural paradigm of personal responsibility, it never would have occurred to me to leave Henry out in the cold. It would not have been an option. I would have responded to his request ("I'm cold, I wanna go home") the same as if it had come from my brother, my wife, or my own child. I would have found a solution and taken Henry home. No hesitation. No excuses.

In the world of education, I think most people (from parents to politicians, superintendents to principals, teachers, counselors, teaching assistants and teaching aides) are also nice people, kind people, who help others, including students, _whenever they can._ But, like my experience with Henry, being stuck in a cultural paradigm of "whenever I can" invites a million reasons (excuses) why students and teachers can be figuratively "left out in the cold." It's time for a reality check.

I was involved in formal education for over 30 years. In that time,

I heard statements like the following ones made hundreds, if not thousands, of times.

"Kids always come first."

"We always do what is best for kids."

"We must make the hard decisions to help all kids succeed."

"We will do whatever it takes to help kids succeed."

If you are involved in education in any way then you have heard (or made) statements like these yourself, many times. After all, there is nothing nobler than to speak out in support of the education of our children. Parents, teachers, principals, and superintendents make statements like these. Board of Education members make these statements. Politicians make these statements. *I* made similar statements. But here is the dark and dirty truth about such statements. There is a distinct difference between _saying_ we will do whatever it takes to help kids succeed and _doing_ whatever it takes to help kids succeed. People's actions often belie what they say. The reality is that most of the time these statements are left unfinished when they are spoken. If they were honestly spoken out loud, they would sound more like this:

"Kids always come first **unless** . . ."

"We always do what is best for kids **unless** . . ."

"We must make the hard decisions to help all kids succeed **unless** . . ."

"We will do whatever it takes to help kids succeed **unless** . . ."

The unfinished parts of the statements above can take many forms depending upon who makes the statement, but all the unfinished segments begin with the word "unless."

"We always do what is best for kids . . . We will do whatever it takes to help kids succeed . . ."

- . . . unless it interferes with my personal agenda.
- . . . unless it costs too much and might impact the school tax levy.
- . . . unless it means we have to do things differently.
- . . . unless the particular kid or group of kids annoys me (or causes problems).

- ... unless it reduces my job security.
- ... unless it hurts my chances of getting re-elected to office.
- ... unless it takes me out of my personal comfort zone.
- ... unless it means that we must backtrack and admit that we were wrong about something.
- ... unless it takes too much time and effort.
- ... unless it doesn't advance my career.
- ... unless it reduces the amount of power and control that I have.
- ... unless it means that my child must sit in class next to one of "those kids" (you can decide who "those kids" are – poor kids, black, Hispanic or Muslim kids, punk rockers, low performing kids, disabled kids).
- ... unless it has the potential to make me or my school look bad.
- ... unless it decreases my (our) ability to make money.
- ... unless it conflicts with my political ideology.
- ... unless it inconveniences me.
- ... unless it upsets or offends someone that I need in my corner, from whom I might need a favor.

There are likely many more finishes to the statement, but you get the idea. We are all too ready to do what is best for kids, *unless* it interferes in some way with what we, as adults, want.

On the other side of the coin, you almost never hear statements like these:

"We always do what is best for teachers."

"We must make the hard decisions to help all teachers succeed."

"We will do whatever it takes to help teachers succeed."

You almost never hear these statements because most people do not equate student success with teacher success. If someone did make such a statement it would have the same qualifiers at the end as statements about student success.

"We will do whatever it takes to provide our teachers with everything they need to help all their students to be successful _unless_ . . ."

The good news is that there are many caring and principled people who truly mean it when they say we should do whatever it takes to help kids and teachers succeed. The best teachers already operate within a cultural educational paradigm of personal responsibility. They feel a deep sense of responsibility for the success of all their students. They take it personally if a student of theirs is failing. They will reach out and try to do "whatever it takes" to help any student or colleague, regardless of who they are, regardless of what others think, regardless of what it may cost (in time and/or money). They are not held back in their efforts by any cultural paradigm.

But we should not kid ourselves. The unspoken "unless . . ." is still found in educational circles. You see the unspoken "unless . . ." in the actions of teachers, parents, principals, superintendents, and board members, with the result that far too many kids and teachers simply do not get what they need to thrive and succeed. We are all guilty at times. It should not happen, but it does. It is our job as educators to make sure that _all_ kids succeed in school and in life. We should all take _full_ responsibility and do "whatever it takes." We should, but we do not always.

Not taking full responsibility for the success of our children is not confined to the halls of our schools. It is a societal issue that reaches into every corner of our country.

Several years ago, I had the pleasure of attending a major fundraising dinner for a local hospital foundation. There were over a thousand guests in attendance at the dinner. It was a magnificent event, a "love fest" of sorts, attended by scores of doctors, attorneys, politicians, and other well-heeled individuals and couples from the community. Anyone who was anybody in the community was there. My wife and I felt more than a little out of place, invited as guests of the local Ronald McDonald House where we both volunteered. There were multiple corporate, business, and individual sponsors and patrons in addition to the thousand people who paid $150 per plate. At one point in the evening it was announced on the big screens that even after all the evening's expenses were paid (food, open bar, entertainment, etc.) the foundation cleared $260,000. The honorees for the evening were the members of the Neonatal Intensive Care Unit (NICU) at the hospital. There were wonderful Powerpoint presentations shown throughout dinner with images of premature babies followed by pictures of the same children when they were older, some even as adults. There were testimonials to the great work the doctors and nurses performed at the NICU to save the lives of the babies in their care. The theme of the evening was "Baby Love." Everyone loves a baby. Babies are like puppies and kittens. They are so lovable. It was a feel-good evening for everyone.

During a speech the head of the NICU, a wonderful doctor who I have the utmost respect for, joked with the parents of one former patient that the "warranty" they received when they left the hospital was now expiring since their child was becoming a teenager. As the doctor said, "You are on your own now." It got a laugh from the crowd because everyone knows how difficult teenagers can be.

As I listened to the joke and took in the entire event, the educator in me could not help but think that there was an underlying unfairness to it all. My mind kept wandering to other places and other people, mostly to schools where I had taught and to students I had known. I thought about all the damaged kids I worked with all week in my job teaching at the juvenile detention center. Throw-away kids to most. Kids nobody cared about. I could not help but wonder if my teenage "throw-away" kids were any less valuable than premature babies or sick toddlers.

Nobody would ever question the importance of caring for a premature baby, or an infant with a heart condition, or a child with cancer. People pull together and support the families of sick young children, and that is how it should be. But when those same children become 12, 14, or 16 years old and are hurting, and their survival is threatened in different but equally dangerous ways (educationally, socially, emotionally, and economically), there is rarely any outcry in the community to "heal" them.

As a society we turn our backs on many of our own children. We do not do whatever it takes to help them. We "leave them out in the cold," like Henry. And why is that?

Is it because babies are cute and loveable, while twelve, fourteen, and sixteen-year-old adolescents are no longer cute little "puppies?" Adolescents can be pimply-faced teens who sometimes sport tattoos and body piercings. They all have "attitudes." They sometimes swear, often lie, and do not always "behave" the way we want them to. They are, after all, adolescents. And they are a whole lot harder to love at times than innocent babies. Is that why we just accept that many of them will fail in school and in life? Maybe.

Or is it because our own children are doing well academically and socially in their schools and already have what they need and want, so why should we be concerned about somebody else's kids? Maybe.

Is it just plain ignorance? Are we so out of touch that we do not even realize that there are thousands upon thousands of kids who are educationally, socially, emotionally, or economically "sick?" Maybe.

Is it because we feel powerless to do anything to help, so why worry about it? Maybe.

Is it that the very thought of all those struggling kids makes us feel uncomfortable, so it is easier to just put them out of our collective mind and passively accept the situation? Maybe.

Or does it have something to do with who the kids are, or where they live, or where they come from, or the color of their skin? Is that why we can casually dismiss their failure? Maybe.

I think the reason we casually accept the struggles and failure of so many adolescents, and all the problems associated with that failure, is some combination of the above plus the following last reason. To me, this last reason is the most dangerous because it provides false justification for individuals, groups, and society, to turn its back on these kids. It is my hope that you never go down this road to explain why you might accept student failure as inevitable, but not the death of sick children. It sounds something like this.

"Well, of course we care more about sick babies and young children. Sick babies don't ask to be sick. They can't help it. But adolescents can choose to fail. They make bad choices that put them into situations that result in them failing. In other words, they make their bed, so now they have to lie in it."

I confess that I get a little angry when I hear this argument. Truthfully, I get a lot angry. My emphatic response is that "_Kids do not choose to suffer and fail_!" I would love for you to just trust me and believe me on this point. If you cannot, then maybe this will help.

I hope you will acknowledge that people prefer feeling good to feeling bad. It is a reasonable assumption. When human beings exert an effort to do something, anything, and are met with success, they feel good, and they like this feeling. It is human nature. You see this in the eyes of a young child taking her first steps, in the face of the high school senior walking across the stage at graduation, and everywhere in between. On the other hand, when human beings exert an effort to do something and they are met with failure, they feel bad. It hurts. It is why people cry when they try to get or achieve something, and they fail. If you have children, think back to all those tears you wiped away when your child failed at something; when your child did not make the team or get a role in the school play, or did not get the grade they wanted on a project they labored over, or when they were shunned by a social group they longed to be a part of. People of any age do not like to fail because it makes them feel bad.

I worked with thousands of children (and adults) over the years and I can guarantee you that none of them ever _set out_ wanting to fail. Even the toughest kids I ever faced in a classroom at the juvenile detention center desperately wanted to succeed and share news of that success with their friends. They wanted to know their grades immediately on quizzes or tests. It was important to them. It is absurd to suggest that a young person's life plan would include consciously choosing to fail. To believe that adolescents want to fail would be to accept as real the following life plan of an adolescent.

"Hey, I have an idea! I think it would be just great to start failing repeatedly in school. After a while I could get emotionally beat-up and start making bad choices that lead to me dropping out of school. Then, if I work at it, I can make more bad choices that will land me in juvenile detention. Or, I could get really depressed and start doing drugs on the street and end up in rehab, or dead. Or maybe I could get pregnant and be a single mom living in a one-room apartment in the projects. Without *any skills I'd have no job and no hope of improving my life situation or the life of my child. Yeah! Now there's a plan!"*

Kids do not <u>want</u> to fail, and teachers do not <u>want</u> their students to fail, any more than Henry wanted to stay on the front porch of Sarah's Place in the freezing cold. Kids want to succeed, academically and in life. Teachers want to succeed, personally and professionally. Yet in every school there are hurting kids who desperately want to experience the good feelings that come with success. And in these same schools there are teachers who feel powerless to help their most needy students succeed because they are not provided with what they need to get the job done. Cultural, structural, and operational constraints within the traditional educational paradigm make it difficult, if not impossible, for teachers to honor their commitment to do what is best for kids. These students and their teachers are all "out in the cold," feeling hopeless, waiting for someone, anyone, to help them, to "bring them home."

Who will do that? Ever the eternal optimist, I believe there are tens of thousands, perhaps even hundreds of thousands, or millions, of individuals willing to embrace a new paradigm in education that takes full responsibility for the success of <u>all</u> kids. These individuals want to do whatever it takes to help kids succeed. They just need to know what it is they can do and how they can do it. I include you in this group. I doubt that you would have read this far if you were not looking for a better way to help kids. I think you and thousands of others will gladly shed antiquated educational structures and procedures and welcome new, more effective educational paradigms that help all students and teachers succeed.

You may wonder why I kept blathering on about this for so long. I blathered on because there are traps that we all must be aware of, and must avoid, if we are to build an educational paradigm in which all students and teachers can thrive and succeed.

This chapter is a cautionary tale. As you read further into this book you will encounter many new ways of doing things in our schools. You may frequently catch yourself saying, "Oh, that sounds good, but it will never happen in my school because . . ." or "That would be great for my students, but it is just never going to happen because . . ."

When you get to one of those inflection points, I want you to stop and ask yourself which way of doing things would be better for kids and teachers. Would it be better for the kids and teachers in your school to do something the way it has always been done, or would it be better for kids and teachers to do it the new way you just read about? And, when you ask yourself this question, clear your head of any clutter that involves economics (How will we pay for it?) or politics (the superintendent will never go for it) or other influences that might bias an honest answer to the question. Beware! There are many biases, both internal and external, that can influence you to not choose what is best for kids and teachers. For a list of biases look back at the "unless" statements from earlier in this chapter.

Because when you say to yourself, "Oh, that sounds good, but it could never happen in my school because . . ." what you are really saying to yourself is "We will always do what is best for kids and teachers **_unless_** . . ."

Major points to take away from *Chapter 1, Bringing Henry Home*

1. There are entrenched cultural, structural, and operational paradigms in education that prevent us from doing "whatever it takes" to help students and their teachers grow, achieve, and succeed. Schools are "stuck."
2. Until we shed the self-centered cultural paradigms of "unless . . ." and "whenever I can" in favor of a paradigm in which we take personal responsibility for the success of every child, we, as a society, will continue to fail to do "whatever it takes" to ensure that <u>all</u> teachers have what they need to help <u>all</u> our children succeed.
3. Kids (and their teachers) don't choose to fail!

CHAPTER 2

A Brief Look in the
Rear-View Mirror

"There is always an easy [well-known] solution to every human problem--neat, plausible, and wrong."
H. L. Mencken, *Prejudices: Second Series, 1920*

HOW DO WE go about the business of educating middle school and high school students today? What are the educational paradigms that our schools are stuck in like cement? You know these paradigms very well. They are the same structural, operational, and cultural paradigms that students and teachers have labored under for decades. You will recognize them because they were in place when you went to school, whether you are a young teacher in your twenties, a forty something parent of a high school student, or an "experienced" seventy something member of the community.

Traditional educational paradigms:

1. One principal runs a school and oversees, supervises, and evaluates a large staff (20 to as many as 60 or more teachers, teaching assistants, and teacher aides) with or without the help of an assistant principal or two, depending upon the size of the school and the wealth of the community.
2. There are discrete, independent teaching/learning units – classrooms – run exclusively and independently by a single teacher working in isolation.
3. Students operate independently within these teaching/learning units, do their assignments independently, take their tests and quizzes independently, and receive grade reports and recognition as individuals.
4. Teachers, principals, superintendents, and board of education members are not required to shoulder complete responsibility for _all_ students' achievement and success (see number 5 below).
5. Teachers, principals, superintendents, and boards of education generally accept a normal distribution of student achievement, i.e., some students will excel, a lot will be average, and some will fail.
6. School staff contact with students' parents is minimal, usually only occurring at report card time and when there is a "problem."
7. School contact and involvement with the larger community (non-parental) is essentially non-existent.

Most of you reading this were probably successful navigating your way through schools operating under these paradigms. You were fortunate. And based upon your successful experience you may be tempted to assume that the existing educational paradigms work fine for everyone. But they do not. Depending on where you lived and what school you attended, anywhere from five to fifty percent of your classmates were _not_ successful getting through school as you did. They did not make it through in large part because the traditional educational paradigms in our schools are flawed.

People in and around education have long recognized that large numbers of students are not successful in school year after year. Even casual observers know that our current educational system does not work well for many kids. That is why educational reformers of all stripes, for as long as I have been an educational professional (and before), have been trying to "fix" education.

To understand exactly where our schools are today there is no need to review all the attempted "fixes" that came down the educational pike between 1958 (when I started first grade) and the year 2000. But we do need to briefly examine what happened to public education in the last twenty years because wide-ranging federal policies and laws dramatically impacted schools in many ways, often not for the better.

In the early 2000's a lot of people were very unhappy with what they saw happening in our schools. People saw low graduation rates in many high schools around the country. They saw schools with such high drop-out rates that they were labeled "drop-out factories." They saw that many students who _did_ graduate from high school were ill-prepared for the workplace or for college level work as evidenced by the number of graduates who had to take remedial courses in college. They saw racial and economic inequities in educational opportunity and achievement. They saw that students in the United States were not scoring the highest on international tests in science and math. And perhaps most troubling of all, people recognized that many of these problems seemed intractable, resistant to previous reform efforts over decades. People were frustrated.

This widespread dissatisfaction and frustration led a diverse group of reformers to seek changes in schools that would produce better student outcomes. Many of these new educational reformers did not come from the ranks of life-long educators as you might expect. Rather, many of the "movers and shakers" who pushed for educational reform were businessmen turned philanthropists, politicians who sensed their constituents' dissatisfaction with education, and young, aggressive educational newcomers looking to shake up the educational establishment. The influence of these new educational reformers helped produce two major pieces of federal legislation that shaped public education in the first two decades of this century.

The first, passed in 2001, was President Bush's signature education law, No Child Left Behind (NCLB). The second, dubbed Race to the Top (RttT), was President Obama's signature educational reform package passed in 2009 as part of the American Recovery and Reinvestment Act. In both legislative initiatives the new reformers touted what they viewed as "common sense" changes to improve education in this country. They believed, in good faith, that these changes would make a significant positive difference in the levels of academic achievement of all students.

NCLB and RttT shared many attributes. Both had worthy and ambitious long-term goals. Both established new, universal high standards for achievement (the Common Core State Standards under RttT). Both identified who would be held responsible for students meeting these standards. Both offered some monetary assistance. Both provided incentives for more school choice options (particularly Charter Schools). Both held a threatening "club" (in the form of negative consequences) over the heads of those being held responsible in the belief that it would motivate them to work harder to solve student achievement problems. And both then leveled consequences (punishments) on those held responsible if they did not get students to achieve at the desired levels.

But Race to the Top and NCLB differed in one important aspect. NCLB ultimately held _school districts_ accountable for student achievement. RttT placed the responsibility for increasing student achievement squarely on the shoulders of _teachers_. The primary focus of RttT became teacher accountability. RttT ushered in the era of teacher evaluation systems based, in large part, on student test score results. Teachers deemed "ineffective" in the new evaluation systems could be fired and replaced by (theoretically) more effective teachers. Financial incentives in the form of salary increases and bonuses could be offered to teachers rated "highly effective."

At first glance, the RttT strategy may sound pretty good to you. After all, everyone knows that having high educational standards is a good thing. And most everyone accepts that the teacher is the most important piece in the education puzzle. And that having skilled and highly effective teachers in every classroom is preferable to ineffective teachers. But remember the quote at the start of this chapter from H.L. Mencken, *"There is always an easy [well-known] solution to every human problem--neat, plausible, and wrong."*

In this instance, Mencken was right on target. RttT and NCLB both seemed like easy, neat, plausible solutions to the problems of high drop-out rates, low graduation rates, and graduates who were ill-prepared for college or the workplace. But they were not.

In the intervening twenty years since NCLB was passed, and the twelve years since RttT was initiated, the educational problems they were both designed to fix remain unsolved. After billions of dollars were spent on developing standards, testing regimens, and teacher evaluation systems, levels of student achievement, graduation rates, and drop-out rates are only marginally improved. Economic and racial achievement gaps remain.

It is important to understand what was wrong with the solutions put forth by RttT and NCLB so that we can avoid making the same mistakes going forward. Let me explain.

First, the solutions offered by both NCLB and RttT were <u>*non-solutions.*</u> Both simply deflected the responsibility for finding solutions onto others. If I am responsible for finding the solution to a serious problem, in this instance getting all students to achieve and succeed, my solution cannot be telling someone else that she must find the solution. In both NCLB and RttT the reformers did just that. They passed the buck, to school districts in NCLB, and to teachers in RttT. Teachers were not told what to do to get all their students to achieve at higher levels and succeed. Teachers were expected to figure it out on their own.

In addition, the strategy of "school choice" was, and still is, also a "non-solution." If students and teachers in our public schools are struggling to achieve and succeed, having them move to another school is simply running away from the problem. And often others are left behind who must still deal with the ongoing issues that led to poor student achievement.

Second, the non-solution solutions of both NCLB and RttT (higher standards, teacher accountability linked to high-stakes testing, and school choice) were based entirely upon belief, not upon scientific data. No large scale (or small scale) field tests were ever performed on these strategies to determine their effectiveness in improving student achievement. Yet, the proponents of these strategies who strongly believed they would work convinced the federal government to design legislation that effectively coerced almost the entire country to get on board with an unproven strategy. We were "all in" with the new reform movement's strategy, like it or not.

Third, and perhaps most telling, in crafting NCLB and RttT reformers made no changes to the basic educational paradigms used in our schools, yet they presumed that student outcomes would change.

Reformers fell victim to their own "magical thinking." They wanted better student outcomes and they thought and truly believed that they would get better outcomes if they held school districts and teachers accountable, even while failing to make any substantive changes to the way schools conducted the business of educating our children. But wanting something to happen, thinking it will occur, and believing strongly that it will materialize, does not magically make it happen.

And finally, the non-solution solution of using teacher accountability to compel teachers to find real solutions produced dangerous and damaging side effects including:

1. *Educational constituencies other than teachers were essentially absolved of any responsibility for their role in finding solutions to our problems in education.* Since teacher accountability was established <u>by law</u> as the way to improve student achievement, the responsibility level of principals, superintendents, and boards of education was reduced to devising, implementing, and administering new teacher evaluation systems. They were able to bury themselves in the task of holding teachers accountable while no longer seeking other solutions to student achievement concerns. Other constituencies, e.g., parents, politicians, community leaders, were similarly absolved of any responsibility.
2. *Once teacher accountability was identified as the primary solution to student achievement issues, it made it less likely that*

*other factors contributing to students' failure to achieve and suc-
ceed would be identified and addressed.* This danger is linked
to the previous one. If the solution to a problem is known, why
would anyone spend any additional time, energy, or money
seeking another solution? It is like the children's riddle: Why
do you always find what you are looking for in the last place
that you look for it? Answer: Because after you find it you stop
looking! Once RttT located the long sought after "solution" to
student achievement concerns – teacher accountability – educators were too busy working through the mechanics of teacher
evaluation/accountability systems to consider the possibility
that other, better solutions existed.

3. *Huge amounts of federal, state, and local resources (money,
    brainpower, human capital, and time) were diverted into cre-
    ating and implementing convoluted and cumbersome teacher
    evaluation systems and standardized student assessments of the
    Common Core.* As everyone who has ever dealt with a fam-
    ily or business budget knows, there are only so many available
    dollars and only so much time to do the things you want to do.
    Spending money and time on one project necessarily means
    that that time and money is not available for a different project.
    To meet the requirements of RttT, federal, state, and local agen-
    cies spent billions of dollars. The dollars and other resources
    that went into the development of new teacher evaluation sys-
    tems and student assessments were dollars and resources not
    available for other initiatives that could have made a more di-
    rect impact on instructional quality and student performance.

4. *A loss of intrinsic motivation for teachers.* The new reformers
    were bound and determined to return to 19th and early 20th
    century "carrot and stick" techniques to try to motivate teach-
    ers. Not only is using threats of punishment not motivating for
    teachers, it actually decreases teachers' own internal motivation
    and suppresses their creativity. You don't have to believe me.
    Read Daniel Pink's book, *"Drive, The Surprising Truth About
    What Motivates Us."* He will help you understand why trying

to motivate professional educators with "carrots and sticks" is a misguided motivational strategy.

5. *A redefinition of what it means to be a good/great teacher from that of an individual who is creative, motivating, and inspiring, to one who is good at drilling students and preparing them to score well on tests.* With teachers' evaluations tied to student test scores, every teacher's job and career became inextricably linked to how well his or her students performed on end of the year tests. When teachers saw other good educators being misidentified as poor teachers and dismissed from their jobs because of low test scores, they woke up to the reality that it was all about student test scores. Teachers then made doubly sure that student test preparation took precedence over everything else in their classrooms. To do anything less would put their livelihood at risk. Sadly, test preparation ability now defined them as teachers.

6. *Many teachers, feeling scapegoated, left the profession, while the number of candidates in teacher training programs declined steadily for a decade.* The teacher shortages around the country today were produced, in part, by the educational community being too eager to point the finger of blame at teachers for student achievement problems.

As it turned out, the strategy of "holding teachers accountable" was not the panacea solution that reformers hoped for and anticipated. If anything, it added additional shortcomings to an already deeply flawed traditional educational paradigm.

But there is hope. That hope rests on our willingness to reclaim our own personal responsibility for the success of our children. It rests upon our willingness to do "whatever it takes" to help all kids succeed in school and in life, regardless of the impact on our own personal agendas. And it rests upon our willingness to get out of our "stuck place," to shoulder responsibility for the design, construction, and adoption of new educational paradigms that will work for all kids. Paradigms built on a foundation of educational truth, not personal belief.

In this chapter I was critical of the educational reforms in NCLB and RttT. Please do not conflate my criticism of these reforms as criticism of the people who advanced them. I respect and admire anyone who genuinely and sincerely works to improve the education of kids. God bless anyone who recognizes that our schools need improvement and who then actually takes some action. I want to pat them on the back, give them "high fives," fist bumps, and whatever other accolades and encouragement that I can. We desperately need people who are willing to give of their time, money, and expertise to make our schools better places for kids to learn and teachers to teach. So, for the record, remember that I respect, admire, and appreciate all educational reformers *even though I may not like everything they propose or do*.

So where does this leave us today?

What No Child Left Behind and Race to the Top did do for us was make clear the nature of the ongoing problem in education. The giant, two-headed, wicked problem that remains unsolved is this. How do we populate *all* our classrooms with outstanding teachers who will get *all* their students to achieve and succeed?

The rest of this book is dedicated to finding a solution to this wicked problem.

Major points to take away from *Chapter 2, A Brief Look in the Rear-View Mirror*

1. The educational paradigms used in schools today are the same as those used more than a half century ago.
2. These antiquated educational paradigms are flawed, as evidenced by the large numbers of students in our schools who fail to achieve and succeed.
3. Federal education reform legislation, *No Child Left Behind* (NCLB) and *Race to the Top* (RttT), did not present real solutions to longstanding educational problems, they merely deflected the responsibility for finding solutions onto schools (NCLB) and then teachers (RttT).

4. NCLB and RttT made no changes to the traditional educational paradigms used in our schools yet still expected significant increases in student achievement and overall student success.

5. RttT's targeting of teachers as both the cause of and answer to educational problems produced damaging and dangerous side effects that ultimately hurt students.

6. The reform efforts of the first two decades of the 21st century clearly identified the giant, two-headed, educational problem that remains unsolved today. How do we populate _all_ our classrooms with outstanding teachers who will get _all_ their students to succeed?

CHAPTER 3

A Foundation of
Educational Truth

A SUCCESSFUL EDUCATIONAL paradigm should meet four basic criteria. First, it should work exceedingly well for *all* teachers and *all* students *everywhere*. Teachers should be successful in helping all students to achieve at high levels and succeed regardless of where the school is located. Why build something new if it is only marginally better for *some* students in *some* locations? Second, people should *want* to use the new paradigm. You cannot drag people kicking and screaming into a new way of doing things. Change makes people feel uncomfortable. The new paradigm must appeal to and meet the needs of teachers, students, parents, and school administrators. If it does this, it will draw people in. No coercion necessary. Third, the paradigm should have "staying power." It should work well for all teachers and all students, year after year after year. And fourth, a successful educational paradigm must be built upon and supported by <u>facts</u>, widely accepted fundamental truths in education, not closely held personal beliefs.

Thirty-six years ago, my wife and I decided to design and build our own house with our own hands (crazy, I know). We had no prior house-building experience, so we took evening classes and read lots of books to gather information about site planning, building design, and home construction. When we started building, we tapped our newfound treasure trove of design and construction truths to inform our decisions about building materials and construction methods. We used 2 x 10 – inch floor joists to span our living spaces and support the anticipated loads. Using 2 x 4 or 2 x 6 – inch joists would have been much cheaper, but our floors would probably have sagged or collapsed. We installed our drain/waste pipes at an exact angle that ensured gravity could do its job carrying waste away from the house. We learned that driving nails into a board too close to the end would split the board, so we blunted the points of the nails or pre-drilled pilot holes. We discovered that we needed strong headers over our windows and doorways so that our windows would not crack from the weight above and our doors would open easily. Armed with these and hundreds of other building and construction truths we built a house that has now served as our home for almost 40 years.

Building a successful educational paradigm is very much like building a house. To construct a new educational paradigm that people will *want* to use, that will work for *all* students and teachers *everywhere*, year after year after year, we must build it on an exceedingly strong foundation of _educational_ truths.

The educational community knows a lot about kids and teachers and the teaching/learning process. We have a knowledge base gleaned from decades of practice using our current educational paradigm and from research aimed at improving this same paradigm. We know a lot that is fundamentally true about education.

In constructing the CP, I first identified 24 fundamental educational truths from this knowledge base that would serve as its foundation. Some of these truths are positive in nature (*Children need a degree of stability to thrive and be successful*), while others are negative (*Teachers work in near total isolation in their classrooms*). In the CP, positive truths are nurtured and reinforced. Negative truths are not disregarded or ignored, but rather confronted head-on and minimized. In a successful educational paradigm, *all* educational truths must be acknowledged and addressed, not just the ones we find convenient to incorporate.

All 24 fundamental truths (FTs going forward) described below are *facts* widely accepted as true by all constituent groups in the education community. These FTs pertain to children, teachers, principals, the teaching/learning process, and schools in general. You may disagree with my categorization of some of the following FTs as "facts." That is understandable since the only proof I offer of the factual basis of any given FT is my personal observations and experience over 60 years as a student, teacher, parent, coach, school administrator, religious education instructor, and youth center director. I encourage you to talk about these FTs with other people who have spent a lifetime, or at least a sizeable chunk of a lifetime, working with young adults and teachers. If you have these conversations, you will come to see that the statements that follow are indeed fundamentally true.

Each FT is explained in detail to aid your understanding of its importance as part of the foundation of the CP. Just as you should not try to build a house without spending many hours learning about masonry, carpentry, plumbing, and residential wiring, so also should we not expect to build a successful educational paradigm without solid knowledge of the educational truths that form its foundation.

I often reference these fundamental educational truths in subsequent chapters when I describe the CP in detail. In Appendix F I provide you with a bullet list of all 24 FTs for quick reference.

Building the CP Foundation – The Fundamental Truths

1) Children need a degree of stability in their lives if they are to grow into successful, high functioning adults.

Many students lack any degree of stability in their lives outside of school. Teachers, guidance counselors, and principals learn over time that many of the children who struggle the most in the classroom are those who come from chaotic and unstable home environments. For many students, school may be the only place where they experience any degree of stability. Experienced teachers know the value of classroom routines and clear and consistent expectations (See FT 2) which provide students with some sense of stability.

Unfortunately, some school environments are anything but stable. In schools where there is high teacher and administrative turnover, where rules, expectations, and points of emphasis are constantly changing or where they are wildly different from classroom to classroom, students have great difficulty adjusting, both academically and behaviorally. Some of the worst teachers I ever observed taught in classrooms with no structure, no routines, and no clear expectations (academic or behavioral). In short, chaos reigned.

A successful school paradigm must have structures, operational procedures, and a culture that provides stability for all students (and staff as well).

2) Students function best and have the greatest chance of succeeding when they know exactly what is expected of them <u>and what they can expect from their teachers, coaches, and the learning environment that surrounds them.</u>
  a. Corollary: Students rarely achieve at levels higher than what <u>*they*</u> expect to achieve and/or what <u>*others*</u> expect them to achieve.

Any discussion of ways to improve education always includes raising expectations of students. Having "high expectations" is one of the sacred cows of school reform, as it should be. No educator worth their salt would dispute the importance of having high expectations of students. But (and you knew a "but" was coming), if those high expectations, indeed any expectations, are not clearly communicated between students and teachers, if they become superfluous window dressing, they are worthless. And if students and teachers are not provided opportunities to meet expectations in a reasonable period of time, the high expectations can prove to be counterproductive.

Perhaps as a parent, or simply as an adult with a long memory of your teen years, you can relate to and/or remember conversations such as the following.

Mom comes home from work to find her teenage son lounging on the couch. There is a perceptible "stink" in the air coming from the kitchen trash.

Mom: Why didn't you take out the trash when you got home from school?

Son: I didn't know I was supposed to take out the trash.

Mom: Can't you smell it? Do I have to tell you everything?

Ouch! Those last two questions from mom are not going to improve the mother/son relationship. Let me answer mom's last question. Yes mom, you need to tell your teenage son everything you expect of him and/or ask him to make a commitment to doing some things on his own, without reminders. At some point in the future, he will hopefully develop into an independent thinker who proactively does things without being told to, but for now you had best communicate clearly to him what you expect.

The brief conversation above is illustrative of "the guessing game" that is played out in our schools a million times a day. Too often principals and teachers have "high expectations" but fail to communicate them clearly to students. The result is that students are left to guess what teachers expect of them, academically, behaviorally, and socially. When students guess wrong, they are punished in some form (poor grades, detention, verbal scolding, etc.) for failing to meet expectations that they knew little if anything about.

You might remember this guessing game. Can you recall taking a class in high school or college where the teacher/professor was throwing tons of information at you? You also had required textbook readings that added to the information overload coming your way. And then it came time for a test/exam, and you had absolutely no idea what you would be tested on. It was never made clear which concepts in the morass of information were most important. You tried to internalize every concept and fact but invariably the teacher would throw in a few questions about some insignificant and obscure facts that were buried in the reading and were never even covered in class. Gotcha!

If you dig deep into why students like some teachers more than others and why students do better in some teachers' classes than others it is often because students do not have to play the "guessing game." Good teachers know about this "guessing game" and do everything in their power to avoid it. At the "macro level" good teachers make their general expectations of students known at the start of the year and then reinforce those expectations repeatedly throughout the year. _Good teachers also inform students of what they (the students) can expect of them as their teachers._ Students never have to guess what is generally expected of them or what they can expect from their teachers. At the "micro level" good teachers clearly communicate to students exactly what they need to do to be successful in each academic unit _on a daily basis_.

Any successful operational paradigm in education must include clearly communicated expectations between students and teachers. When students know what to expect it helps foster the important sense of stability described in the preceding FT.

3) Students inherently understand the concepts and value of team and teamwork and benefit greatly from working in a team setting.
   a. Corollary: Students are drawn to activities that stress team and teamwork.

The benefits of teams and teamwork are many. Students working in a true teamwork setting feel a strong sense of mutual responsibility for the achievement of team goals. They perform at their best so they will not let their teammates down. No one wants to be the one who keeps the team from reaching its goals. Teammates help each other to improve their performance since they are not competing against one another. Members of teams "pick up" and encourage their teammates when they have tough days. And lastly, even though conflicts between students still occur in a team setting, their frequency is much less than what you see in "every man for himself" settings.

We see students realize these benefits in sports, musical performing groups, drama, Model UN, mock trial teams, Science Olympiad teams, etc. As teachers we praise these activities for "teaching kids the value of teamwork." And yet, in the academic classroom we essentially ignore the value of team and teamwork. Even though we know that students are drawn to activities that involve teamwork and that they benefit greatly from them, the overarching paradigm in our classrooms remains that of "every man for himself." We pay lip service to teamwork in the classroom via occasional brief forays into cooperative learning which, unfortunately, are rarely true exercises in teamwork.

Teams and teamwork are a cornerstone of the CP. Much more about them later.

4) Students (and people in general) rise to the top and put forth the greatest effort to succeed when they have a goal, a higher purpose, that is outside and beyond that which they want to achieve for themselves.

This fundamental truth is linked to the previous one regarding teamwork. We see manifestations of this FT on every well coached athletic team where the coach has been able to successfully "sell" his/her players on the team goals. Players buy-in and do "whatever it takes" individually, including sacrificing personal statistics and glory, to help the team reach its goals. This FT is also a foundation building block of successful businesses, military organizations, musical and theatre companies, charitable organizations, even political campaigns.

Similarly, leaders in some of the best schools get the faculty, support staff, students, and even the parents, to buy into a shared vision of what the school can become. Everyone's efforts are channeled toward realizing the school vision – a "higher purpose," a "greater good."

Tied to its emphasis on team and teamwork, the CP uses the concept of a higher purpose to engage and motivate students, teachers, and the school community at large.

5) Students and teachers need to belong, to be a part of a family, to have a strong affiliation with a group.

This is another FT that applies not just to students, but to all people. Decades ago, William Glasser, in his book *Control Theory* (1985), identified "the need to belong – to love, share, and cooperate" as a basic human need. This sense of belonging, being a part of a family, includes many of the same attributes associated with teams, a common history, rituals and traditions, a group identity, effort, and pride. But the sense of family goes beyond what we normally associate with sports teams, although some sports teams can and do meet this need for students. Family implies closeness, a caring concern for others in your group. In a group where a true sense of belonging exists group members care deeply about the well-being of other members of the group.

The sense of belonging to a "family" may be lacking in a young person's home life. To meet this need students sometimes turn to gangs or other unsavory groups. Say what you will about gangs, they certainly offer a strong "family" bond. Gang members protect one another. They "have each other's back." Kids need a sense of belonging, a family, and they are going to find it somewhere. Yes, we prefer that kids join a sports team or the band or some other constructive group to meet their need for a sense of belonging. But such constructive groups may not be an option for many kids. How about our classrooms?

Your first reaction to this question may be, "Come on now, schools can't be all things to all people." You are probably right to some degree. But consider this. Students already assemble at school 180 days a year. From September through June most students spend more waking hours at school than any other place, including home. What a tremendous opportunity we possess to create a culture where students experience a sense of belonging, of family. Many educational and social benefits could be realized for students if our educational paradigm included an emphasis on creating relationships in a family atmosphere. This happens in the CP. In the CP students and teachers find the positive group affiliation they need. In the CP, students and teachers *belong!*

6) Students' <u>perceptions</u> of how much the adults in their lives (parents, teachers, coaches, etc.) love and care about them directly influence their behavior, motivation, decision-making, *and their ability to learn*.

  a. Corollary: A teacher can do everything right in her teaching from a technical standpoint, but if she does not demonstrate through her words and actions that she cares about her students she will <u>*not*</u> be highly successful as a classroom teacher.

When students *perceive* that the adults in their lives do not genuinely love and care about them it can impact how much they love and care about themselves. How much students love and care about themselves, in turn, directly influences their behavior and decision making. Self-destructive behaviors often result when young adults perceive that no one really cares about them. "If nobody cares about me, why should I give a damn about myself?"

Caring is reflected in virtually every aspect of good teaching. In a study at the University of Memphis[1], Susan Thompson concluded that "the personal characteristics of effective teachers . . revolve around an encompassing theme of caring." She goes on to say that teachers who care are fair and consistent in their treatment of students, they are well prepared, have a positive attitude, and they respect students and are respected in return. Caring teachers are forgiving; they do not hold grudges and they start fresh with students every day. Teachers who care have a sense of humor (they can laugh at themselves), they are willing to admit when they make mistakes, and they show compassion for the feelings of their students. It boils down to this. *Students will work harder and achieve more in classrooms where they know the teacher cares about them.*

In our schools today little attention is paid to this fundamental truth and the impact it has on student motivation and, subsequently, student learning and achievement. Not easily quantified, and seemingly impossible to legislate, dictate, or put into formal policy, the impact of caring is usually simply ignored (if it is not "measurable" why bother with it?).

When hiring, human resource departments rarely make any attempt to assess, formally or informally, whether teacher candidates will exhibit behaviors that demonstrate to students that they genuinely care about them.

However, we can (and in a successful educational paradigm we must) create structures within the teaching/learning environment, and a culture that permeates those structures, which afford teachers the opportunity to communicate more readily, via words and actions, that they care about their students as full and complete human beings, not just as test scores. It can be done. Stay tuned.

7) Kids need a nurturing and <u>safe</u> environment to grow, develop, and learn. The environment must be physically, emotionally, and educationally safe.

It is critical that classrooms be not only physically safe places (a given), but also emotionally and educationally safe places where students can take good educational risks. Students need to feel comfortable asking questions or offering opinions without fear of ridicule. Teachers, by virtue of the cultural paradigm that they construct within their classrooms, can ensure such safe learning environments.

In my classroom I never let my students develop the classroom rules, as is often suggested in the ivory towers of university teacher training programs. I had only two rules in my classroom. I confess that I stole the first rule (slightly modified) from a priest who ran a retreat center in Binghamton, New York. Rule #1: "In my class you may put down, mock out, make fun of, or make judgments of, only one person . . ." Before identifying that one person I always enjoyed asking the class, "And who might that one person be?" When I taught middle school classes the students' answer was usually, "You?" I always laughed, wondering in my mind why they thought it was OK to mock out or make fun of the teacher. I then straightened them out, telling them that the one person was themselves. I added that I preferred they not even do that. High school students usually figured out right away who that one person was.

To help my students understand the importance of Rule #1 I told them this story.

Imagine that you are in a classroom and there is a student you know who rarely ever speaks up. The student is shy and very unsure of himself. He doesn't say anything in classroom discussions and won't volunteer to answer the teacher's questions because he is fearful of being wrong. One day the teacher asks a question, and this student feels 100% sure that he knows the answer. He raises his hand and the teacher, thrilled to see this student participate, calls on him. The student gives his answer which, unfortunately, is not correct. As a matter of fact, the answer isn't even close. It's way off. In the back of the room another student, trying to get a few laughs from his friends, says under his breath, "What an idiot!" And the laughs come.

At that point I ended the story and asked my students, "How long will it be before this shy student attempts to answer another question?" Every class I ever taught knew the answer. They always responded, "Probably never." Adolescent students understand better than anyone the pain that comes with ridicule, sarcasm, put downs, and judgments, because virtually all of them have been on the receiving end. They "get it." This behavior is rampant in our society – call it "put-down" humor. Almost every sit-com on TV is one long string of put downs, mock outs, making fun of, and judgments. Great for laughs on TV, but in a classroom, it is incredibly, and sometimes permanently, destructive. From day one my students knew that our classroom was an emotionally and educationally safe place where they could take good academic risks without fear of ridicule. After a couple weeks of regular enforcement of Rule #1 (students policed the room themselves for violations) the <u>absence</u> of put-downs, mocking, and judgments became the norm. That must be true of all classrooms in a successful educational paradigm.

You may wonder about Rule # 2. Rule #2 was "In our classroom, anything that interferes with your learning, or anyone else's learning, is against the rules." Pretty broad and all-encompassing, I know. But it was effective.

8) Students exert tremendous influence on their peers, and in return can be strongly influenced by their peers.

This influence (generally referred to as "peer pressure") can be negative or positive. In most instances the term "peer pressure" conjures up images in people's minds of teenagers leading each other astray into a dark world of drug use or any of a host of other illicit behaviors. Forever and a day the media have bemoaned the impact of (negative) peer pressure on the behavior of adolescents. However, positive peer pressure can be (and is) just as strong an influence on adolescent behavior as negative peer pressure.

Knowledgeable and skilled teachers have mined this resource for years and effectively use it to help students be successful. Unfortunately, this has generally been done in a very "hit and miss" fashion, without the benefit of any school sanctioned formal structures or procedures to encourage it. In the CP formal structures foster positive peer pressure so that over time it becomes an integral part of the school culture.

9) Shaming and public humiliation do _not_ motivate people to work harder, not students, not teachers, not principals.

When a teacher uses public humiliation to try to motivate students all she gets are angry, <u>unmotivated</u>, students. Shaming is also sometimes used by teachers to punish students, or to establish or reestablish superiority in the classroom. Teachers who shame or humiliate their students for _any_ reason get students who hate them for what they are doing, who have no respect for them, and who will do less work, often completely shutting down, as in zero effort. Students who are humiliated in front of their peers will even take an active role in sabotaging anything the teacher is trying to accomplish in class. "Humiliate me? I'll show you!"

I included this as a fundamental truth because so many people cling to the belief that shaming and public humiliation <u>is</u> a way to increase motivation. Not only do some teachers cling to this belief, so also do some people in positions of power in large school districts. Several years ago, the Los Angeles and New York City school districts decided that it would be a good idea to publish teacher rating scores so that teachers with low ratings would be shamed and humiliated and want to work harder. This practice only served to alienate teachers. Its use indicates to me the frustration that comes with the inability of school leaders to address the problems of student achievement and teacher effectiveness in the classroom. District leaders were frustrated and looking for any way to improve student achievement. Unfortunately, they chose a strategy that only made the problems worse.

Shaming and public humiliation as a motivational technique, for students or teachers, should be relegated to the dust bin of educational history. They have no place in the CP.

   10) Students need to experience some level of success to build confidence in their ability to succeed.
       a.   Corollary 1. Without a belief in their ability to succeed, students will not exert a consistent effort.

There are two spirals in education that every good teacher is aware of. One spiral goes up; the other goes down. The spirals work like this. If a student experiences a little academic success in school, he begins to develop some confidence (belief in his ability to succeed). That belief leads to the student exerting a little more effort, which in turn leads to more success. Liking the feeling of success and buoyed by additional confidence, the student then works harder, has even more success, gains more confidence, and so on and so on. The spiral goes up and up.

The downward spiral is simply the reverse of the upward one. A student who is not experiencing any academic success loses confidence in his abilities. Without confidence in his ability to succeed he does not feel like it is even worth putting in the effort (since he feels pre-destined to fail). With little effort being expended the student experiences more failure, which lowers his confidence even further, which leads him to work less, more failure, and so on and so on.

In the CP I do not advocate for lower standards, grade inflation, sugar-coating failure, or cheating for that matter. What I do advocate for is an educational paradigm (remember, "a way of doing things") that recognizes and addresses both the upward _and_ downward spirals described above. We _can_ have high expectations and get students to reach them if we take our time and do things correctly. If we rush and beat kids up with repeated failure, we lose any chance of getting them to reach higher standards. Go slowly. Guarantee some early success. Build confidence. Then, and only then, will you get students to work harder toward the achievement of higher standards.

> 11) For learning to take place, students' <u>brains</u> need to be fully and consistently engaged.
>
>   a. Corollary: Students' brains can only be engaged if students are in the classroom.

On the surface this fundamental truth and its corollary may appear to be (pardon the pun) "no-brainers." However, you would be surprised at the number of people, both inside and outside the education community, who make erroneous assumptions about what does and does not constitute engaging students' brains. For example, people look askance at teacher lecture, assuming that lecture is not a valid strategy for engaging students' brains, that students in a lecture setting are passive observers. However, a teacher can utilize a host of different techniques to ensure that her students' brains are fully engaged throughout a lecture. On the other hand, people assume that if you assign "seatwork" or plop students down in front of a computer that their brains will be engaged. Big mistake.

Any successful educational paradigm must make sure that teachers are trained and highly skilled in designing (or finding) and executing teaching/learning strategies that actively engage students' brains at all times. Teachers also need to be expert at continuously assessing the degree of student engagement as well as in techniques to refocus students.

The corollary to this FT, _students' brains can only be engaged if students are in the classroom_, is all about attendance. Obviously, students need to be in class if they are to learn. Students with high absentee rates are prime candidates for failure.

As a high school softball coach, I did a lot of fundraising for my program, and I was pretty good at it. I can recall many people kiddingly saying to me that I should have gone into sales instead of education. My response was always, "I am in sales. I am a teacher."

Education is a product, and we (teachers and principals) are the salespersons. No one can stuff knowledge and skills into students' heads. Students must put forth an effort to acquire knowledge and skills and no student will do that unless they want to. Students may be required by compulsory education laws to attend school until they are 16, but that does not guarantee that they will "buy" our product, education. An appealing educational experience (see the Timeout after FT #12) will bring students into school and get them to engage their brains while they are there.

> 12) Students sometimes give up, on a variety of different levels and for a variety of different reasons. They may give up on individual tasks, on a specific learning unit, on a subject, on the entire educational enterprise (dropping out mentally and/or physically), or on life as a whole.

In the first chapter I referenced people who believe that students choose to fail. These people point to students giving up as evidence that they are "choosing to fail." What those pointing the accusatory finger at students do not realize is that a student who "gives up" has already failed and may have been failing for a long time. In general, students give up when they feel helpless, that no amount of effort will break them free of a hopeless life situation that includes repeated failure.

Students give up for many reasons. Students give up because they get frustrated when they try hard and cannot "get it." They give up because they get bored. They give up if they see no connection between what they are doing in school and their own personal reality. They give up when they fail repeatedly. Students give up when the learning environment becomes socially painful to them. They give up when they are not supported in their learning at home or at school. They give up when they *feel* or *perceive* that they are not being supported in their learning at home or at school. The student's perception of a lack of support can be just as destructive and damaging as a <u>real</u> lack of support.

No child starts out wanting to fail and wanting to give up. All children start out wanting to learn, anxious to learn, wanting to succeed. If you do not believe this then you have not spent enough time with young children. Something happens over time that leads many students to give up on their education, in part or with the whole. Sadly, most of the events that lead to students "giving up" take place *in school*. Since we, as educational professionals, have control over what takes place in our schools, it makes sense that we should also have control over the types of events that lead students to give up.

After first acknowledging the existing factors and events within schools (structures, operations, and culture) that contribute to students giving up, the CP then puts in place new structures, strategies, and supports to counteract the influence of these factors and events.

Timeout

You are now halfway through my description of the fundamental truths of education upon which the CP is based. You probably noticed that the first twelve FTs primarily focused on students. This is a good time to pause and reflect upon opposites. Imagine two school settings where students experience opposite sides of each FT we have discussed so far.

First, imagine a school that is chaotic, where academic and behavioral expectations of students are not clearly communicated or simply non-existent, where students feel adrift. Imagine a school where students feel no connection to other students, no sense of belonging or family, and are resigned to having to go it alone. Imagine a school where students do not feel physically, emotionally, or educationally safe, a place where they are shamed and humiliated. Imagine a school where students do not feel supported and encouraged by their peers and/or teachers, where they feel like no one cares about them as people. Imagine a school where the struggle for daily survival (academic and otherwise) pushes any thoughts of a greater goal or higher purpose out of students' heads. Imagine a school where students are not engaged in their classes and have little confidence in their ability to succeed simply because they have experienced so little success in the past. And then if you can, imagine how students in such a school setting would feel. Are students in this school setting likely to "buy" the product they are being sold in school? Is the product appealing to students? How likely is it that these students will be successful? Might these students feel like giving up?

Now imagine the opposite. Imagine that a school provides a stable environment where academic and behavioral expectations are clearly and routinely communicated to all students. Imagine that students are made to feel that they belong, that they are part of an educational family, as they work together with fellow students and staff toward the achievement of individual _and team goals._ Imagine that students feel physically, emotionally, and educationally safe in school and know that their teachers and peers genuine care about them as people. Imagine a school in which students are never shamed or humiliated but rather supported and encouraged by their peers, teachers, and community. Imagine that students _want_ to come to this school because they are confident in their abilities having experienced success in classes that fully engage them as students. In such a school, students do not give up. In such a school the entire educational experience appeals to students. As a result, they "buy" our product, education. When a school paradigm acknowledges and appropriately addresses the fundamental truths of education regarding students, we create an educational experience that is so appealing to students that the probability of student success skyrockets.

Time to move on.

13) Teachers are most successful when they use a variety of methods and strategies to fully engage their students. Having a large repertoire of teaching techniques is essential for success.

This is another fundamental truth that is lost on "reformers" looking for a "quick fix" who impose a particular teaching methodology on all teachers because they (the "reformers") are convinced that it is the one and only best way to teach. I am not sure what I feel more, sadness and disappointment, or frustration and anger, when I read about teachers following, word for word, precise scripts for lessons to make sure that they are "properly" teaching to some new standard. The skill and art of teaching lies in a teacher using her knowledge, experience, and creativity to identify effective strategies to teach specific concepts. One day it may mean an "active lecture" where information is presented by the teacher and frequently processed by the students. Another day students may be kinesthetically modeling a science concept. Groups of students may formulate arguments and then debate the pros and cons of an issue in Social Studies. Or students may create visual presentations to teach other small groups of students.

Any successful educational paradigm must give teachers the opportunity to develop an extensive repertoire of teaching strategies and the freedom and support to use that repertoire in the manner they feel best meets their students' needs.

14) Great teaching comes in many different "shapes and sizes." There is no one best way to reach and teach kids in a particular discipline or at a particular level. Unorthodox, or very orthodox; both can be very effective.

When I accepted a position as the principal of a Catholic junior-senior high school I inherited a school in great financial difficulty. I was forced to deal with several staff cuts made by my predecessor just prior to his departure. One of the teachers cut was M.R., a 22-year veteran who was still low man on the seniority totem pole. When word got out, parents came out of the woodwork to complain and threatened to pull their children out of the school if this teacher was not reinstated.

Fortunately, I was able to reinstate M.R. and then observe him during the school year. I told M.R. after one observation that I would never recommend that any new teacher imitate his style and techniques of teaching. Every textbook on teaching pedagogy (instructional methods) would say that M.R. did a lot of things wrong. Current teacher evaluation systems would probably peg M.R. as "below average" or even "unsatisfactory." He lectured from yellowing notes and didn't use cooperative groups, project-based learning, jigsaw, or any other "modern" teaching strategies. All he did was keep every student in his classes totally engaged for the entire period and, as a result, he had some of the best results in the school on end-of-year state Regents exams. His methodology may have appeared antiquated, but he communicated high expectations to the students. His gruff exterior belied one of the most caring teachers on the staff. And he worked hard. Students loved and respected him. No wonder parents were ready to pull their children out of the school if MR left. If ever there was a poster child for a "do not mess with success" teacher it was M.R.

For an educational paradigm to be successful with all students it must guarantee the presence of high quality, engaging instruction in every classroom. This comes from the ongoing support of skilled veteran teachers as well as energetic new teachers, of traditional style teachers and "off the wall" unorthodox teachers. Structures and procedures must be present that insure the growth and development of _all_ teachers into highly effective instructors.

15) In most schools, teachers work in complete and total isolation.

Most people outside the world of schools might find it difficult to believe such a statement. After all, teachers are almost always in a classroom with 20 to 30 students. Teachers work in school buildings with dozens of other teachers. However, teachers may be in the same building as other teachers, but each teacher does her work alone in a classroom with her students, isolated from any other adults.

Consider this. In most states a school year consists of about 180 days. Teachers teach on average six classes a day. Do a little math and you find that an average teacher teaches around 1080 classes per year. On maybe three occasions during the year a principal or other school administrator will come into a class to do a formal observation/evaluation of a teacher. With rare exceptions (such as special education teachers), other teachers are never in class observing, assisting, or co-teaching when a fellow teacher is teaching. Teachers are alone in their classrooms with students the other 1077 periods, or 99.7% of the time.

Put another way, an average teacher is fortunate to have another educational professional in her classroom less than one half of one percent of the time she is working.

This severe isolation is both disheartening and destructive. Indeed, isolation may well be more damaging to teachers than any other aspect of the traditional educational paradigm. It negatively impacts teachers (and ultimately students) in many ways.

- The first casualty of isolation is collaboration. Yes, occasionally two teachers may have a shared planning period during which they can talk about topics related to their teaching. But this is the rare exception, not the rule. Few schools provide structured time for teachers to collaborate with one another, which is sad. Sad because when teachers collaborate, instruction improves on many levels. See FT # 16 for more on collaboration.

- Teaching in isolation diminishes any sense of shared responsibility between teachers for the success of the students. Shared responsibility is a powerful motivator. Imagine that two teachers are responsible for making sure that students learn a particular set of concepts. If these two teachers plan to execute a lesson together to teach these concepts, I guarantee you that both teachers will make doubly sure that their part of the lesson is ready and that it is of the highest quality. No teacher wants to be seen in their colleague's eyes as the one who did not do their part and who let the students down. When you know that someone else is counting on you, you do your best. (See Chapter 18, Accountability in the CP)

- Isolation eats away at a teacher's confidence and hurts teacher motivation. After operating alone for long periods of time (years) teachers may begin to question their abilities. "Am I doing a good job? Should I be doing things differently?" I taught with an outstanding and dedicated chemistry teacher (I knew this because my daughters were in her class, and I taught in the classroom directly across the hall from her) who always questioned her worth and value as a teacher. She did not have the benefit of working closely with another educational professional who could point out the many great things she did to help her students learn and thus validate her worth as a teacher. Good teachers need affirmation that they are doing a great job. When they do not get it, they can begin to question, "Does anyone really care what kind of job I do?"

- On the flip side, isolation can also create a false sense of confidence in a teacher that is not warranted. At one school where I worked as a teacher, we hired a young physics teacher who outwardly displayed tremendous confidence in his abilities as a teacher. Never having been in his classroom I had no reason to doubt his capabilities. The following summer this teacher was hired to teach 8th grade Physical Science at the summer school where I served as summer school principal. When I observed this teacher, I was shocked to see that his perception of his teaching skill did not match with reality. Not only did he lack basic teaching skills, but I also observed him teaching science concepts incorrectly. Isolated in his own classroom no one really knew what was going on.

- Teacher isolation makes it virtually impossible to evaluate teachers accurately and fairly. One simple question should suffice to understand why this is so. Think back to the numbers described above. If you had an employee who worked for you in your business for 180 days in a year and performed 1080 "service calls," would you feel confident evaluating that employee based upon your observation of him doing between one and three service calls? I think not. Any system that attempts to evaluate teachers in the existing educational paradigm (where teachers are isolated for 99+% of the time) will be fatally flawed.

- Teacher isolation makes it difficult to know when a teacher is feeling "beat up," overwhelmed, and/or on the verge of "giving up" on some level (See FT # 19). Teachers are so isolated that when they have a bad day (or days) in the classroom there are often no other adults they can go to in school who know and understand what they are going through. There is no one there to provide support and help a teacher through difficult times. Suggesting that teachers "go see the principal" when they are having difficulties is presupposing a level of trust that may not exist. After all, the principal is the person who will be writing the teacher evaluations after only a few visits. Teachers are loath to show any weakness to the person responsible for evaluating them. Without help and support a teacher's problems might go away. But it is more likely that they will remain and increase in magnitude, and then everyone loses.

- Teacher isolation makes it virtually impossible to build capacity in the teaching ranks, that is, to help teachers grow and develop as professional educators. Without regular, direct contact in the classroom with other educational professionals who can provide feedback and interaction, teachers can become stale in their teaching or develop and cement bad habits. Contrary to what many people believe, practice does _not_ make perfect. Practice makes _permanent._ A distracting verbal mannerism, poor questioning technique, or ineffective strategies for refocusing students that are repeated by a teacher over and over become solidified as part of that teacher's practice. If there is no one to help a teacher identify and correct such deficits, that teacher cannot grow.

Equally harmful is the fact that outstanding teaching methods, effective motivational strategies, superb classroom management skills, innovative techniques for handling classroom logistics, and other "great teaching stuff" that teachers possess _never make it beyond the walls of their classrooms._ Other teachers are rarely if ever in the classroom when great teachers are teaching. Teachers do not get to see and learn from other teachers because they are isolated within the four walls of their classroom.

I have a unique perspective on this because of my personal career path. In my career I moved back and forth between teaching and administration several times. This permitted me to view scores of teachers in action. When I returned to teaching I "borrowed" many of the great teaching ideas, skills, and techniques I had seen and incorporated them into my teaching. I had an opportunity that few teachers ever get. I had the opportunity to not only observe, but also dissect, provide feedback on, and discuss scores of classroom lessons with other teachers. By the time I finished my last year of teaching I had spent 7½ years as a principal. This opportunity to observe and interact with teachers made me a far better teacher at the end of my career than I would have been had I spent my entire career isolated in my own classroom.

In summation, not only does isolation fail to promote the development of highly effective teachers but it can slowly tear down and destroy good teachers over time. It even violates my own classroom Rule #2. Teacher isolation most definitely interferes with student learning. That changes in the CP.

16) Teachers (and other professionals) work best and are more creative, innovative, and effective when they are afforded opportunities for collaboration with others.

Education, like so many other professions, is about problem solving. Virtually everything we do involves finding solutions to problems; how best to design a lesson to engage students; how best to assess student progress; how to modify negative student behaviors; how to create a welcoming and supportive culture in the classroom; how best to motivate students; how best to reach students with different learning styles; how best to refocus students; how to build confidence in a struggling student. The list goes on and on.

When you put two or more heads together you get better, more imaginative, creative, and effective solutions to problems. The simple act of sharing and bouncing around ideas generates new thoughts and ideas which can then be modified on the way to finding the best solutions. This type of collaboration is a centerpiece, a cornerstone, of every professional enterprise (medicine, engineering, architecture, business, the law, etc.). Sadly, it is a cornerstone of every professional enterprise except education. The CP dramatically changes that.

17) Veteran teachers have a wealth of knowledge and experience that usually remains confined within the four walls of their classrooms.

People looking to reform education often presume that older, veteran teachers are "stuck in their ways," less energetic, and less effective than young, energetic, and <u>compliant</u> new teachers. Many reformers equate veteran teachers' doubting and questioning of new reforms with an unwillingness to consider new ideas. Nothing could be further from the truth. Over the years veteran teachers have seen many reform "trains" come down the tracks loaded with the latest fads in education. They have seen most of these fads wither away and disappear, succumbing to a lack of resources (often time) to follow up. It is understandable that veteran teachers view new ideas with a certain degree of skepticism. Skilled and effective veteran teachers are our best resource for evaluating and predicting the efficacy of new reforms. Any attempt to improve student achievement that does not tap into the knowledge, expertise, experience, and institutional memory of veteran teachers is wasting a valuable resource.

18) Teacher candidates fresh out of undergraduate training are ill-prepared for what they will face as teachers in traditional school settings.
   a. Corollary: Most students exiting Masters Degree programs in education are _still_ inadequately prepared for the challenges of the classroom.

This statement is not intended as a criticism of teacher preparation programs, but rather as a simple statement of fact. The art and craft of teaching is not something that can be mastered within a college classroom or through brief stints as a student teacher. Teacher training programs can give prospective teachers a good foundation in the knowledge and basic skills needed for teaching. However, applying that knowledge and those skills effectively in the classroom takes years to master. In the process, classroom teachers acquire other skills that are never taught in teacher training programs. Unfortunately, some of the other FTs of education (teacher isolation and limited collaboration with skilled veteran teachers) hinder the acquisition of these skills and overall teacher development. Is there more that colleges and universities can do to develop highly skilled teachers more rapidly? I believe so. But, just as many elementary, middle, and high schools are locked into ineffective paradigms, so also are many colleges and universities locked into teacher training paradigms that are less than ideal.

As a case in point, there are literally hundreds of institutions of higher education that grant Masters Degrees in education. Among these institutions you would be hard pressed to find more than a handful that include any significant amount of clinical experience in the classroom as a part of their Masters programs. In most Masters degree programs in Education you complete 30 hours of graduate level coursework, write a thesis and/or take comprehensive exams at the end, and you can walk away with a Masters Degree in Education. Holding a Masters Degree in Education cannot be equated with being a master of the craft of teaching. It should be, but it is not. That needs to change (See Chapter 22, The University Connection).

A successful educational paradigm must first recognize the limits of what colleges and universities currently can do to prepare teaching candidates and then put in place structures, procedures, and programs to build capacity in the teaching workforce over time. Welcome the CP!

19) Some teachers "give up" on a variety of levels for a variety of reasons.

Teachers may give up on individual students, on a whole class, on a particular group of students in a class, on a unit, on an entire grade, for a day, a week, a month, for a year, or in total (just going through the motions). They may give up because they are frustrated, having worked hard for days, weeks, and months, doing their best, and having their kids still not "get it." They may be frustrated that their kids do not seem to care and are not even trying so why should they care as teachers. Teachers may be frustrated with the apparent lack of parental support or involvement in their students' education. Teachers may feel over-whelmed with the workload. They may lack the educational resources needed to do a quality job. Teachers may be frustrated with having to deal with so much student misbehavior that "they can't teach." They may feel like they are not making a difference in kids' lives, and that is what they really want most. Teachers may feel that their principal is not supportive, by choice or by default (see Chapter 5). More recently, teachers may be frustrated with the time they must spend recording data, doing test preparation, and jumping through the "hoops" of new teacher evaluation systems based on student test results.

Make no mistake about it, teachers giving up is wrong at any level. It is bad for students and bad for the profession. It is imperative that this FT be addressed. Currently, the formula for addressing this FT is simple. If test scores indicate a teacher is not "effective," fire them and replace them with someone who will hopefully prove to be better. No attempt is made to ad-dress the root causes that lead teachers to give up at some level.

The CP confronts this FT head-on. The CP provides a highly sup-portive, collaborative, and professional environment for teachers that precludes them from ever giving up. Teachers grow and develop into highly effective teachers in this environment. If they do not, their posi-tions are not protected. As you will see, compared to current efforts to hold teachers accountable, in the CP there is a higher level of _profes-sionally appropriate_ teacher accountability that uses far greater amounts and kinds of data gleaned from significantly more direct contact with teachers in their classrooms. (See Chapter 18, Accountability in the CP)

20) Tenure is both a blessing and a curse, essential for the protec-tion of good teachers (and principals) and an artifact that can be used to shield poor teachers (and principals).

When I first started constructing the CP, I asked myself the following question at each juncture. "Is this aspect/part of the CP truly what is best for kids or is it designed more to advance the agenda of some group of adults?" Regarding teacher tenure this litmus test required that I answer two questions. 1) Is lifetime tenure for teachers what is best for kids?

And 2) Would eliminating tenure be what is best for kids? Based upon my experience, the answer to both questions is an emphatic "No!"

There is no question that lifetime tenure is sometimes abused by teachers. A teacher who shuts down completely for some of the reasons described in FT # 19 may decide to simply "ride it out" to retirement under the protection of tenure. Ineffective teachers may use lifetime tenure as a shield against disciplinary action. As a teacher and principal, I personally witnessed a few teachers abusing tenure. Seeing a colleague take advantage of tenure was painful to watch because I knew it hurt kids, plus it reflected badly on the rest of the teaching community. You may have had similar experiences or heard horror stories about ineffective teachers that school districts could not get rid of because of the difficult process and expense needed to remove a tenured teacher.

But what you probably have not heard about or experienced (unless you are an educator yourself) are the abuses that occur on the other side of the tenure issue. And I believe they happen with equal or greater frequency. Good teachers without tenure are dismissed for reasons that have absolutely nothing to do with the quality of their teaching, and everything to do with political issues and administrative power and control.

In my first teaching assignment in a public school, I shared a classroom with another science teacher. Prior to the start of the school year this teacher warned me, "Whatever you do, never teach sex education in your science class (it was not taught in that conservative rural community) and _never question the superintendent in public or you will not get tenure_." I had just spent four years teaching in a K-8 Catholic school where everyone worked together (teachers, administration, parents), and I confess that I was rather naïve when it came to the adversarial relationship that exists between teachers and school administration in many public schools. I did not fully believe what my teaching colleague said, but I kept my mouth shut regardless, just to be safe. My wife and I had a new baby in the house, and I could ill afford to lose my job.

Over the next two years I watched another new teacher, who perhaps was not lucky enough to be forewarned, speak out against some of the actions and policies of the superintendent that negatively impacted kids. It turned out that my classroom-mate knew what she was talking about when she warned me. The superintendent made the outspoken teacher's life miserable, to the point of what I would call harassment or abuse, and then summarily dismissed her after two years. This was not an ineffective teacher, or even an average teacher. This was an outstanding choral music teacher who went on to have a distinguished 35-year teaching career in other public schools. Her only "crime" was that she spoke up for what was right, for what was best for kids.

You will better understand why tenure cannot be eliminated after reading Chapter 5, on Principals and School Administration. To eliminate tenure for teachers would hurt kids. Current educational reforms espouse the need to populate our classrooms with highly effective teachers. We can all agree on that. We should also all agree that any policy or procedure that results in the removal of _any_ highly effective teachers from classrooms is bad for kids. That is exactly what eliminating tenure protection can do.

The form of teacher tenure proposed in the CP will likely not make teachers' unions _or_ school administrators and boards of education completely happy. That is because it is not designed to make either group completely happy. It is designed to be what is best for kids.

21) Teachers generally know little about their students' lives other than what they learn about them in the classroom.

This is a "sad but true" FT. When you teach anywhere from 100 to 150 students in a day, and you have only 40 to 45 minutes to spend with each class, it is impossible to get to know very much about your individual students, even if you want to. It is not a criticism of teachers. It is just the way things are in our existing paradigm. As teachers we accept it because there is little we can do within the current school structure to get to know our students better. But would it be helpful if teachers did know more about their students' lives outside of school? I think so. Without question.

Twenty-five years-ago I was teaching in a junior-senior high school (grades 7-12) in a small rural community. After teaching there for six years I made the decision to drop to part-time status to run a local youth center. In my role as a youth center director, I became more familiar with the lives of many of my students. One young man, Bill (not his real name), was a regular at the center. He was one of our most dedicated student workers. Any job he was asked to do he did well. He painted. He cleaned. He worked in the kitchen.

Over time I learned that Bill's home life was not so great. It was chaotic at best. The idea of him finding a quiet time and place at home to do his homework was absurd. As a result, his homework often did not get done. Back in the faculty room at school Bill was raked over the coals by some of my colleagues. I remember one teacher who had strong views about Bill. "That Bill is such a lazy asshole. He never does a lick of homework and then he just makes up lame excuses." My knowledge of Bill's situation allowed me to make adjustments so that he could be more successful in school. My colleague did not have the benefit of knowing what I knew.

Expecting a teacher to be successful with students without knowing something of their "history" is like expecting doctors to treat their patients without knowing their medical history. If a doctor, lacking knowledge of a patient's history, prescribes a drug to which a patient is allergic, that patient may become very ill or die. Similarly, a teacher, lacking knowledge of a student's history, can say or do something to a student that will trigger emotional pain, anger, or resentment and result in that student completely shutting down – becoming academically "dead."

We become more effective as educators when we know more about our students' lives. This FT must be addressed in a new educational paradigm if we are to reach all our students and help them to succeed.

22) Principals and assistant principals cannot adequately supervise and evaluate an entire faculty of teachers *for professional growth and development*, nor can they effectively motivate an entire faculty on their own.

This is one of the most significant fundamental truths that is addressed by the CP.

It is incredibly unfair to expect principals to oversee, evaluate, grow, and develop a staff of 40, 50, or more teachers while also doing everything else they are required to do in their job descriptions (See Chapter 5). This expectation is unfair to principals. It is unfair to the teachers in their charge. And it ultimately hurts kids. Unfortunately, this expectation is one of the most rigidly cemented stones in the traditional school paradigm wall. It is a boulder of a problem.

I understand that proclaiming this statement as a fundamental truth of education might initially offend dedicated, hard-working individuals in school administration. I apologize. It is certainly not my intent to "throw stones." If you are a principal, please understand that I walked in your shoes for many years. When you read Chapter 5, Principals and School Administration, you will better understand why I believe we must confront this and other unsettling realities and identify solutions to long-standing problems in education, even if the solutions initially take some of us out of our comfort zones. That includes finding a better system for supervising, evaluating, and growing our teachers that does not overwhelm our principals. In the long run, the CP will help principals be better school leaders, and teachers and students will reap the benefits.

23) Any reform or change in education, regardless of the degree of merit it contains, will meet a great deal of resistance, and will ultimately fail or fade away, if it is forced upon teachers and principals.
   a. Corollary: Even with teacher and principal "buy-in," reforms fade away if both resources (including time) and support are not provided and then maintained going forward.

Another way to say this: "Do not shove reforms down teachers' throats and then expect them to implement the reforms without adequate resources and ongoing support." This fundamental truth (and its corollary) pretty much explains why for decades many school reforms have sprouted, briefly bloomed, and then faded away. The reforms were either overly "top-down" or resources and support for maintaining the reforms were few and short-lived, or non-existent from the start. Both are mistakes that cannot be repeated if we want to effect long lasting positive changes in our schools and their surrounding communities.

24) Teachers make the difference.

People everywhere can point to a teacher or teachers who impacted their lives in some way, either positively or negatively. I vividly recall my high school physics teacher who was awful, and I mean just terrible. Knowing what I now know about teaching after a career in education I cannot recall anything that he did right. His ineptitude was reflected in my grades in the course (low C's and D's). What he did accomplish was turning me off to physics so strongly that I avoided taking any college courses in physics until my junior year. I needed two physics courses for my science major, and I absolutely dreaded taking them. I was convinced that I hated physics. Shockingly (to me), I took the courses and loved them both. I had great instructors, looked forward to every class, and ended up with A's in both (4.0's!). The teachers made the difference.

This was the first time in my life that I can recall recognizing the impact that teachers make in the classroom. Sure, there were some teachers I liked more than others in middle school and high school. And yes, the same was true of professors in college. But now I can look back and identify specific teachers who truly shaped who I am today. I would not be a Biology and Earth Science nut were it not for a couple of great science teachers. I am guessing that you can also point to teachers who made a difference in your life.

This is the one fundamental educational truth about which I expect to get little if any blowback. The entire teacher accountability reform movement in education is built upon this FT. Teachers agree, students agree, parents agree, principals agree, school boards agree, even politicians (for the most part) agree. Everyone knows that it is better to have a good or great teacher than an average or poor teacher. Teachers can make or break students, everyone knows that. For good or for bad, teachers make the difference.

With that said, and although everyone reading these words spent a large portion of their waking lives between ages 5 and 18 with teachers, you probably know less about teachers and the world of teaching than you think you do. Even many teachers do not realize everything that they do in their classrooms every day. Please do not be offended. Just turn the page and step into the world of teachers and teaching – and be surprised.

Major points to take away from *Chapter 3, A Foundation of Educational Truth*

1. Successful educational reform must be built on a strong foundation composed of the fundamental truths in education.
2. All fundamental educational truths, even those we may not want to talk about, need to be acknowledged and addressed in a new educational paradigm.

1. *Highly Qualified for Successful Teaching: Characteristics Every Teacher Should Possess,* Susan Thompson, John G. Greer, Bonnie B. Greer, The University of Memphis www.richlandone. org/cms/lib/SC02209149/Centricity/Domain/158/12_ characteristics_article.pdf

CHAPTER 4

On Teachers and Teaching

"I've come to a frightening conclusion that I am the decisive element in the classroom. It's my personal approach that creates the climate. It's my daily mood that makes the weather. As a teacher, I possess a tremendous power to make a child's life miserable or joyous. I can be a tool of torture or an instrument of inspiration. I can humiliate or heal. In all situations, it is my response that decides whether a crisis will be escalated or de-escalated, and a child humanized or dehumanized."

Haim Ginott

WE HAVE A serious drop-out problem in education in this country, and it is likely not the drop-out problem you are thinking of. Depending upon which source you deem most accurate, somewhere between thirty and fifty percent of new teachers leave the profession in the first five years. Teachers are dropping out of the profession at an alarming rate, resulting in shortages of qualified teachers in districts across the country. This is a serious problem in education. And it is a problem that is only getting worse over time.

A March 2021 nationally representative survey conducted by the Education Week Research Center found that 54% of *all* teachers were "very likely" or "somewhat likely" to leave teaching in the next two years. On the surface this does not seem to make any sense. After all, why would young new teachers throw away a career after spending or going into debt for $60,000 (a lot more at private colleges and universities) for tuition, fees, books, and room and board for four years of college to become a teacher? Why would teachers give up a job where they work 8 to 3 and get summers off and week-long vacations at Christmas and in the spring (and even in the winter in some northern locales – we call it "winter break")? Why would teachers give up a "cushy" job where they get to hand out assignments and let their students do all the work?

If you find it hard to believe that *anyone* would give up such a job, then perhaps you do not know as much about teachers and the teaching profession as you thought you did. Do not feel bad. You are not alone. The overwhelming majority of the population believes they know and fully understand the teaching profession. After all, high school graduates spend seven hours a day, one hundred and eighty days a year, for 13 years, in constant contact with teachers. Surely, they must know all there is to know about teachers and teaching. Right? Right? Umm, no. I hate to burst the collective bubble of high school graduates everywhere, but unless you spend several years in the classroom *as a teacher*, you have no idea what teachers and teaching are all about.

Imagine that you had a job that required an inordinate amount of air travel, perhaps flying 180 days of the year. Would you presume to know all there is to know about being a pilot and flying a plane? I do not think so. Yet the jobs of airline pilot and teacher have more similarities than you might think. Both individuals are charged with taking groups of people from point A to point B. Airline pilots are charged with taking groups of people safely from one geographic location to another.

Teachers are charged with shepherding groups of students safely down a long and sometimes perilous educational road. Both jobs appear quite simple on the surface. Passengers get on the plane, the pilot starts the engines, gets the plane in position for take-off, gives it "the gas," and off they go. Teaching appears just as simple. Students come into class, the teacher points the students in some direction (dispenses new information, gives them some assignment, or administers a test), and then corrects the assignments or tests and gives the students a grade. If you find yourself thinking, "Oh no, a pilot's job is a lot more complicated than that," and "Yeah, that sounds about right for teaching," then you are one of the millions of people who believe they know and understand teachers and teaching having only experienced it from a student's perspective. Believe me, there is a lot more.

A Day in the Life:

Eight years into my teaching career I was working in a school district where the teachers' union and administration were at odds. I was asked by my union leadership to do a presentation for the Board of Education to help them understand the role of teachers. Since most of the members of the board were businesspeople, I decided to use a business analogy to help them understand teachers and the teaching process. I will do my best to recreate it.

Businessmen and women are occasionally asked to do instructional presentations. They may have to present to a Board of Directors, to department heads, or to the workforce in a particular department. Regardless of the audience, the businesspeople I know always speak of the anxiety associated with the preparation for and anticipation of doing such a presentation. They speak of (and complain about) the time they spend putting together Powerpoint presentations and talking points.

Now imagine that you, as a businessperson, are asked to do not one, but five or six presentations _in one day,_ all to different groups of people, with two or three of the presentations being different from one another. You are expected to produce presentations that are interesting to the attendees and that will keep them focused and motivated. There is also an expectation that attendees will actively participate during the presentations so you must plan activities accordingly. You need to be aware of the attendees' learning styles (auditory, visual, kinesthetic, etc.) and make adjustments if someone is not "getting it." You are expected to constantly monitor your audiences to make sure they are focused and have strategies at the ready to refocus anyone whose attention wanders. Not only will you have to present the information, but you will also have to plan some way to assess how well the attendees are internalizing (learning) that which you are presenting. _And then the next day, you need to be prepared to do five or six more presentations, all new, and all with the same general expectations as the previous day, followed by five or six more presentations the day after that, and so on and so on (25 to 30 presentations each week for months on end)._ You will be afforded precious little time during the day to work on these presentations, or on the tools you will use to assess the attendees' knowledge, or to evaluate the attendees' assessments and provide written feedback when they are completed. If the participants fall behind in meeting the goals of your presentations, you are expected to remediate them and bring them up to speed. This is the case even if the participants miss presentations due to illness. Oh, and your personal evaluation will be based in large part upon how well the attendees perform on their assessments.

If I were a manager in a business and I put these kinds of expectations on an employee I would either be laughed at or told I was out of my mind, or both. But this is exactly what teachers do with their students, day in and day out, 180 days a year. And this is just the tip of the iceberg when it comes to understanding teachers and teaching.

In that same district the following year the teachers' union put on a program in which members of the community were invited to come in and teach for a day. The regular classroom teachers met with their guest teachers in advance, did the lion's share of the planning for them, and remained in the classroom as the guests taught. After just one full day of teaching the guest teachers were dragging. They could not believe how mentally and physically exhausted they were. What they did not understand about teaching going in was that teachers receive, interpret, and respond to thousands of visual and auditory stimuli during the day and make literally thousands of small decisions to facilitate learning in their classrooms.

"What analogy or example should I use when a student does not understand the concept? Which students are not focused? How can I best refocus them without embarrassing them or losing their respect? What questions should I ask to assess learning? How should I best respond to student questions? Who needs more individual attention? Where should I stand in the classroom? How often do I need to move near a particular student or student group? How can I best re-explain a concept? Are the students getting bored? How and when do I "shift gears" to keep my students energized and engaged? How and when should I praise a student for their effort? How do I respond to a student's incorrect answer? How can I lead that student to an understanding of the concept with additional questions? Should I reteach a concept to the entire class or move on to a new topic? Do I let the student who just came from lunch go to the lavatory at the beginning of class? Do I respond or not respond to a minor class disruption, or do I just give them "the look?" If I choose to respond what will be my best strategy to elicit the behavior I desire? Is that student copying another student's work? Should I move closer and raise their level of concern?" _All day long teachers monitor and adjust, making thousands of decisions along the way. It is exhausting._

Remember that "8 to 3 workday?" Most middle school and high school teachers teach six periods a day, are assigned a duty or two (study hall, lunch duty, hall monitor, bus duty, etc.), get a period to eat lunch and a "planning period" of 40 to 45 minutes. The most fortunate teachers might get a second planning period each day or every other day. So, when do teachers plan and put together all those presentations? When do they create and/or assemble the materials for a lesson? When do they make photocopies of handouts? When do they grade homework, quizzes, tests, labs, and projects? When do they meet with students who need extra help? When do they make those calls home to students' parents about academic or behavioral concerns? When do they record their grades and fill out and submit the myriad forms required by administration? For that matter, when do they go to the bathroom? When? Teachers do all these things during their 40 to 45-minute planning period of course, or on their lunch break. And if they cannot get everything done in 40 to 45 minutes (and that is a physical impossibility) they better plan on spending a _lot_ of time at school after the students leave or before they arrive, or plan to take a _lot_ of work home.

What I just described are "average" days in an "average" school with "average" students; days when everything goes reasonably well. But no class of students and no day is ever "average" in teaching. All students have special "needs," not just special education students. Teachers had best identify and address those needs if they want to be successful. Some students are English Language Learners, and some have disabilities. Other students have behavioral issues and may disrupt class, throwing off a teacher's entire plan of scheduled activities.

In "high needs schools" with large percentages of "high needs students" the challenges that teachers face are greatly magnified. An "average class" in an "average school" might have a half-dozen "challenged" students that need special attention in a class of 24 to 30 students. In a "high needs school" the number of "challenged students" in a class may increase to 20 or more, with a corresponding quantum leap in workload for the teacher.

And then there are the bad days. The presentations do not flow as planned; a piece of instructional technology does not work and the teacher has to scrap her entire plan and "wing it;" a student comes to class angry and behavior issues boil over requiring administrative intervention; another teacher holds on to his students after class and they arrive 10 minutes late, throwing the lesson plan off schedule; there is an unplanned period-long assembly that the principal neglected to inform the teaching staff about so now a teacher's two 10th grade English classes are not at the same point in the curriculum; a parent calls and berates a teacher for not doing more to help her child.

Remember that through all this, the multiple presentations to plan, prepare, and execute, the thousands of stimuli to receive, interpret, and respond to, the myriad student needs to address, the unexpected challenges, and all the additional tasks a teacher has to squeeze into precious little time; through all this the teacher is totally and completely alone, isolated from her peers within the four walls of her classroom (recall the isolation of teachers described in FT#15). Are those teaching jobs still looking "cushy" to you?

Growing Teachers

The teacher is the pivotal factor in the classroom that determines whether students succeed or fail. It is a fundamental truth that," Teachers make the difference" (FT #24). But teachers can only make a positive difference if they first develop their teaching skill sets to the point where they are highly effective in the classroom. Also recall FT #18, that new teachers fresh out of college still have much to learn if they wish to be successful teachers. These fundamental truths beg the question(s); When, how, where, and from whom will teachers pick up the additional skills they need to survive in the classroom and make a positive difference in the lives of students?

One would assume that when a recent graduate takes her first teaching job her employer would take responsibility for continuing her professional growth and development. Not so. There are a lot of things we presume will happen in the world of education that just do not happen. It's time to learn about some dark and dirty secrets about the professional growth and development of teachers in our schools.

Dark and Dirty Secret #1: Most principals contribute very little to the growth and development of their teachers. This is true because:

- Principals do not have the time to work with and grow their teachers' skills, or
- The current educational paradigm in which principals work does not prioritize building capacity in the teaching ranks (the emphasis of many of today's teacher evaluation systems is rating teachers, not growing them), or
- Principals may not have the expertise to work with and grow their teachers' skills, or
- All the above may be true.

This may seem like a harsh statement to make, but it is true. Principals I worked for had precious little time to work with teachers to improve their skills. Even from the best principals who have the desire and skills to help their teachers grow, the most a teacher can expect are a few discussions with the principal in post-conferences following observations of a few isolated lessons. Hopefully in these conferences, and in other passing interactions, a teacher can pick up a few valuable tips that will help her grow as a teacher.

Unfortunately, some principals and superintendents are ill-equipped to observe and analyze lessons and provide meaningful feedback to teachers that will help them grow as professionals. Time crunched school administrators frequently rely upon "check-list" rubrics to identify areas where the teacher is "proficient" and other areas "in need of improvement." They then dispense pro forma advice that often has little value to the teacher. Much more on why principals contribute little to the growth of their teachers in Chapter 5, "Principals".

Dark and Dirty Secret #2: New teachers (and all other teachers) rarely derive any professional benefit from the three or four inservice/conference days allotted each year in the school calendar for staff development.

For starters, staff development days are often hijacked for other purposes. Required trainings ("Right to Know" regarding toxic substances in the workplace, mandatory child abuse reporting updates, etc.) and informational meetings on new mandates from state education departments are just a few of the many things that can cut into the few days available for staff development.

If a day of professional development is scheduled, teachers are often less than fully enthusiastic about it. The prospect of having something else new thrown at them that they are expected to do or attempt to do in the middle of a school year is not appealing. This response is understandable considering the intense and demanding nature of the job. While teachers cherish the break from their everyday teaching duties, they often enter these days feeling overwhelmed and would much rather use the time to catch up on backlogged grading and other tasks that need to be done. You may be thinking, "Well, then teachers should not complain about a lack of staff development if they do not embrace the few opportunities that they do get."

The teachers' mindset regarding staff development days is not shaped solely by their workload and the time constraints they feel, but also by knowing how these days play out historically. Enter "the drive by shooting." Veteran teachers know about "drive by shootings." This now antiquated and probably inappropriate expression has nothing to do with the horrific violence visited on schools over the last several years. The expression refers to the way professional development is carried out in schools year in and year out. It goes something like this.

A principal, superintendent, or a committee of teachers and administrators decides upon a topic for one of the three or four in-service/conference days allotted for teachers' professional development in a year. The topic and accompanying skills are taught to the teachers by an individual or group of individuals brought in for the day who are deemed as "experts." These experts may or may not have seen the inside of a classroom for many years. The expression "drive-by shooting" is derived from the fact that <u>after</u> these in-service days there is rarely any follow-up with the teachers. The outside staff development "experts" go into a school, spray teachers with "educational bullets," and then move on to their next faculty victim at another school. The teachers, thus sprayed, are expected to magically internalize and apply that which they are exposed to on the staff development days. Since there is no time in either the principal's or teachers' schedules for follow-up, little of what is "learned" on these days is ever incorporated into a teacher's repertoire in the classroom. "Drive-by shooting" professional development does little to improve teacher competencies and build capacity in the teaching ranks. And over time teachers grow understandably cynical of staff development done in this manner.

Dark and Dirty Secret #3: Most new teacher mentoring programs (should a school even have one) consist of little more than a weekly (at best) sit-down meeting between a new teacher and a more veteran teacher designed to answer questions.

These scheduled meetings between new and veteran teachers are more like a short-term orientation program than true mentoring. They help new teachers in a school deal with all the logistical issues associated with a new position; what forms need to be filled out and where to find them; how to submit attendance through the computer; how to get access to copy services; technology questions, etc. Questions rarely come up regarding the art and craft of teaching. After logistical concerns are taken care of, subsequent meetings usually consist of exchanges something like this:

- Mentor: "How's it going?"
- New teacher: "Good!"
- Mentor: "Any questions or problems?"
- New teacher: "Nope"
- Mentor: "Great! Let me know if there is anything I can do for you.

Both teachers then exit, happy to get back to what they need to prepare for the next day, or their next class, because they are pressed for time as always. Remember, both the mentor and the teacher being mentored have full class loads to teach.

There are undoubtedly mentor programs out there that do more for teachers than what I have described, but I have not been privileged to experience or view any. My guess is that mentor programs that involve intensive interaction between teachers, including regular classroom visits followed by debriefing sessions to discuss pedagogy (the art and science of teaching), are few and far between.

Dark and Dirty Secret #4: Teachers that survive and become successful in the classroom pick up the post-college, requisite skill sets they need on their own in a "hit or miss" or "trial and error" fashion.

This secret follows rather obviously from the first three. If your school is not helping you to develop the skills and strategies you need to survive in the classroom, then you must acquire them on your own. Through luck, chance encounters with colleagues who offer constructive advice, and much painful trial and error, teachers may slowly grow into seasoned professionals. Or they may not.

All four of these "dark and dirty secrets" about professional development in our schools help us to understand why the _teacher_ drop-out rate is so high. Poor professional development for new teachers, along with the heavy teacher workload and stress level, along with the general lack of support, and along with the isolation, together create a perfect storm for teacher attrition. And every one of these factors is locked, cemented, into our existing school paradigms.

The job of teaching has always been tough. But over the last decade it was made even more difficult as teacher accountability based educational reforms targeted teachers as the root cause of the failures of students and schools. These reforms so changed the climate and culture of teaching that more and more people are actively discouraging young men and women from pursuing careers in teaching. I feel deep sadness when I hear great teachers that I know say that today they would never encourage their students – or their own children – to become teachers, not while teachers continue to serve as scapegoats for all the problems in our schools.

Reforms that focus heavily on teacher accountability, while well intended, are inherently damaging and dangerous. Such reforms do not focus on building capacity in the teaching ranks as they should. Instead, they focus on rooting out teachers perceived as "bad" or "ineffective" using policies and procedures which, at the same time, drive out good teachers and scare away prospective new teachers from entering the profession. Just look at the headlines.

"Enrollment in Teacher Preparation Programs Plummet," _Stanford Center for Opportunity Policy in Education,_ September 24, 2013.

"Steep Drop Seen in Teacher-Prep Enrollment Numbers," _Education Week,_ October 21, 2014.

"Where Have All the Teachers Gone," _nprEd,_ March 3, 2015.

"Who Wants to Teach," _Detroit Free Press,_ April 25, 2015.

"Teacher Prep Enrollment Continues to Decline," _Education Week,_ March 29, 2016.

"Education Pipeline at Risk," _Center for American Progress,_ report issued September 2016.

"Enrollment is Down at Teacher Colleges, So They Are Trying to

Change," *Education Week,* August 9, 2018.

It is a sad irony that teacher accountability reforms aimed at ensuring the presence of a highly effective teacher in every classroom are ultimately reducing the number of quality teachers in the workforce. We can agree on the importance of having great teachers in every classroom, but we disagree on _how_ to reach that goal.

If we want all children to achieve and succeed, we need to attract the best and brightest teacher candidates, 4 and 5-star recruits, and treat them as professionals. Teaching can and should be a revered profession that talented young scholars are clamoring to get into.

Treating teachers professionally translates into providing teachers with a work environment that fosters professional growth <u>every</u> day of the year, not just on four isolated staff development days. It means providing professional incentives (not necessarily monetary) that will motivate teachers to <u>want</u> to grow and develop into outstanding educational professionals. And most importantly, it means giving teachers an educational paradigm to work within that provides them with the <u>best</u> opportunity to be successful with <u>all</u> their students, because that is what teachers want more than anything else. The CP provides all of this for teachers.

One final note on teaching.

I know that I just painted a bleak picture of the teaching profession. If the job is that difficult why would anyone want to teach? Good question. The answer lies in the knowledge that, in addition to being difficult and challenging, teaching is also an incredibly rewarding and deeply satisfying profession. Good teachers' students become "their kids," even if the teachers have biological children of their own. Good teachers derive incredible pleasure from seeing these "other children" of theirs succeed. They thrive on the high of seeing the light bulb of understanding go off in their students' heads when they "get it." They are as proud as a parent when they see struggling students turn it around and succeed, especially when they know that they had a part in that turn around. Where else can a "helping professional" make such a huge difference in the lives of kids?

Major points to take away from *Chapter 4, On Teachers and Teaching*

1. The teaching profession is more complex, difficult, and demanding than most people realize.
2. After a teacher takes a teaching job, ongoing professional growth and development is, at best, a hit or miss proposition.
3. Large numbers of new teachers drop out of the profession within the first five years, while many other teachers quit long before retirement.
4. Despite the difficulty, demands, and complexity of the job, teaching can also be an incredibly rewarding and deeply satisfying career.
5. Attracting and retaining the best teaching candidates will require making significant changes to our existing educational paradigm.

CHAPTER 5

On the Role of Principals

SOMETIMES NECESSARY BUT uncomfortable tasks are best done quickly. Like tearing off a band aid or delivering bad news. "Sorry, but we did not choose you for the position."

So, here we go.

Reimagining our middle schools and high schools so that we can do what is best for all kids and their teachers will require some major changes to the role of the principal. *In a reimagined CP school, the principal will continue to be responsible for all activities in her school, but she will no longer be directly responsible for teacher supervision, evaluation, and professional growth.* Bam! There it is.

Unless you are a principal yourself, your reaction to this statement is probably something like, "Well, if principals do not have to supervise and evaluate teachers, then what else are they supposed to do with their time? They don't teach. Can we just get rid of them to save money?"

This is most people's normal response to the "bad news" statement above that principals will no longer be directly responsible for teacher supervision, evaluation, and professional growth in the CP. People think this because, unlike the job of teacher which everyone believes they know and understand, virtually no one knows and understands the job of principal because no one spends much (or any) time around principals while they are in school.

To understand why this change is an absolute necessity, why it is critical that someone else be directly responsible for growing and developing teachers in our schools, it will help to have at least a superficial understanding of the job of principal within the traditional educational paradigm.

Short of job shadowing a principal for a year, or serving as a principal yourself, the best way to get a passing knowledge of the job is to look online at job descriptions for high school and middle school principal positions. These job descriptions are compiled by school districts to inform potential principal candidates of the expectations of the Superintendent and Board of Education. They also serve as templates for evaluating principals. I selected one job description which I felt was representative. It is an actual job description from a public high school in New England. The school's home page proudly describes the school as "a four-year comprehensive high school of approximately 600 students [with] 63 professional staff members; 71 percent have advanced degrees."

I know that you will be tempted to skip reading this. I know that it is long, but I ask that you persevere and take a few minutes to read through the job description once. Just once. You do not need to study it, and I certainly have no expectation that you memorize it. But one read through will be most helpful when I explain _why_ the principal's position must be reimagined in the CP. Here it is, unedited, except for the name and location of the school.

TITLE: *High School Principal*
QUALIFICATIONS:
Education /Certification
- *Department of Education certification as Principal or equivalent*
- *Minimum of Masters Degree*

Special Knowledge/Skills
- *Successful experience working in a leadership role in education*
- *Working knowledge of curriculum, professional development and assessment*
- *Excellent skills in communicating and collaborating with staff and parents*
- *Excellent skills in supervising and evaluating staff*

REPORTS TO: *Superintendent of Schools*

SUPERVISES: *Faculty and Staff of _____ High School*

JOB GOAL:
To use leadership, supervisory, and administrative skills to develop, achieve and maintain the best possible educational program for the students of _____ High School that support the mission, vision, and beliefs of the _____ School District.

PERFORMANCE AREAS:
- **Administration/Organizational Management** – *The ability to practice participatory management; possession of good organizational skills and the knowledge of effective administration of school operations.*
- **Budgeting, School Finance, Plant Management, Business Services** – *The ability to effectively and efficiently utilize and manage the facility and assigned support services through responsible stewardship of school*

resources and a working knowledge of school finance, such that the needs of his/her school can be effectively represented in the budgeting process, including budget development, acceptance, and implementation.

- ***Communications*** *– The ability to articulate effectively, both orally and in writing, the successes and needs of the school with the school committee, central administration, staff, students, parents, and the general public - in large and small groups and with individuals.*

- ***Community Relations*** *– The ability to relate positively to the public; a view of the community/school relationship as a partnership; recognition of the need to be visible and active in the community and understanding the importance of considering community needs and wants.*

- ***Curriculum/Instruction*** *– The ability to work with staff to identify assessments, concepts and skills related to learning results, and to contribute guidance and assistance to staff in planning and implementing curriculum utilizing appropriate instructional strategies.*

- ***Educational Leadership*** *– The ability to inspire, motivate, guide and direct staff in setting and achieving the highest standards of educational excellence for the school and district.*

- ***Educational Renewal*** *– The ability to contribute to constructive educational change and demonstrate knowledge of current practices and research in school improvement.*

- ***Involvement in School and Community*** *– The ability to perform responsibilities as a visible presence in the school and to be aware of community developments, participating in and attending school events to the extent possible.*

- ***Personnel Management*** *– The ability to recognize school staffing needs, to perceive in candidates the potential for suitability, and to contribute to an effective recruitment/selection/retention process.*

- **Professional Development** – *The ability to contribute to the development and implementation of professional growth and staff development programs that raise both aspirations and expertise.*
- **Supervision/Evaluation** – *The ability to supervise and evaluate staff and all activities through knowledge and the commitment to contribute to the improvement of instruction and the effectiveness of programs in general.*

SPECIFIC PERFORMANCE RESPONSIBILITIES MAY INCLUDE BUT ARE NOT NECESSARILY LIMITED TO:

Administration/Organizational Management

- *Plan, organize, and direct (or oversee/approve) implementation of all school activities.*
- *Oversee the school's administration and instruction; make recommendations when central office or school board authorization is needed.*
- *Work with other members of the leadership team (central office and other administrative staff) on matters and issues of more than individual school import, such as curriculum, special services, transportation, and the like.*
- *Budget school time to provide for the efficient conduct of instruction, co-curricular activities, and operational business.*
- *Schedule the school day and classes within established guidelines to best meet students' instructional needs.*
- *Maintain high standards of student conduct, and enforce discipline as necessary, affording appropriate due process to students and parents.*
- *Establish positive guides for proper student conduct and the maintaining of fair, consistent discipline.*
- *Supervise the maintenance of accurate records on student progress and attendance.*

- *Conduct staff meetings as necessary for the proper functioning of the school.*
- *Plan and supervise fire drills and emergency preparedness program in accordance with legal requirements and established school system procedures.*
- *Participate in principals' meetings, negotiations meetings, and in such other meetings as may be required or appropriate.*
- *Serve as an ex-officio member of all committees and councils within the school.*
- *Delegate authority to appropriate personnel to assume responsibility for the school in the absence of the principal.*

Budgeting/School Finance/Plant Management/Business Services

- *Prepare and submit the school's budgetary requests, and monitor expenditures of allotted funds.*
- *Supervise the maintenance of all required building records and reports.*
- *Oversee appropriate accounting and control of school funds and student activities accounts.*
- *Assume responsibility for the safety and administration of the school plant.*
- *Oversee the daily use of the school facilities for both academic and non-academic purposes, including by school staff, students and the community.*
- *Provide for adequate inventorying of school/school system property, and for the securing of and accountability for that property.*

Communications

- *Keep the Superintendent informed of the school's activities and problems.*
- *Respond to written, oral, and electronic requests for information from appropriate sources.*

- *Develop and implement a plan for communicating with parents on a regular basis.*

Community Relations
- *Act as liaison between the school and the community, interpreting activities and policies of the school and encouraging community participation in school life.*
- *Assume responsibility for all official school correspondence and information.*

Curriculum/Instruction
- *Assume the responsibility assigned by school board/ administrative policy in the development, revision, and evaluation of the school curriculum.*
- *In coordination with appropriate members of the leadership team, supervise the guidance program and other instructional and student support services to enhance individual education and development.*

Educational Leadership:
- *Establish and maintain a school climate that enhances teaching and learning.*
- *Lead in the development, determination of appropriateness, and monitoring of the instructional program.*
- *Assert leadership in times of crisis or civil disobedience in school in accordance with established policy and procedures.*
- *Assume responsibility for the interpretation and implementation by the school's staff of all school board policies and administrative procedures/regulations.*
- *Serve as a member of such committees and attend such meetings as the superintendent may direct.*
- *Assume an active role as a member of the District Leadership Team providing input to district-wide decision making.*

Educational Renewal

- *Assist in the organizing of District renewal efforts and strategic planning.*
- *Work with building principals and team leaders to design meaningful ways to monitor the implementation of improvement programs and strategies.*
- *Keep abreast of educational changes and developments by attending appropriate meeting, reading professional journals and other publications, and discussing problems of mutual interest with others in the field.*

Involvement in School and Community

- *Maintain active relationships with students and parents.*
- *Participate in special events to recognize student achievement, as well as in typical school sponsored activities, functions, and extra-curricular events.*
- *Establish and maintain relationships with local community groups and individuals:*
  - » To foster understanding and solicit support for overall school objectives and programs.
  - » To interpret school building policies and procedures.

Personnel Management

- *Coordinate personnel needs with appropriate other members of the administrative team.*
- *Participate in the recruiting, screening, nomination, training, assigning, and evaluating of school building personnel.*
- *Cooperate with college and university officials regarding teacher training and preparation.*

Professional Development

- *Orient newly assigned school staff members and assist in their development, as appropriate.*
- *Participate in the in-service orientation and training of school staff.*

- *Assume responsibility for monitoring own professional growth and development through participation in professional organizations, through attendance at regional, state and national meetings, through enrollment in advanced coursework and the like.*

Supervision/Evaluation

- *Assume responsibility for supervision of all administrative, certified, and support staff attached to the school.*
- *Supervise the school's instructional practices.*
- *Assume responsibility for evaluating and counseling of all staff members regarding individual and group performance.*
- *Recommend, according to established procedures, the dismissal or non-renewal of a staff member whose performance is unsatisfactory.*
- *Assume responsibility for supervision and evaluation of the school's extracurricular and athletic programs.*

Other

- *Provide for regular and special conferences between parents and teachers.*
- *Prepare or supervise the preparation and submission of reports, records, lists, and all other paperwork required or appropriate to the school's administration*
- *Perform such other tasks as may be assigned.*

EVALUATION:

The basis of the evaluation will be the extent to which the performance responsibilities of the job are successfully completed and the extent to which yearly job goals are met. The Superintendent will perform the evaluation.

NOTE: *The above job description reflects the general requirements necessary to describe the principle functions or responsibilities of*

the job identified and shall not be interpreted as a detailed de-
scription of all work requirements that may be inherent in the job,
either at present or in the future.

If, as I portrayed it in the previous chapter, teaching is one of the most demanding and difficult jobs on the planet, then the job of principal is, quite simply, impossible. And you should note the line above that states, "Specific performance responsibilities may include but are not limited to:" which means that there can be (and usually are) more than the 52 "specific performance responsibilities" already listed.

At one point in my administrative career, I shared my job description with an experienced business executive in the private sector, a regional president for a large, national health insurer. At the time I was the principal of a rural middle school with 450 6th, 7th, and 8th grade students. I did not have an assistant principal. I had a staff of 44 teachers, 4 teaching assistants and teacher aides, one guidance counselor and a school social worker. I also had an administrative intern (an administrator in training) who I was responsible for overseeing. My job description was not unlike the one above.

I asked the business executive, "How many people are you directly responsible for in your job, that is, how many employees report directly to you that you supervise and evaluate?" After a little thought she responded, "Um, about eight, no, maybe as many as twelve at times." I then asked her what she thought of one individual overseeing and evaluating 51 educational professionals, plus clerical staff, in addition to all the other duties in the job description. Her facial expression said it all. It was a combination of disbelief and shock, as if she couldn't believe I would ask such a ridiculous question. Her response was, "That's impossible. You can't do that. Nobody can do that." And of course, she was right. Any businessperson knows that it is absurd to expect one or two administrators to supervise, evaluate, grow, and develop, a staff of 50 or more professionals in addition to all their other responsibilities.

Principals are a dedicated, incredibly hardworking bunch. But no principal, regardless of how many hours they dedicate to the job of middle school or high school principal, can complete all the tasks that are required of them at a quality level.

And here is the kicker. The huge, unwieldly, and impossible to complete job descriptions of principals do not even include the task of growing and developing teachers from "rookies" fresh out of college to outstanding/great classroom teachers. What all principal job descriptions require of principals is that they supervise and evaluate the teachers in their charge using the model or instrument they are provided. In almost every instance that means the principal is required to perform one to three observations a year to assess whether the teacher, during those few close encounters, is adhering to some predetermined list of teacher qualities and practices. So, when I say in FT #22 that, "Principals and assistant principals cannot adequately supervise and evaluate an entire faculty of teachers _for professional growth and development_ . . ." I am **not** saying that principals are not doing their jobs. On the contrary, principals generally do their jobs well, but the job of supervising and evaluating their teachers only encompasses observing each teacher teaching between one and three of the 1000+ classes they teach each year and then providing feedback. Even if an outstanding principal recognizes the need to do more to grow her teachers into outstanding instructional professionals, she simply does not have the time to do it.

Let me take one last stab at helping you to understand why this change (the principal no longer being directly responsible for teacher supervision, evaluation, and professional growth) is so critical. The teacher in me is hoping that an analogy will help you understand. My apologies in advance if you are put off by sports analogies.

Principals, superintendents, school boards, everyone, wants outstanding, highly skilled teachers in every classroom. Owners of major league baseball teams want outstanding, highly skilled players at every position on their teams.

Both school districts and major league baseball teams look to hire the most talented individuals they can find, the ones with the most potential to become great. A baseball team drafts players out of college or high school after a lengthy scouting process. School districts also "draft" young talent but through a different process. Districts take applications for positions from candidates fresh out of college or graduate school. The applications are reviewed carefully, references are contacted, interviews are conducted, and then a decision is made regarding which candidate to hire.

The similarities between the two personnel development systems ends there. The roads to greatness in teaching and baseball diverge in two very different directions.

Under the assumption that they are ready to teach, newly hired teachers are thrust directly into the "major leagues" of education. They are assigned full teaching loads, put through a brief orientation program, and (if they are lucky) assigned a mentor. After that, as described in the previous two chapters, their development is, for the most part, left up to chance. Limited professional development opportunities (at most maybe three or four days a year), limited nurturing by the principal through required supervision and evaluation, and limited contact with other educational professionals, all hinder the growth and development of newly hired teachers. Most growth occurs through painful trial and error.

Newly hired (drafted) baseball players are recognized as the raw talents that they are, nowhere near ready to perform at the highest level. They are assigned to a minor league team where regular coaching begins. The players go through intensive training and practice before playing in any games, even though every new draftee has already played baseball for anywhere from 12 to 16 years. Once a minor league season starts, player performance is constantly observed and evaluated. Regular coaching by the manager and position coaches adds to players' development. And ongoing interaction with team members provides additional feedback to new players.

In baseball, player development continues for many years. If growth is apparent a player may be promoted to a higher level minor league team. Eventually, if a player develops enough, they may make it to "The Show," that is, be promoted to the Major Leagues. All along this path to a Major League team, and throughout a player's career in the major leagues, practice, training, and coaching with lots of feedback, are constants.

Starting to get the picture? What if baseball players were developed the same way we develop (or do not develop) teachers?

Imagine a coach saying to a player, "I'm going to come to three of your games during the entire 150 game season. At those three games I will watch your second at-bat, and then I will watch you play in the field for an inning or two. Afterwards we can talk about what I saw, and I can give you a few pointers. Other than that, you are on your own."

How far do you think a major league prospect would advance with this kind of coaching? I can answer that. Not far at all. And teams cannot afford to let that happen. Teams invest too much money on prospective talent. Baseball teams need great players if they are to compete and win.

Two or three observations. Two or three written evaluations. Two or three conferences. In our schools this is the only kind of "coaching" that our principals can do with our teachers. It is also the only kind of "coaching" that principals _are asked and required to do_ with their teachers. That is a sad indictment of our existing educational paradigm.

In education we cannot continue to approach teacher growth and development in the haphazard manner that we do. With everyone acknowledging the importance of having a great teacher in every classroom it is time to reimagine our schools to make this a top priority. It is time to stop setting up our principals for failure. It is time to give our principals the resources (including staff), tools, and time to focus on growing and developing all their teachers into great teachers. This happens in the CP. It must. To do anything less is to acknowledge that we are not willing to do what is best for kids, to do whatever it takes to help every student achieve and succeed.

Major points to take away from *Chapter 5, On the Role of Principals*

1. In the traditional educational paradigm, no middle school or high school principal, regardless of how many hours they dedicate to the job, can complete the huge number of tasks that are required of them at a quality level.
2. The huge, unwieldly, and impossible to complete job descriptions of principals do not include the task of growing and developing teachers from "rookies" fresh out of college to outstanding/great classroom teachers.
3. In a reimagined CP school, the principal will continue to be responsible for all activities in her school, but she will no longer be directly responsible for teacher supervision, evaluation, and professional growth.

CHAPTER 6

Our Teenage (and near teen) Students

BEFORE WE DIVE headlong into the CP, I think it is important for you to know as much as possible about these wonderful, annoying, lovable, irascible, beings we call teenagers (and "near teens" – those 11- and 12-year-olds qualify in my book).

I toyed with the idea of writing a long narrative for you about students. But then I recalled the hundreds, if not thousands, of works out there about the sociology and psychology of adolescents, some of which I was required to read when I was working on my Masters degree (while also teaching full time). I remember thinking, "Wow. Great stuff, but how am I going to apply this to what I am doing in the classroom tomorrow?" With that in mind, I thought it better to go down a different path and give you something which I hope you will find more useful.

I decided to record everything I could remember about my interactions with students and other adolescents over the last 35+ years.

I literally sat down at my computer and started thinking about students who I taught, and what they taught me. I thought about students I coached and advised. I thought about students who attended and worked at the youth center that I directed. I thought about students I had to see for disciplinary reasons as a principal, and students in juvenile detention where I worked. I thought about my own daughters. There is no rhyme or reason to the order in which these factoids are presented. I simply wrote them down as they spilled out of my memory.

My hope is that this chapter will help you realize how much you value and love the kids in your life, as a parent, teacher, principal, or community member. Kids are worthy of our best efforts.

1. Middle school and high school students travel on the emotional roller coaster that is adolescence every single day of their lives.
   a. Students can love you and the entire world one day (or one hour), hate everything about the world the next day (or next hour), and be back again loving you the next. Their emotional swings defy understanding at times.
   b. We need to be the steady presence in their lives and love them no matter what, no matter where they are on their emotional roller coaster ride. This can require great patience and emotional strength on our part, but that is what is expected of us as adults.

2. Students' actions are directly linked to their needs and wants of today, and only rarely linked to where they see themselves five, ten, or twenty years from now.
   a. If you are trying to motivate students, it does little good to tell them that if they work hard in school they will be able to get a good job down the road. Young students see little connection between what is happening today and what their lives will be like ten years from now. From the perspective of our life experience we can see the connection, but students often cannot. If we can help students to achieve and succeed while also meeting their needs today, we can

slowly get them to see the connection between their actions in school today and their future.

3. Students do whatever they have to do to get their needs met and survive. If they are not able to get their needs met in a manner we deem socially acceptable they will often make poor choices to satisfy those needs.
    a. We need to be understanding when students make bad decisions for the right reasons (survival).

4. Students' lives outside of school often suck. Students deal with more issues and problems in their lives outside of school than you can ever imagine.
    a. Many students come to school with so much personal baggage, even at a young age, that it is a wonder that they can function at all. As educators we cannot excuse or accept the dysfunctional behaviors related to this baggage, but we can understand. And armed with that understanding we can (and must) use all our skills and do everything possible to help our students succeed _despite_ all the baggage they bring to school every day.
    b. Students may share something about issues or problems they are dealing with at home or a tragic event in their life. Whatever you do, please, please, please never say "I know exactly how you feel," even if you had a similar experience in your life. Perhaps try, "I cannot begin to imagine what it feels like to be going through what you are right now. Maybe you can help me to understand better so that I can help."

5. Students sometimes bring those issues or problems into school. Their attitude, demeanor, or behavior in school sometimes reflects that which they are dealing with on the inside.
    a. When I was a Dean of Students an 8th grade special education student was sent to me by his teacher for insubordination,

refusing to follow directions or do anything constructive in his resource class. This was very out of character for the student, which I noted. Did his apparent insubordination warrant punishment? Not when I learned that his mother's boyfriend had assaulted him the night before and left marks on his neck. There was no way the young man could function normally in school that day. Empathy and a call to Child Protective Services were warranted, not punishment.

6. Students are brutally honest when providing feedback.
   a. Ask students for feedback and they will tell it like it is. Knowing this, why not tap students for feedback to help us improve our performance as educators. Not doing so is wasting a valuable resource. After all, who has more direct contact with teachers than students?

7. Students will respect you if you value them and always treat them with respect.
   a. When, as educators, we respect students and gain their respect in return everyone wins. In an environment of mutual respect teacher and students can work together toward the mutual goal of student academic and life success. Disrespect students and you will create a hostile environment in which everyone loses.

8. Students care deeply and will respond as individuals or as a group to help meet the needs of others.
   a. Knowing this, why would we not provide students the opportunity to come together to lend support and assistance to worthy causes within their school or community. Through such actions students grow and develop into caring and contributing members of society, a goal certainly no less important than scoring well on a mathematics assessment.

9. Students do _not_ respond well to sarcasm directed their way.
    a. Teachers may think they are being funny when they are sarcastic with students, but to students, sarcasm aimed in their direction is perceived as anything but funny, even if they laugh on the outside. Students are hurt by sarcasm, they hate it, and they hate the teachers who engage in it.
    b. Leave your sarcasm at home. Do not risk using it in school. You never know when you will step over the line with students and turn them off.

10. Students need to exert some degree of power and control over their environment.
    a. Young children become accustomed to having virtually all life decisions made for them (what to eat, what they can wear, where they can go, who they can spend time with, etc.). As children approach adolescence and enter middle school and high school they want and need to start making some decisions for themselves.
    b. In schools we need to give students some opportunities to do this.

11. Students want to succeed.
    a. Do not believe for a moment that any student ever entered school wanting to fail. Succeeding feels good. Failing hurts. Who would choose the pain of failure over the joy and pleasure of success?
    b. Students do get to the point where they feel their situation is beyond hope. It is at this point where they may stop trying entirely. To keep trying and repeatedly fail is too painful. It is easier and emotionally safer to not try, pretend not to care, and then fail.
    c. When you hear a student laugh about failing a test, when he says he did not study and does not really care, know that what you see and hear is a defense mechanism being employed to minimize the pain of failure.

    d.   Do not confuse the overwhelming hopelessness that may lead a child to give up with "choosing to fail."

12. Students need to succeed. See FT #10

13. Students who fail repeatedly will eventually give up, shut down, and stop trying entirely. See FT #12
    a. If students reach this point, we have failed them, and our job to help them be successful becomes that much more difficult. Just as it is easier to provide simple, regular maintenance to keep a car running well, so also it is better to put energy into ensuring that students experience some degree of success so that they will continue to work hard. Once the car breaks down, or the student shuts down, repair is more difficult and costly.

14. Students desperately want and need to belong. See FT #5
    a. Adolescents are incredibly social. Those who appear to be "loners" desperately do not want to be. All students need to be part of a group and experience the support of a family, a group, a team, a gang – some group, any group.

15. Students will often work harder to achieve a group goal than they will to achieve a personal goal. See FT #4

16. Students can tell if you really care about them as individuals or if you are just "doing your job" and/or faking it.
    a. Teachers and other educational professionals need to genuinely care about the young people they work with and demonstrate that caring through words and actions. If they have trouble doing that, they should perhaps rethink their career choice.

17. Students who perceive that you care about them are more likely to work harder. FT #6
    a. As an educator, genuinely caring about your students makes you more susceptible to sorrow and disappointment if they

fail. But genuinely caring for your students also increases the likelihood that they will achieve and succeed and bring you joy.

18. Students can be incredibly cruel to other students who they perceive to be different in some way – too short, too tall, too skinny, too fat, too smart, too dumb, too "cool," not "cool" enough, bad skin, the wrong color skin, the wrong religion, or came from the wrong place.
    a. As educators we need to model acceptance, not simply tolerance, and acknowledge that we are all "different" in some way. We need to welcome and celebrate diversity in our schools because many students do not see and experience such acceptance and welcoming behavior at home.

19. Students will sometimes bully, harass, and intimidate other students to push them down, believing (subconsciously) that lowering others somehow elevates themselves. See #18 above.

20. Students need to know what you expect of them. FT #2
    a. Do not play the "guessing game" with students. Let them know every day what you expect of them, and what they can expect from you in return. Hold them accountable for what you expect of them and ask them to hold you accountable for what they can expect from you in return. There is no shame in having a student say, "You know Mr. Czarniak, you told us that you would always correct and return our quizzes the day after we took them, and lately you have not been doing that."

21. Students like structure with some variety mixed in. Students do not do well with chaos but really like the occasional "out of the blue" unexpected event to break things up.
    a. Structure is critical in classroom settings. Students need established routines to help them know what to expect day

to day. But the once-in-a-blue-moon special learning event can have a lasting impact on students.

22. Students hate to be bored.
    a. A good rule of thumb? If a lesson or activity seems a little boring to you, it is probably deadly boring to your students. Not every lesson has to be "the best ever," but each should engage students in a constructive manner.

23. Students are very susceptible to the "disease" of teacher enthusiasm and excitement for a topic.
    a. There are always topics in a curriculum which do not naturally elicit excitement in students, but which still need to be taught. The teacher has a choice. She can be a moaning and groaning "Eeyore" and drag students down into the abyss of boredom. Or she can spread the "disease" of excitement and enthusiasm for the subject through her words, tone, and actions.
    b. I taught Earth Science. On the surface, the topic of rocks might not appear to be the most exciting thing to learn about. But, if you hold a rock up to your ear and tell your students that rocks can talk to you, and that you can hear what they have to say if only you listen carefully, you might begin to grab students' attention (yes, I did this. I can be a little crazy). Students can be drawn to any topic in any discipline if the teacher is willing to spread the "disease" of enthusiasm.

24. Students like working _with_ you more than they like working _for_ you.
    a. Students like working alongside you toward the achievement of a common goal. Regardless of the setting, if they see you as a hard-working partner, they will put forth a stronger effort. This is true in the classroom, on the athletic field, during a fundraiser, at an extracurricular activity, anyplace.

b. On the other side, if students see you simply as a "dispenser of tasks" who then sits back and takes it easy while they work, they will not like it and you will not get the best effort from them.

25. Students will always remember the great, crazy things you did with them to help them learn and grow.

a. Sister Josetta Jones, my principal at a small K-8 Catholic school, told me, "Curt, your students are never going to remember exactly what you taught on March 5, 1982, but they will always remember the above and beyond special things you do to make learning fun and exciting." She was right. Whenever I run into a former student from those days it is always those special things they bring up – the nature trail we built, the lunch corporation we ran, the solar ovens. A couple years ago one former student from out of state asked me out to lunch. At the lunch he shared that when he was in 7th grade, I helped launch him on his career in acting. I was incredulous (I taught him Science, Reading, and Religion). I did not remember the Christmas play we did that year, a play which this former student remembered in minute detail and credited with changing his life. You never know the impact you will have on kids. The kids remember.

26. Students like to have fun.

a. Learning activities can sometimes be fun, but often they are not. There is a reason they call it "work." But that does not mean that students and teachers cannot have a little fun while they are working. Sometimes something as simple as adding a little humor to the class (a "goofy" science teacher simulating an amoeba's movement or an English teacher role playing a comedic passage from Shakespeare) can be enough to break the monotony and add a little fun to a lesson.

27. Students like to eat.
    a. In education we refer to this as the "M&M school of education." Even if it happens only a few times a year, students will always remember those times when a teacher figured out a way to incorporate food into a lesson. And yes, a good teacher of any subject can figure out how to incorporate food into a lesson.
        i.   Foreign languages – Easy! International foods
        ii. Science – Foods flavored by microorganisms (cheeses, yogurt, etc.)
        iii. Social Studies – Irish immigration, the great potato famine
        iv. Math – Fibonacci numbers in fruits and vegetables
        v.   English – A Charles Dickens lunch

28. Students influence, and are influenced by, their peers, both in negative and positive ways. See FT #8
    a. Most people think only of peer pressure with negative connotations. Positive peer pressure is as strong, or stronger than, negative peer pressure. Ask any advertising expert. They all know we mimic what we see other people do. Why do you think companies pay millions of dollars for celebrity endorsements of their products? Positive peer pressure between students is an educational gold mine waiting to be tapped.

29. Students are often the best teachers of other students.
    a. And when students teach concepts to other students those same concepts are cemented into the brains of the students doing the teaching.

30. Students like to move (because they rarely get to do so in most traditional classroom settings).
    a. Would you like to spend your day sitting passively for eight 45-minute periods punctuated only by three to

four-minute intervals when you move to your next sitting location? Not a lot of fun. Design or locate activities that allow students to move in class. Again, not all the time, but often enough to break up the monotony of sitting and sitting and sitting.

31. Students appreciate adults who do not take themselves too seriously, who can laugh at themselves.
    a. I always introduced myself on the first day of class as a teacher with enormous feet (size 15), lifting one up onto a desk to demonstrate. I encouraged students to keep their feet out of the aisle and under their desks lest I crush them with my monster feet as I walked around the room.

32. Students do _not_ like to be put down, or mocked out, or made fun of at any time. FT #7

33. Students _really do not_ like being put down, mocked out, or made fun of _in front of their peers._ FT #11
    a. Any successful educational paradigm needs to address the ubiquitous put downs found in our culture. Students may laugh when they are the target, but they still hurt when they are put down, mocked out, or made fun of. And they hate it!
    b. Students will do _anything_ to avoid being embarrassed in front of their peers.

34. Students have an incredibly well-developed sense of justice and fairness!
    a. See # 35 below

35. Students like to see consistency in the way they and their peers are treated by adults.
    a. Be fair, just, and consistent in your dealings with adolescents and you will greatly enhance your chances of success.

36. Students need to save face in front of their peers.
    a. Do not back students into a corner, literally or figuratively. When students make mistakes, even serious ones, provide them with a path to take responsibility for the mistake while at the same time maintaining their dignity.

37. Students will win (and you will lose) if you get into a "pissing match" with them in front of a class (see items #33 and #36 above).
    a. Some of the worst teacher/student conflicts I dealt with as a principal were over relatively minor transgressions. These minor transgressions exploded into major issues when the _teacher's_ initial response effectively threw gasoline on a minor fire by choosing a strategy that humiliated students.

38. Students love being part of a team, a group effort to perform or achieve something (strongly linked to students' need to belong). See FT #3

39. Students can "smell" a fake a mile away. If you are not genuine with them, they will sniff out your BS in a hurry.
    a. See #42 below. Being a fake, not being genuine, lacking sincerity, is essentially a lie. Any adult demonstrating such behaviors can kiss any student respect goodbye.

40. Students (all adolescent students) lie at times, especially when they need to protect and preserve their parents' image of them as "a good kid."
    a. A wake-up call for parents: When dealing with student discipline issues as a principal and dean of students I had many conversations with parents. I often heard parents say, "My kid may not be perfect, and he/she might lie to you, but he/she would never lie to me." The truth is that kids do lie to their parents, even "great kids." Kids do not want to

disappoint their parents. They desperately want to preserve their parents' image of them as a good kid. Parents, they lie to you sometimes because they love you and are trying to protect your relationship. Remember, adolescence is an emotionally confusing time for kids.

b. Kids also lie to avoid embarrassment.

c. Telling a lie does not make a student a bad person. Have any of you, my adult readers, ever lied? Did you ever lie to protect a relationship or to avoid causing another emotional pain? (Does this outfit make me look fat?) Kids do not only lie to avoid getting into trouble, although they do a lot of that as well.

41. Students at some point begin to believe that our love for them is conditional, that they must be perfect to be deserving of our love. Children will do whatever it takes to maintain that image of perfection. See #40 above.

a. If a student believes that our love and caring is conditional, that they can never make a mistake without risking the loss of our love, then we can expect that they will lie to us whenever they do make a mistake.

b. Better to say to your child or student what I must have said a thousand times to students during the years I spent as a principal and dean of students. "I have no expectation that you be perfect because I am certainly not perfect. But I do expect that if you make a mistake you will 1) own up to your mistake, 2) take responsibility for the mistake and accept any consequences, 3) put it behind you as I will, and 4) learn from your mistake, because the only dumb mistakes are the ones we repeat over and over. If you can do this, I will respect you and always be in your corner going forward." Working through mistakes, even big ones, can make your relationship with your child/student stronger, with more mutual respect, if you can say this and truly *mean* it.

c. I would also say this to my students. "I will tell you the same thing I tell my own daughters, 'I love you dearly, but I don't necessarily love everything you do.'" It helps to separate the person from the act.

42. Students may lie with some degree of frequency themselves, but they are intolerant of adults who lie to them.
   a. If a student knows that a teacher lied to them, the student and his/her peers will cease to have any respect for that teacher.

43. Students, when they do something wrong, often have absolutely no idea _why_ they did what they did.
   a. I learned a long time ago that it does absolutely no good to let anyone (parents or teachers) berate a child in a parent conference with questions like, "Why did you do that?" or "Why didn't you do your assignment?" Kids usually cannot answer those questions because they truly do not know the answer. Kids just do things. They have no idea why. Remember, we are dealing with adolescents. If you try to force an answer out of them they will just tell you what they think you want to hear.
   b. Students may know the answer to the "why" question but still not answer to avoid embarrassment.

44. Students really appreciate it when a teacher or other adult can admit a mistake and say, "I'm sorry."

45. Students are incredibly protective of their peers.
   a. Beware, the walls have ears. I caution all teachers (and others working with students) to never say anything out loud anywhere that they would not want their students to hear. If a teacher trashes a student in private it can be overheard or in some way get back to the student. If that happens the teacher loses all credibility with the student and his/her peers. The teacher is toast.

46. Students (adolescent students) appreciate a little "corniness" from their teachers. They may groan about it, but they love it.
    a. I never met a student who did not complain about corny teacher jokes. Nor did I ever meet a student who did not laugh and enjoy corny teacher jokes, even if their laughter was as much at the teacher for telling such a corny joke as the joke itself.

47. Students like when teachers share a little bit about themselves with them.
    a. Do not confuse this with trying to be the students' friend. A teacher cannot and should not try to be the students' friend. It is important to maintain professional distance. But, if during a lesson a teacher shares something about his life, his interests, or his travels, it makes him seem more human and accessible.

48. Students like to see teachers outside the classroom as human beings.
    a. I resided, grocery shopped, went to church, and pumped gasoline, in the same small community where I taught for many years. While some teachers do not like the feeling of "living in a fishbowl," I relished seeing my students outside of school. But not nearly as much as my students seemed to enjoy seeing me. Again, it pays dividends in the classroom if students see you as more human and accessible, not some wax figure in a shirt and tie bound to a classroom.

49. Students will often surprise you and "step up to the plate" to meet your high expectations of them.

50. Students will also disappoint you and fail to live up to your expectations of them. When they do
    a. Do _not_ take it personally. Remember that kids are goofy. They do things for unknown reasons.
    b. Be forgiving. Always be willing to give kids another chance at redemption.

51. The kids who you find hardest to love are the ones who need our love the most.

Well, did it? Did reading this chapter help you realize how much you value and love the kids that you work with and for? I hope so. Because loving all our kids unconditionally is central to our role as educational professionals (or our role as parents, or even as community members). Kids deserve our caring concern. They deserve our best.

I hope that you will come back to this chapter often to remind yourself of both the beauty and paradox of these remarkable creatures. Whenever your kids are driving you crazy, pull out this chapter and read through it again before you say or do something you will regret later.

Major points to take away from *Chapter 6, Our Teenage (and near teen) Students*

1. These wonderfully complex, sometimes lovable, often irascible, eternally frustrating, heartwarming, and heartbreaking human beings we call students . . . these are the people we work for. As teachers we do not work for the school board, or the parents, or the superintendent, or the principal. We work for the kids. They are the reason we are here.

Part II
The CP

CHAPTER 7

An Introduction to the CP

THE DESIGN OF the CP is not particularly fancy or complex. Even though the design includes many changes and additions to the traditional educational paradigm, the basic concept is quite simple.

- Assemble a group of nine teachers (five full-time, one part-time and three shared full-time, seven FTE's) and 100 students and designate them as a Learning Community.
- Give the nine teachers complete and total responsibility for the academic, social, and emotional growth of _all_ 100 students _over two years_.
- Establish goals and objectives that _all_ teachers and students are to meet over two years.
- Delineate clear performance expectations for all members of the Learning Community.
- _Provide teachers and students with the_ **_resources_** _they need to meet these goals and expectations._

The key bullet above is the last one, and the key word in that last bullet is "resources." When most people think of educational resources they think of desks and chairs, textbooks, workbooks, paper and pencils, computers and software, internet access, media access, chalk boards, white boards, or smart boards. But this entire section, where I describe the CP in detail, is all about providing teachers and students with different kinds of resources, the structural and operational resources they need to be successful.

Describing the CP to someone who has never heard anything about it is challenging, in part because of the sheer volume of changes and additions to our existing educational paradigm, but more so because the elements and attributes of the CP are so inextricably linked to each other. All the interconnections make it difficult to choose a starting point. Because writing and reading are such frustratingly linear processes, when you hear me describe the first few resources/elements of the CP you will, unavoidably, be forced to view them out of context. And when viewed out of context any one element of the CP may seem unnecessary or impractical. But as you read further the connections between various elements of the CP will become apparent and the value of the CP as an educational paradigm will become clear, much like the image of a jigsaw puzzle slowly comes into view as you put the pieces together.

To assist you in gaining an understanding of the CP as quickly as possible I decided to first tell you, in general terms, everything that changes in the CP. Consider the following list of "puzzle pieces" a preview of coming attractions.

In the CP . . .

- The philosophy of education changes.
- The school culture changes.
- Relationships change: the nature of the interactions that take place in each school relationship changes.
- The roles of students, teachers, and principals change with new responsibilities accompanying these changes.
- Completely new positions/roles are created, each with their own new set of responsibilities.

- Higher and more clearly defined expectations are created for all parties (students, teachers, principals).
- New systems are created for determining if individuals are meeting these expectations resulting in an increase in accountability across the board for all parties.
- Supervision and evaluation systems for teachers and principals change.
- Systems for teacher professional growth and development change.
- Teacher and student schedules change.
- Teaching loads change.
- Teacher duty assignments change.
- The length of the school day changes.
- A teaching career ladder is added.
- Teachers pay scales (linked to this career ladder) change.
- Tenure changes.
- Grade reporting systems for students change.
- Student recognition systems change.
- Student organizational structures change.
- Systems for community connections change.

In designing the CP, I assumed that the most fundamental want and desire of every parent, community member, teacher, principal, school board, and politician is to have _all_ students grow, develop (academically and otherwise), and succeed, in school and in life. I further assumed that we do _not_ want schools where students, might, can, or simply have the opportunity to succeed, but rather schools where _all_ students _do_ succeed. There is a big difference.

Going forward, everything in the CP targets two goals: the production of successful students (all of them), and the production and retention of highly effective and successful teachers.

As you read through the following chapters that describe the CP in detail your mind is likely going to bubble over with multiple reasons why the CP will never happen. You will envision obstacles of all types and sizes coming from every direction. My suggestion, at this point, is to not focus on all the reasons why the CP cannot become a reality. Rather, I encourage you to focus on the positive outcomes that will likely result when it does become a reality. In Section 3 I address the path to CP pilots and adoption, including obstacles and resistance that need to be overcome.

CHAPTER 8

The CP Philosophy and School Culture

"If there was little they could do individually to turn the situation around, perhaps there was something they could do collectively. Perhaps the seeds of redemption lay not just in perseverance, hard work, and rugged individualism. Perhaps they lay in something more fundamental – the simple notion of everyone pitching in and pulling together."

The Boys in the Boat, by Daniel James Brown

IF YOU ACCEPT the premise that we need to make changes in education such that our schools will better serve *all* our students, where should we begin? The history of recent educational reforms teaches us that perhaps we should *not* look to the same "experts" who gave us No

Child Left Behind or Race to the Top. Who, then, knows how best to reimagine our schools? Who can point us in the right direction?

Twenty-six years ago, I was fortunate to attend a summer principals' institute where I learned the value of having a faculty and staff describe their vision of a "dream school," a school that both students and teachers look forward to coming to every day, a school where teachers enjoy teaching and are successful, and where students are enthusiastic and successful participants in the learning process. It made sense to me in 1996, and it makes sense to me today, that we should tap into the knowledge and expertise of our most valuable resource, our teachers.

Teachers know and understand schools and children better than anyone. They spend their entire lives working with and for students. They know what kids need to be more effective in the classroom. They know what it will take to help students grow into successful and productive adults. *Teachers know kids.*

I tapped this resource when I served as a principal. To start painting a picture of their "dream school" I asked faculty and staff members to complete sentences like those below.

1. At "Our Town" Jr/Sr HS I would like to see more . . .
2. Students would really look forward to coming to "Our Town" Jr/ Sr HS if . . .
3. I could be more effective in my job if . . .
4. I would like to see relationships between students and staff characterized by . . .
5. As an educator, I feel proud when . . .
6. What bothers me the most about the old "picture" of "Our Town" Jr/Sr HS is . . .
7. I know it will probably never happen, but in my dream school I'd like to see . . .

Over the years I gleaned responses from teachers with well over a combined thousand years of teaching experience. My teachers' written responses produced a huge amount of data which, being a true educator/packrat, I saved. What teachers wanted to see in their dream schools, what they believed would make them more effective, and what they felt would make them and their students look forward to coming to school every day, was not what I expected. Their responses had almost nothing to do with facilities or curricula or scheduling. They did not emphasize larger classrooms, smaller class sizes, better textbooks, or more technology. They did not mention merit-based salary increases for themselves or school choice for their students. What their responses screamed for was a new school culture where they and their students could all work together and succeed. Here is how the process played out.

Key descriptive words and phrases were pulled from the hundreds of responses teachers submitted. Faculty and staff teams placed the descriptors into a small number of groups (3 to 5) based on similarities and then distilled out one word that summarized all the descriptive key words in each group. The goal was to find a "bullet version" of our school vision that could be easily communicated and understood by all constituent groups in our school community. In each school where I went through this process the results were strikingly similar. When the teachers and staff members described their "dream school" they identified a school culture of total responsibility that would simply not accept or tolerate student or teacher failure. This culture, which forms the philosophical basis of the CP, has four key attributes.

Belong

At the heart of what constitutes a great school, a school where teachers _want_ to teach and where students _want_ to learn, is the sense of _belonging_. The descriptive key words that my teachers grouped under the summarizing word "belong" included the following:

- unity
- connection
- family
- respect
- acceptance/tolerance
- caring
- equal

- trust
- kindness
- teamwork
- thanks/appreciation
- support
- welcome
- relationships
- openness
- peace
- wellness
- cooperation
- school spirit
- tradition
- pride
- all "glued" together
- love
- recognition
- sharing
- older students standing up for younger
- ownership
- community
- safety
- open communication
- a love for one's school
- involvement

If you look back at the 24 fundamental truths in education that form the foundation of the CP (Chapter 3) you will find that 16 of them are fully or partly linked to the sense of *belonging*. To be a part of a family with some stability *is to belong*. To work together with teammates, class-mates, or colleagues toward the realization of a larger goal or higher purpose *is to belong*. To know that people care about you and that you are in a safe teaching/learning environment free from shaming or humil-iation *is to belong*. To be supported and encouraged by your peers/col-leagues when you struggle and feel like giving up *is to belong*. To share rituals and traditions while working together as a member of an educational family *is to belong*. To be valued, appreciated, and recognized for your skills, talents, and what you can bring to the table *is to belong*. To always be trusted and treated with respect *is to belong*. All these links to *belonging* pertain to both students <u>and</u> teachers. <u>*Belonging*</u>, with all its many attributes, is of paramount importance in CP culture.

Believe

Other descriptors and key words identified by my teachers included being <u>hopeful</u> and <u>positive</u>, knowing that you and others have the <u>courage</u>, <u>self-assurance</u>, and <u>self-confidence</u> needed to drive forward, as well as <u>faith</u> in your <u>ability to change</u>, <u>improve</u>, and succeed. These descriptors together define a second, no less important, part of CP culture – that of *believing*.

A person's belief in their ability to succeed is directly related to the amount of effort they are willing to put forth. Greater confidence translates into more effort. Similarly, if a person doubts his ability to succeed, and if no other members of the learning community bolster him by encouraging him and expressing <u>their</u> belief in his ability to succeed, it is unlikely that he will regain the confidence he needs to press on.

Work Hard

The third and most "Captain Obvious" part of CP culture is the necessity to *work hard*. Years ago, when I explained my personal classroom philosophy to my students, I would always pose this question to them. "If you are a solid, contributing member of a sports team, a true team player who supports his teammates (you *belong*), and if you truly *believe* that you can win, is that enough? Is being a team player and having confidence enough to ensure that you will win?" Students never failed to identify the missing piece to being successful. They would say, "No. Even if you are a good teammate and believe you can win you still have to practice and work hard to be good enough to win." Students know. They get it. Even in the most collaborative and supportive team-oriented culture, where individuals have great confidence in their abilities, people need to work hard to succeed. The descriptive key words of my teachers were in lock-step agreement with my students on this point. Their feedback included the following.

- Have a unified direction, purpose, and goals
- Work together
- Be willing to try very hard
- Challenge yourself
- Be energetic
- Show excitement and enthusiasm
- Display creativity and innovation
- Have high expectations
- Be motivated
- Don't shy away from difficult work
- Achieve personal bests
- Be diligent in your work
- Exhibit professionalism
- Develop camaraderie and collegiality

Succeed

The fourth and final attribute of my teachers' dream school was that _everyone_ should be successful in doing their jobs, students, teachers, counselors, administrators, bus drivers, cafeteria workers, custodial staff, etc. Their specific feedback included:

- Feeling important and purposeful
- Know you are making a difference
- Positively change the world
- Breakthrough – seeing the "light bulb" of understanding go on
- Success

In the CP culture, where belonging to a caring and supportive learning community takes center stage, success is expected. Everyone's success is expected. But no teacher or student is expected to succeed entirely on his/her own. In a CP learning community, every teacher and student supports every other teacher and student, sharing responsibility for the success of each individual. No student or teacher is permitted to fail because others in the learning community will not allow it. Teachers and students succeed when those with whom they have built relationships also succeed. This concept can be summarized by the simple yet profound philosophical statement that within the CP . . .

I succeed when we succeed.

In the CP culture *every* member of the learning community shares a sense of belonging, has confidence (belief) in their ability to succeed, responds to challenges with hard work, and celebrates success together.

Belong, Believe, Work Hard, Succeed

Take a few minutes to digest this. Is such a school culture even possible? Or is it pure fantasy, an old man's pipedream? If you think the latter, you would not be the first person to suggest that I am overly imaginative, not grounded in the real world of education. I have been figuratively patted on the head and sent on my way with a "Nice idea, dreamer boy, but you can't create the kind of culture you describe in the real world of schools." If you share this sentiment you may be surprised to hear me say that you are correct, sort of. Let me explain.

In almost every endeavor in our society – business, law, medicine, sports, aviation, the military – individuals on teams are driven to higher levels of performance by the support of their teammates, the desire to meet team goals, and shared accountability. In business, an individual may come up with an idea for a product but the ultimate success of the company rests on the shoulders of teams of designers, detailers (who create the manufacturing specifications), manufacturing, marketing and sales, and shipping. Successful (and safe) air travel is a result of teams of pilots, flight engineers, ground crews, flight attendants, gate agents, air traffic controllers, security personnel, and more that I am not even aware of, I am sure. A sports team wins when everyone does their job successfully. If a halfback rushes for 200 yards but his team loses, did he succeed? I think not. He succeeds when the entire team succeeds. Individuals on legal teams, medical teams, and military teams all succeed when the team succeeds. The solitary successful man or woman is a fading myth in today's world. A person succeeds when she can surround herself with a strong team that works collaboratively to reach shared goals. The CP culture I described above is not a pipedream or a fantasy. It is an effective and practical organizational culture that already exists in successful organizations everywhere in our country. *Everywhere, that is, except in education*, where isolation and individualism reign.

I hope that you will at least acknowledge that the pipedream/fantasy of the CP culture in education is something that teachers and students want in their schools. If nothing else, it's a great pipedream; all teachers and students working together, doing their part to make sure that everyone succeeds, feeling a strong bond to a learning community where everyone supports, cares about, and helps one another. Great dream, yes?

Imagine for a moment that you are a teacher and that a group of students knocks on your classroom door. When you answer the door the students say, "We want and need a school culture like the CP culture that we just read about." What do you say to them? A fair and honest response would be, "I'm sorry, but we can't do that. It's just not possible in today's world of education." You would be speaking the truth. The students would be disappointed. They would amble off and try to figure out another way to get what they want and need. And you would feel bad, but there was nothing else you could do or say. You did not want to give them false hope.

You can probably see where I am headed with this. I just returned you to the front porch of Sarah's Place. Henry – aka: the students – told you what they wanted and needed – a ride home on a bitterly cold night / a school culture where they will all thrive and succeed. And you said exactly what I said, "I'm sorry. I can't help you. I'd like to, but I can't." And you said it for the very same reasons I did. You and I and just about everyone in the world of education are stuck, locked into a certain way of doing things in schools, the traditional educational paradigm. In the context of that traditional educational paradigm the emergence of CP culture is indeed a pipedream, sheer fantasy, the product of an overactive imagination. I acknowledge that we cannot create and sustain the kind of culture that students and teachers want and need in the real world of schools **_as they are structured and run today._** We need to make significant changes that will allow us to say to kids (and teachers), "Yes, we can do that for you."

The CP philosophy and school culture are critical resources for students and teachers. Without them all other aspects of the CP crumble and fail. If we want to make the "fantasy" CP culture a reality we need an equally fantastic set of structures, policies, procedures, *and people,* to foster that culture. Making major structural, organizational, and operational changes in schools to support a culture that will virtually guarantee that <u>all</u> students and teachers are successful will not be easy. It will require creativity and innovation and lots of people who are willing to do "whatever it takes" to help kids succeed without any "unless" statements to hold them back. It can be done. <u>We</u> can do it. Let me show you how.

Major points to take away from *Chapter 8, The CP Philosophy and School Culture*

1. The overarching educational philosophy in a CP school is that teachers and students succeed when those with whom they have built relationships also succeed. **_I succeed when we succeed._**

2. In the CP culture <u>every</u> member of the learning community shares a sense of belonging, has confidence (belief) in their ability to succeed, responds to challenges with hard work, and celebrates success together. **_Belong, Believe, Work Hard, Succeed_**

3. The CP philosophy and CP culture will not emerge in the real world of schools as they are structured and run today.

4. Making the CP philosophy and CP culture a reality will require major changes to school structures, policies, and procedures.

CHAPTER 9

House

"Never be afraid to do great, crazy things."

Dr. Lorraine Monroe

I LEARNED A long time ago to never hesitate to do great things for kids, even if people look at you like you have a few screws loose. Use saws, lopping shears, shovels, and other tools to build a nature trail with my 7th graders? No problem. Have groups of 9th graders and parent chaperones out to our house in the country for a night lab on the apparent motion of stars? Works for me. Take sixty-five 7th graders on a two-day outdoor education experience and sleep in tents? Guilty as charged. When I heard Dr. Lorraine Monroe speak the words above in 1996, she reaffirmed what I already knew and strongly believed. If you know something is good/great for kids, if you know it will help them learn, grow, and be successful, do not let other people's stodgy attitudes prevent you from moving forward.

Moving forward with the creation of the CP culture in our schools means putting in place "great, crazy" structures, policies, and procedures that foster a sense of belonging. *Belonging is the lynch pin*. Recall that sixteen of the 24 fundamental truths in education that form the foundation of the CP (Chapter 3) are fully or partly linked to the sense of belonging. The 200+ teachers I surveyed placed tremendous emphasis and importance on all the attributes related to belonging. And students, in all the years I worked with them in many different capacities, wanted more than anything to feel the closeness and connection of a group/team/family.

In the CP, the focus on belonging begins with the creation of a new structure and a new role for teachers that produce the following numbers.

12 : 19260 : 1 : 2

12 students : 19260 minutes : 1 teacher : 2 years

In the CP, the same 12 students spend 19,260 minutes together with one teacher over 2 years in something called House. That is 321 hours over two years. These direct contact hours are above and beyond the time teachers spend with students in their regular classrooms teaching Math, English, etc. It is in House that students begin to experience the sense of belonging that carries over into every other aspect of a CP school. *These hours spent in House over two years become the most important hours in the academic and social development of every student*. An outrageously strong statement, I know.

House is not a traditional homeroom or study hall. Nor is House an "advisory period." House consists of designated times each day during which students develop a sense of belonging through shared experiences, the majority of which revolve around academics.

Skeptic Sidebar: Don't our schools already foster a sense of teamwork and family?

You may question the need to reimagine school structures, policies, and procedures to promote belonging. After all, don't our schools already foster a sense of teamwork and family? The simple answer to this question is "No, they don't." You likely never thought of your children's schools in this way, but our existing school cultures and structures are <u>not</u> designed to pull students together. Rather, they often push students apart. Schools in our current educational paradigm are set up to help students identify themselves as superior (or inferior) to other students. Our grading systems, honor rolls, top ten lists, even the competitions that many teachers use in class to make learning "fun," produce winners and losers. They promote feelings in students that say "I am better than you. I am smarter than you. I am a winner." The leap is not too great then from "I got better grades/I won the competition/I am smarter than you," to "You are dumb/You are stupid/You are a loser."

There is a terrible irony at work in our schools today. School boards, school administrators, and teachers all decry the scourge of bullying, yet the very schools where we send our children provide a fertile ground for bullying to thrive. It is within our schools that many students become shunned and isolated. It is within our schools that some children feel the need to demonstrate their superiority over others. And bullying is just a crude way for one student to tell another that they are superior, better in some way than the person they are bullying. Heaven forbid that some students are a little quirky or "different." They don't stand a chance in our existing school cultures. Absent structures and operational procedures that promote acceptance in <u>every </u>class <u>every</u> day, such students are quickly ostracized, too often with painful, even tragic, results. Once the bullying snowball starts rolling downhill it can easily morph into "I am a better person than you (I am superior), you are ugly, you are weak, you are worthless, we hate you, you don't deserve to be alive." Is there any chance that our traditional schools have helped produce those lonely, disaffected, angry young people who snap and vent their anger on those around them and on themselves? I think maybe so. Do our existing schools promote a sense of teamwork and family? Not really.

For you to understand House I need to first explain some basic structures of a CP school. Students first encounter the CP in their schooling in either 5th or 7th grade. For the purpose of this narrative, I arbitrarily choose a grade 7-12 CP school. In a CP school the basic instructional unit is a Learning Community. A 7th grade Learning Community (LC) is made up of the following:

- Between 96 and 104 7th grade students
- Five full-time core academic teachers,
- Three full-time special area teachers who are shared with another Learning Community
- One half-time teacher
- Special Education teachers, teaching assistants, and teaching aides, as needed.

The 100 students in the Learning Community are divided up into eight Houses, each with 12 or 13 students. Each House is assigned a Housemaster (one of the students' teachers) and a House Steward (a member of the community – more about them later). Each House meets early in the school day for 40 to 45 minutes and then at the end of the day for another 10 minutes. The 12 or 13 students in each House *remain with the same Housemaster for two years* – through 7th and 8th grades (think stability. FT #1).

The Housemaster (HM)

The Housemaster is *totally responsible* for the academic success and social development of every student in her House for *two years.* This is true of HMs at every grade level. The role of the HM is part salesman, part facilitator, part cheerleader, part teacher/coach, part counselor, and part student advocate.

The job of HM is challenging (and rewarding) at any level, but it is most difficult in 7th grade (or whichever grade that students first experience the CP and House concepts). When a new group of students enters a CP school for the first time, they are a blank slate. Students accustomed to functioning as discrete educational units, concerned only about their own individual success, find themselves immersed in a new and different school culture. Everything about the CP is new to them.

On Day 1, a 7th grade Housemaster starts selling the students in her House on the CP culture and the philosophy of "I succeed when we succeed." *Belong, Believe, Work Hard, Succeed,* becomes the mantra of each House. The HM repeatedly voices the expectation that each person in the House will succeed with the help of everyone else. A sense of common purpose is promoted while emphasizing that, unlike in sports, every individual and every team (House) can succeed and win. Success in the CP is not a zero-sum game.

But putting the same twelve students together in a room for 19260 minutes over two years does *not* guarantee that these students will develop a sense of belonging with each other. Nor will you get a group of young people to truly feel that they are a part of a team (family) by standing in front of them and preaching about the importance of being a team. The sense of team and family is created <u>through shared experience</u>. Shared experience is the glue that connects members of any group. And it is the Housemaster who serves as the grand "conductor" of all activities in House, all shared experiences, that over time lead to the development of a sense of belonging.

Shared experience takes many forms in House. Students share social experiences, service opportunities, and a variety of other activities designed to bond House members together. These types of experiences are enumerated later in this chapter. But the shared experiences at the core of House revolve around the common purpose of academic success.

Common Purpose: Grade Reporting Structures in the CP

When students first enter a CP school, they are accustomed to the "every man for himself," individualistic nature of the traditional educational paradigm. The concept of a common academic purpose is foreign to them. To embrace the CP culture students must be given a compelling reason to work together and help (or get help from) their fellow students. What drives collaborative efforts between housemates and classmates in the CP is a significant change in the grading and academic recognition systems.

In the CP, teachers calculate individual numerical grades for all students as they do in traditional schools. Teachers evaluate student work (quizzes, tests, essays, lab reports, projects, etc.), assign a grade, and provide feedback so that students can improve. Grades are then entered into a computer grading program. At the end of a marking period grading software takes these individual grades and generates report cards for each student. These report cards include the individual student's average in each course, *the student's House average in each course* (a combined average of all 12 or 13 students in the student's House), and *the entire Learning Community's average in each course* (a combined average of all 100 students in the LC).

When the computer generates a student report card it looks something like this.

Course	Individual Grade	House Grade	LC Grade
Algebra	93	76	82
Biology	95	83	80
English	75	80	84
History	78	88	80
Spanish	83	82	81

In the traditional educational paradigm, a student would only receive the grades in the first column. Questions between students would sound something like, "How did *you* do in Spanish?" or "What did *you* get in Math." A student might say to himself, "I'm doing well in Algebra and Biology, and fairly well in Spanish, but if I ever expect to make the Honor Roll, I'm going to have to work on my English and History grades." That is about all the information the student could glean from the individual grades.

In a CP school, much more information is communicated to a student by adding House and Learning Community averages to the student's individual grade report. The conversation changes. New questions between House members sound more like, "How did *we* do in Math? How does *our* grade in science compare to the LC's grade?" The students' focus expands from the individual to the individual *and the group*. With the additional information (House and LC grades), and with the help and guidance of his Housemaster, a student might reach the following conclusions:

"*My House* is really struggling in Math. If *we* can get *our House Algebra grade* up to 80, *we* will be on the *House Honor Roll*. I should help some *other students* in Algebra during House to pull up *our House average*. Biology is my best subject. I could definitely help *other students* in *my House* in Bio. English is my worst subject, and *our House grade* is below the LC average and right on the borderline for qualifying for House Honor Roll. *We* are all going to have to *help each other* improve *our English grades*. *My House* is "kicking ass" in History, but not me. I shouldn't have any trouble finding someone in House to help me improve my History average." (The *italics* in the two previous paragraphs highlight the shift in student thinking from the self to the group.)

Consider a second student with the following report card. This individual would come to very different conclusions when he looked at his individual, House, and LC grades.

Course	Individual Grade	House Grade	LC Grade
Algebra	66	76	82
Biology	72	83	80
English	80	80	84
History	74	88	80
Spanish	81	82	81

He might say to himself, "I am holding my own in English and Spanish, which are my best subjects. I could maybe help someone out in those subjects. But I am struggling bigtime in Algebra. Our House Algebra grade is keeping our House off the House Honor roll and my grade is part of the problem. I need to get some help and pull up my grade in Algebra. And I need to work on my Bio and History grades as well. Those are our House's best subjects, so I shouldn't have any trouble finding someone to work with me."

These mature and appropriate interpretations of students' individual, House, and LC grades are only possible against the backdrop of the CP culture (belong, believe, work hard, succeed) and philosophy (I succeed when we succeed) that is constantly reinforced with students in all classes and House periods. It is linked to academic recognition systems and goal setting practices unique to the CP.

Academic Recognition in the CP

Virtually every school has some form of academic recognition program that acknowledges individual student achievement. These programs usually take the form of an Honor Roll which may or may not be broken down into multiple levels – honors, high honors, principal's list, etc. At the end of a marking period when reports cards come out student averages are calculated. Based on these averages, some students are placed on the Honor Roll.

In the CP, in addition to individual recognition, Houses are also recognized for academic achievement. Criteria for House Honors are set school-wide and, when these criteria are met, Houses are placed on the appropriate House Honor Roll (House Honors, High Honors, and Principal's List). Similarly, an entire Learning Community can be recognized for academic achievement.

House Honor Roll recognition can be broken down by subject. For example, a House can earn Math Honors or Math High Honors, for its performance in Math during a marking period. Such a recognition system would permit a House that was particularly strong in Math/Science (or English/Social Studies) to be recognized with Honors even if the overall House academic average was not high enough to qualify for general Honors.

The addition of House and House Honor Roll to students' school experience does not denigrate the value of individual effort and accomplishment. Students and teachers can and should be recognized for their individual accomplishments along with the accomplishments of their teams. Having a House Honor Roll does not preclude schools from continuing with Honor Rolls and other forms of individual academic recognition for students. Both types of recognition can and should exist side by side.

Goal Setting

The establishment of individual and group goals is an important part of the CP. Having clear goals, both short and long range, helps teachers and students to focus their efforts. Goals also provide Housemasters with a vehicle to help motivate students and, when goals are achieved, the opportunity to celebrate group accomplishments.

Having an academic recognition system like the one described above helps students set realistic and meaningful academic goals. Students in a new 7th grade House, along with their Housemaster, may agree that a realistic yet challenging House goal for the first marking period of a school year might be to make the House Honor Roll in one subject (not specified). Subsequent marking period goals could be more specific as a House identifies its strengths and weaknesses. Once group goals are identified and posted the HM helps students maintain a constant focus on the realization of those goals. The achievement of the group goals becomes a central common purpose in House life. The HM's task of keeping her students motivated is made easier by the presence of goals.

In addition to long range marking period goals, HMs can also work with their students to establish short-range goals. A House may decide to set a goal of achieving a specific grade average on an upcoming assignment or test. The flexibility of CP grading software makes it easy for the HM to quickly determine if a short-range goal has been met. In addition to determining an end-of-marking-period average for a House in each subject, the grading software can instantly calculate House averages for any test, paper, lab report, or other assignment once grades are entered into the computer. For example, after a science teacher gives a test and enters student grades, all Housemasters can look in the computer to see how well their House performed on the test. Success or failure in reaching a short-range goal can be assessed instantaneously.

Such instant feedback not only helps evaluate goals, but it also allows HMs to track how well their House is doing on all their assignments, quizzes, and tests across all subject areas. Which brings us to what shared academic experiences look like in House.

Shared Academic Experience

No student is ever abandoned in a CP House. Students who might otherwise founder in the old "every man for himself" paradigm know that they have a support system of fellow students and teachers who will help them to achieve individual and group goals. They know they will not be made fun of or mocked out for struggling in a subject. Students can be confident that they will find encouragement and active assistance from everyone in their House. Maybe.

I say "maybe" because anyone who has ever taught middle school knows that it would be crazy to assume that students have even the slightest idea how to assist another student who is struggling ("helping" does not mean doing someone's work for them). Students at just about any level are clueless as to how to actively assist their classmates. *If we want students to help each other on their academics in House, if we want them to work together to achieve individual and group academic goals, we must show them how.* This is where the HM steps into her role as teacher/coach. In CP training all HMs learn strategies which can transform their students from "have no clue how to help" zombies into competent peer tutors and cooperative learners, ready and willing to help their fellow students while also growing academically themselves.

Here is how this can play out in a House. A Housemaster (not the Math teacher) knows from regular interactions with fellow teachers in her Learning Community (see *Chapter 13, Growing Outstanding, Highly Effective Teachers*) and from looking at grading program output that the students in her House are struggling in Math. She also learns that they have a test coming up at the end of the week. The teacher shares with the students in her House something like this. "I know that we have been struggling a little bit in math as a group, and that you have a test coming up on Friday. How about we set a short-range goal for the test and then get after it the next three days in House? I'm not a math expert but I will learn alongside you. What do you say?"

After she gets her House to agree and a goal is set, the HM can model new practice strategies that students can use with partners or in small groups. The bulk of House time that week is devoted to Math peer tutoring and practice. More often than not, if a realistic short-range goal is set and if a concerted team effort takes place, the House will achieve its goal. When the goal is achieved, House members should celebrate along with the HM. Visual reminders of all achieved goals can be placed on House walls.

The ramifications of achieving a modest goal on a math test extend far beyond a small celebration. Recall the upward spiral I described earlier in Chapter 3 – FT #10. Students need to experience some level of success if they are to develop a little confidence, confidence which then leads to greater effort and even more success. There is no question that students reap benefits when they experience *individual* success. *But these benefits are magnified many times over when students know that they made a meaningful contribution to group success.* What runs through the minds of students when they contribute to group success? It is something like this. "_We_ did it! _We_ put ourselves out there and *we* kicked ass. _We_ reached our goal. Man, _we_ can do anything _we_ set our minds to." These are powerful, positive emotions that we almost never see in our classrooms. You might see them on the athletic field when a team succeeds, or at the end of a school drama production or concert, but in the classroom? No. And that is a terrible loss that needs to be corrected.

You may be concerned that the members of a House will have their spirits crushed if a goal is not reached. Not to worry. Failing to reach a short-term goal can be a valuable opportunity for growth. If a House misses a short-term goal, a skilled HM should conduct an honest debrief with her students. She should validate the House's strong effort (if it was) and discuss with House members what they could do differently next time to achieve their goal – without resorting to finger pointing. Above all, the HM needs to be honest in her assessment of her own efforts and the students' efforts, even if it means saying, "You know, I think we all could have worked a little harder, myself included." It is important that the HM emphasizes that _all_ House members need to shoulder personal responsibility for both team success _and_ team failure.

Coordinating and facilitating the academic experiences in House as a teacher/coach is a critical role of the Housemaster. But there is much more.

Skeptical Sidebar: Uncomfortable with the "I succeed when we succeed" philosophy?

Are you a little uncomfortable with the whole concept of "I succeed when we succeed? Does it not sit quite right in your mind? Does the idea of your child having to spend time and energy helping other students in his/her House leave you feeling a little "off?" If you feel that way you are not alone. Let me try to help you work through your discomfort.

Believe it or not, when your intelligent, high achieving child helps other students in her House _she benefits as much or more than the person she is helping._ In education we have something called the learning pyramid. This pyramid, which is based on solid research, shows the percentage of material that will be retained in the brain when that material is encountered and processed in different ways. Turns out that we retain only about 10% of what we read and 30% of what we see demonstrated. But we retain 75% of what we practice by doing and (wait for it), 90% of what we teach to others. So, when your child is working with another student as a peer tutor, she is cementing the required subject matter into her own brain more strongly than if she had studied and practiced alone. This is the reason why all students in a CP school will be taught peer tutoring strategies and encouraged to use them to help others (yes, even those students you might not think worthy of being a tutor). _When students work together and lift each other up to reach shared goals, everyone benefits._

Other Shared Experiences

If all shared experiences in House revolved around academics, House would be a very boring place indeed. House, especially morning House, should be a time of day that students enjoy. We want students to look forward to coming to school and being an active participant in all school activities. To that end, the HM must make House a special time by occasionally planning and conducting other, non-academic experiences that tap into the Fab Four: _Fun, Food, Friends, and Feeling Good._ Some activities need to have elements of fun. Other activities need to include a food element. All activities need to include friends. And some activities need to make students feel good about themselves (e.g., performing service or working side-by-side on a non-academic project with classmates and receiving some praise/recognition when it is completed.).

It is beyond the scope of this book to describe in detail all the possible activities that can be included as part of a quality House program. This is due, in large part, to the fact that the number and types of activities available are limited only by the imagination, creativity, and the resourcefulness of the Housemaster _and her students_, and by the imagination, creativity, and resourcefulness of the HMs and students in all the other Houses in a Learning Community (Houses share!). In other words, the number and kinds of activities that can take place in House are essentially limitless.

There is nothing I enjoy more than recalling great shared fun experiences I had with groups of students, except maybe brainstorming more new ideas for positive shared experiences. Perhaps someday in the future I will write another book that is exclusively about House where I can spend pages and pages describing scores of House activities. Better yet, maybe you will write that book after you and your coworkers spend a few years working in a CP school.

In the meantime, to whet your appetite, I will provide you with a bullet list of some non-academic (and marginally academic) activities and events which can be shared as a part of a House program. This will give you a feel for the possibilities. These experiences may or may not become part of any given House, depending upon the likes and dislikes of the members of the House.

Some of the activities I list might become simple daily or weekly House routines. Others could develop into House traditions or rituals that become a part of the very fabric of a House's identity. And still others may be so impactful that they become rites of passage for members of a House at a certain grade level.

Some activities/events will take little or no time to plan and execute. Others will consume a great deal of time. Most activities will take place during the House periods. Others not (like eating lunch together as a House).

If you are concerned about the time needed for any of the following suggested activities/events remember this. It is the job of the HM to find the right balance between different types of activities in House. Academic activities need to be central, but at times they can take a back seat to other, more fun, activities. The team-building benefits of having a House spend 20 to 25 minutes working together to solve a fun, Project Adventure initiative problem would likely outweigh any loss of shared academic experience time. Taking a few extra minutes around a holiday for some special event that will draw the students closer together is, in my mind, a no-brainer. Remember: *"Never be afraid to do great, crazy things."*

Here are some other possible non-academic shared experiences:

- Team building activities such as Project Adventure initiative problems.
- House awards and recognition ceremonies/rituals.
- A weekly or bi-weekly donut morning with the House Steward – a "working breakfast."
- Guest speakers (on virtually any topic) who are formally introduced by students.
- Designing (and then conducting) a welcoming ritual for a new student or new teacher

- A monthly "Service Day" when the House performs community service
- Sharing a weekly or bi-weekly school lunch meal in House
- Fun, non-academic competitions and challenges with other Houses.
- College and career search: Students research possible future career choices and colleges they may want to attend and present in House (or to another House as a guest)
- Establishing a "moving up" or "pass the torch" tradition for when the House moves on to the next grade.
- Spring Field Days competition where all Houses (including the HMs) compete for the honor of having their name engraved on the House Trophy which is then displayed in the winning House for the next year.
- House outings on weekends
- Decorating a designated area in the House classroom seasonally
- Working on a science challenge together (e.g. bridge building)
- Writing and performing skits.
- Have students design a House logo and/or write a House song.
- Working on the House record or other activities related to the House identity (see below).
- Students conduct a "get to know you" interview with the House Steward, the Master Teacher, principal, school counselor, or others in the school community.
- Write pen-pal letters to students at the elementary school.
- Students teach a skill they have to the House (or a guest House).
- Go on an outdoor education field trip and camp overnight in tents (yes, I know this one is "over-the-top," but I did this at two different schools with 7th graders and it was fantastic, socially *and* academically!).
- Conduct a mini-debate on some topic of interest.
- Have occasional "music mornings" where students can listen to music while they work in House.
- Have students buddy up with elementary students as readers or tutors.

- Group problem solving/brain teasers. Short, mental exercises that students can work together to try and solve.
- Current events/news presentations. Pairs of students take turns summarizing the week's news in presentations to the House.
- School calendar update. Pairs of students share all the events taking place in school during the coming week, including sports events, club meetings, etc.

Some of the activities listed above that are designed to take place during the school day would take more than the 40 minutes available in morning House. These activities, if judged to be important, should be green lighted, even if they take up to 80 minutes. In middle school and high school schedules it is relatively easy to "borrow" a few minutes from each period of the day to create a longer period for a valuable monthly assembly or other event. It happens all the time.

Students come and students go.

One shared experience – developing a welcoming ritual – is particularly important. One of the goals of the House program is to provide students with a degree of stability that may be lacking in their home life. Stability is important to young students. But families move. Students come and go in schools. And transitioning to a new school with all new teachers, new schedules, and new classmates can be traumatic, especially for middle school students changing schools in the middle of the year. Houses can mitigate the impact of a mid-year change of schools by developing a ritual that immediately makes new students feel welcomed and valued. Instead of feeling like a stranger or uninvited intruder, new students are accepted as a valuable addition to the Learning Community and to House.

Ten Minute end-of-the-day House Period

The end of the school day at a middle school (or high school) is bedlam, total chaos. When the last bell of the day rings, students blast out of their last class and hurry to their lockers, ecstatic that the school day is over. Lots of social interactions with peers take place along the way. At their lockers, questions fly back and forth as students try to re-call and/or find out what, if any, homework they have and what books, notebooks, or other resources they need to complete the homework. "Do we have any Math? When is our Science Lab due? Did Ms. Johnson say we are having a quiz in History tomorrow? Oh God, where is that permission slip I was supposed to have signed for the field trip?"

Books, notebooks, papers, and clothing are stuffed into or feverishly grabbed from lockers. Locker doors crash closed by the score while others are frantically reopened to retrieve forgotten items. All of this is done under an exaggerated sense of time pressure as students, in seeming desperation, hurry to get to their buses, sports practices, or other after school activities. Madhouse is not too strong a term to describe this time of day in middle schools and high schools.

This frenetic and disorganized end of the school day creates a great deal of stress in students which can ultimately set a negative tone for the next day. Middle school students, who by their very nature are some of the most disorganized living creatures on the planet, often arrive home either not knowing what assignments they have for the next day or not having the materials they need to complete their assignments, or both. If some social media communication does not rectify the situation, for-getful/disorganized students may arrive at school the next day with-out completed assignments or ill-prepared for a test or quiz, a major stressor (how many of you have had classic stress dreams about arriving in a class only to discover you must take a test that you knew nothing about?). Faced with these situations, students have decisions to make, and they sometimes make poor decisions (like copying assignments or cheating) that make the situation worse. Just reading my own descrip-tion of the end of the school day raises my blood pressure. There must be a better way, and there is.

In a CP school, students return to their House for a brief, but impor-tant, 10-minute period at the end of the school day. This end of the day ten-minute House period provides a calm, organized end to the school day. Students go directly to House from their last period class. They do not stop at their lockers. The Housemaster briefly summarizes the day's events and perhaps offers some praise or encouragement for jobs well done. She emphasizes what students need to do to be prepared for classes and House the next day.

Student helpers post any assignments in each subject, including upcoming quizzes, tests, and project due dates, so that students can check to make sure that homework assignments are written in their agendas. This can be done in low-tech (white boards and hardcopy agendas) or high-tech fashion (electronic posting and student cell phone agendas). Students identify what materials they need to complete their homework and are organized and prepared for when they head off to their lockers. The Housemaster's parting words may reflect her role as cheerleader, encouraging her students to stay focused on House goals.

This ten-minute long House period at the end of the day is the school day equivalent of closure at the end of a lesson. Good teachers know that quality lessons have some form of closure at the end which reinforces or summarizes what students were learning during the class. Closure also sets the stage for what will take place in class the next day. In the same way each ten-minute end of day House period forms a calm and organized bridge between two consecutive school days, ensuring that students will be better prepared and more motivated to learn when they return to school the next day.

House Stewards

Schools may physically exist within a community, but they are often no more connected to the community than water is to the glass that holds it. Community members are asked to vote on school budgets, but often know little or nothing about what takes place in the schools they are being asked to support. And it is fairly safe to assume that students and teachers go about their business having no idea whether or not community members really care about what is being accomplished in school.

This lack of community connection to schools is problematic for both schools and the communities they serve. Community connections have the potential to make a _huge_ positive difference in the overall success of students and teachers. At the same time, communities can reap many benefits, both short and long term, from a close association with their schools. In CP schools, close community connections are maintained through the presence of **House Stewards.**

Recall that when a new Learning Community is formed in a CP school at the start of 7th (or 5th) grade, the students are divided up into eight new Houses. Each of these Houses has a teacher serving as the Housemaster for 12 or 13 students. In addition, *a person, or persons (ideally two or three persons) from the community are linked to each House and serve in the role of* **House Steward.**

House Stewards are asked to make a voluntary six-year commitment to the students in a House, beginning in 7th grade and carrying through to high school graduation. This commitment is not as overwhelming as it first appears, for two reasons. First, the actual time commitment of a House Steward is minimal; ten to twenty minutes with the House every other week and a longer visit a few times each year for special events. And second, House Stewards are encouraged to sign on as pairs or trios. If two co-workers from a local business serve together as House Stewards for one House, they can alternate visits to the House if necessary. Having two or three individuals sharing the role of House Steward also lessens the likelihood that a House will ever feel abandoned if one of two House Stewards cannot show up at a special event for some reason.

House Steward Expectations

What exactly does the volunteer job of House Steward entail? When an individual (or individuals) sign up to serve as a House Steward they are asked to make a commitment to meeting the following expectations.

As the House Steward of Murphy House you can expect that I will:

- Participate in a 90-minute orientation/training session prior to the start of my first year as a House Steward.
- Stop in, show interest, and connect with the students in my House at least twice each month for 10 or 20 minutes.
- Stay in touch with my Housemaster regarding possible participation in future House events.

- Whenever possible, be present during special House events, e.g.
  - » Working side-by-side with students on a community service project
  - » Assisting at an awards ceremony
  - » Participating in spring Field Days.
- Demonstrate to students via words and actions that
  - » I care about the students unconditionally, and about their future.
  - » I believe the students are an important part of the community's future.
- Be a solid role model for the students in my House.
- Share a little bit about myself, my history, and my career, including why I decided to become a House Steward.
- Be a resource for students, teachers, and the school at-large.
- Occasionally (a few times a year – no specific timetable) do something special for my House. I understand that it can be a surprise for students, but it must be cleared with my Housemaster in advance.
- Communicate with other members of the community regarding my experience as a House Steward. (Talk it up!)

Why House Stewards?

Virtually everyone in the greater school community benefits in some way from the presence and involvement of House Stewards. Teachers and Housemasters benefit. School counselors and administrators benefit. The community benefits. Even the House Stewards themselves benefit. But, without question, students are the most direct and significant beneficiaries of the presence of House Stewards.

The primary benefit to students comes from the presence of yet another caring adult in their lives, someone willing to give of their time (and sometimes treasure) to help students succeed. The message sent to students by House Stewards is in some ways even more powerful than the one sent by Housemasters. Housemasters are on the staff of the school district. It is their job to teach and to serve as a Housemaster. They get paid. House Stewards, on the other hand, inexplicably agree to voluntarily provide support and encouragement to students they initially do not know _for six years._ They receive no compensation other than the good feelings that come from making a difference in the lives of young people. For some students (like the young woman quoted later in this chapter) the caring message delivered loud and clear through the regular presence of the House Steward can be life changing, even lifesaving.

The House Steward also sends the message to students that they (the students) are an important part of the community. _They belong!_ Stewards make it clear that the future of their shared community is intimately linked to the success of every student and the contributions they will make down the road. The community needs the students' best efforts in whatever careers they choose to pursue.

It may be difficult for you to grasp the strength and importance of this message. To young adults, knowing that the community values them and is willing to support and encourage them gives them a reason to work hard and persevere in their studies. Recall this fundamental truth; _Students rise to the top and put forth the greatest effort to succeed when they have a higher purpose that is outside and beyond that which they want to achieve for themselves._ A strong sense of connection to the community can provide students with that higher purpose. And who better to convince students of the value of their contributions to the future of the community than individuals from that very community, especially ones who graduated from the same high school?

The other major beneficiary of a strong House Steward program is the community at large. I spend an entire chapter later in this book describing what I call "additional beneficial outcomes" associated with the adoption of the CP in schools within a school district. Not wanting to steal the thunder of Chapter 20, for now let's just state the obvious. The existence of a CP culture, of which Housemasters and House Stewards are an integral part, can significantly increase the number of successful, community connected, students graduating from high school. If a district's schools can produce nearly 100% successful students with a strong connection to the community, those successful students will be much more likely to return when they finish their education as solid, involved citizens to live, work, start families, buy homes, shop, and pay taxes. All good things for a community, yes?

So, if at some point in the future you consider becoming a House Steward in a CP school, recognize that as a House Steward you would be a community's best, low-cost, long-term investment in the future.

The numbers. How many House Stewards will we need going forward?

The number of House Stewards needed in an entire school (or school district) might at first seem overwhelming. A grade 7-12 junior/senior high school with 600 students (100 at each grade level) would have 48 Houses. That translates into between 48 and 96 House Stewards, depending upon the number of singles and pairs that are recruited. A tall order if you needed to find them all at once. But schools do not jump into the CP and the House system all at once. As you will learn in Part III, Making it Happen, schools grow into the CP slowly, adding one grade each year, starting with 7th grade. In the first year of implementation eight House Stewards are needed, one for each 7th grade House. The next year those House Stewards move on with their House into 8th grade. Eight new House Stewards are then needed for the incoming 7th grade. The third year all the House Stewards move on with their Houses and yet another eight House Stewards must be recruited for the next 7th grade. A school this size never needs to recruit more than eight House Stewards (or eight House Steward pairs) in a given year.

Sources of House Stewards. Where are we going to find them?

Finding eight individuals, pairs, or trios to serve as House Stewards is not difficult if the "job" is sold correctly to the right people in the right places. In any community the pool of potential candidates is vast. School alumni are ideal targets since the role of House Steward can be sold to alumni as a way to give back to their alma mater. But any individual who is reasonably successful, and who can be a good role model for students, can serve as a House Steward. Potential sources of House Stewards include:

- School alumni
- Retired teachers and administrators from the school (and retirees in general)
- Successful local businesses (owners or workers)
- Local churches and church organizations
- Fraternal organizations
- Police benevolent associations
- Local unions of all types (trades and professional).
- Local clubs
- Parents and relatives of students currently in school (including retired grandparents of students who likely have more time to volunteer). Think of the old "room mother" concept in elementary schools, except that House Steward volunteers can have a much greater impact than baking cupcakes for student birthdays (although they can do that if they want to as well).

House Steward Training and Guidelines.

Potential House Stewards must complete an application with references and then interview with the Housemaster and Master Teacher (or her designee). Once selected, House Stewards do their "job" under strict guidelines. In the 90-minute orientation/training I mentioned earlier, House Stewards learn their boundaries. They learn that their contact with students is restricted to the school under the supervision of the Housemaster who must always be present. They learn that contacts through email, text, or social media are not permitted. And they learn what they may, and may not, discuss with students. House Stewards are required to report to the Housemaster whenever a student raises any subject or issue that is outside the guidelines for House Steward – student contact. In addition, House Stewards are made aware of their obligation to report to the Housemaster any information about a student or students that might impact their health and/or safety.

House Identity

As students in a House accumulate some shared experiences the group begins to develop its own unique identity. While there is no absolute best time to start the process of establishing a formal House identity, students invariably want to name their House relatively early in the school year. Under the guidance of their Housemasters the students can research possible names. It is important to remind students that they will be carrying their House name forward for six years, so deciding upon a name that carries some significance is important. Students may request to use a House Steward's last name to honor his or her commitment to the House, or they may choose the name of a national or local historical figure.

In addition to a House name, students may want to identify or create a House crest, logo, symbol, motto, slogan, song, or mascot. Houses can get matching tee shirts to wear at House competitions or other special events (sometimes supplied by a generous House Steward). As a House accumulates more shared experiences, they may choose to create a House scrapbook, journal, notebook, or other record of their experiences. This record can include photographs, written entries, profiles of the HS, HM, and individual students, and mementos from events throughout the year.

A House record serves many purposes. It can solidify the sense of belonging and family within the House. It serves as a source of pride to be shared with guests and visitors. It preserves memories which become a part of the House identity. It can ease the transition of a new member of the House by helping them to learn about the House and House members. It helps House members see their growth and development as individuals and as a group. It is a future source of nostalgia and laughter (e.g., at graduation). And it is an historical record for House (and school) alumni to tap in the future.

A strong House identity dovetails with a Housemaster's efforts to have students develop a sense of _group_ pride in their accomplishments. "_Our_ House has been on the House Honor Roll for three straight marking periods." Students can take special pride in their collective skill in a subject area. "In Murphy House _we_ are the best at Science!" And most importantly, a strong House identity ensures that nobody in the House will slip through the cracks, academically or otherwise. "In Murphy

House _we_ look out for each other." The development of a House identity helps shift students' focus from being all about "me and my success" to "my success as a part of _our_ success."

The Housemaster as Student Advocate, Coach, and Counselor

"It is very easy to make all the right decisions when you have had even one person rooting for you all your life. In my case, it was clear to me that nobody gave a damn about my siblings and me."

This was written by an anonymous young woman in a letter to the editor as she reflected on some of the poor life choices she made as a teen. Her words speak to how desperately she wanted someone, anyone, to care about her at a critical point in her life. That is often all that it takes. One person. One person, a little time every day, some encouraging and supportive words and actions, and you change a young person's life forever.

Most people know at least one inspiring story about a young person who escaped a challenging or seemingly hopeless life situation and turned her life around through a connection made with a teacher, coach, or school counselor who cared enough to make a difference. Politicians love to cite examples of turnaround success stories when trumpeting their education agendas. Hollywood makes movies about these stories. You may have your own story of a connection you made with a teacher that changed your life for the better.

Unfortunately, these life-changing/lifesaving "connections" that sometimes occur between students and caring adults are entirely random events. They are "hit or miss." They happen all too infrequently. A typical high school teacher will see 120 to 180 or more students in a day. Students are shuttled in and out of classrooms for 40 to 45-minute classes in groups of 20 to 30 (or more). This is hardly a prescription for making life-changing connections with kids. Even the most caring educators can only get a small peek into the lives of their students. Most of our students travel through their school lives in relative anonymity.

For every kid lucky enough to make a random, life-changing connection with a significant caring adult there are scores – if not hundreds – of other students who are not as fortunate. We _know_ the value of these connections. Teachers know. Parents know. School administrators know. School boards know. And yet we don't promote these connections. _Within the traditional educational paradigm, structures that foster these relationships simply do not exist._

"Wait!" you say. "Isn't that the job of school counselors, to make connections with students? Aren't school counseling offices set up to promote connections with students?" The answer to both questions is yes. But consider the following opening paragraph from an article titled _"The Troubling Student-to-Counselor Ratio That Doesn't Add Up"_ published in Education Week in August 2018.

> _"Nationwide, public school counselors are overworked and under-resourced. The average student-to-school counselor ratio is 482-to-1, nearly double the 250-to-1 ratio recommended by the American School Counselor Association. In fact, only three states—New Hampshire, Vermont, and Wyoming—have statewide averages that fall at or below the recommended ratio."_

Take a moment to wrap your head around these numbers. The nationwide _average_ student-to-school counselor ratio is 482 to 1. I hope that strikes you as insane. An average of 482 means that around half of all school counselors are assigned to _more_ than 482 students. Even the "recommended ratio" of 250 to 1 is disturbing.

The article goes on to state that, _"Many school counselors do their best, but . . . the fact is that even the most dedicated, high-quality professionals can't give every student the necessary attention when juggling an unmanageable workload."_

It does not take a degree in education or counseling to recognize that it is impossible for school counselors to provide students with the support they need given counselors' workloads. Even the most outstanding school counselors (and I have worked with many) fall short when trying to meet the needs of all the students in their charge. The reality is that many students fall through the cracks, some very large cracks, because of counselors' absurd caseloads.

Earlier I stated that at some point(s) in their middle school and high school careers students will feel like giving up (FT #12). Recall that adolescence is an incredibly difficult time for even the most well-adjusted students. So, what happens when students experience difficulties with friends, or at home, or with their studies? What happens when they feel like "throwing in the towel?"

Each student's situation is unique. Some students have families that provide the support they need to hang in there. Others develop positive peer relationships in which each party provides the other with strength and resolve. Still other students may tap into mentors at church or in the community. But sadly, many students, including some of our most needy students, have few if any external resources that can provide them with support, or they fail to tap into available resources for whatever reasons. The result is they give up; on school, on family, on friends, on themselves, on life. And the consequences of giving up often produce a collage of poor life choices. Not a pretty picture.

Enter the House System. In the CP, vital connections between students and caring adults are not left to chance. The roles of Housemaster and House Steward are specifically _designed_ to fill the massive cracks in the existing school paradigm. With a "caseload" of only 12 or 13 students, and with 371 non-classroom contact hours over two years, Housemasters know the students in their Houses better than anyone in the school. HMs are required to make one visit to the home of each student in their House each year, a manageable expectation for one HM with a dozen students' homes to visit. HMs are also required to make at least one contact with students' parents each month by phone or email. As a result, HMs also know their students' home situations better than anyone in the school.

When students have academic issues or issues with another teacher, with peers, or at home, the students know they can approach their HM for help and guidance. Students know that they do not have to compete with hundreds of other students for their HM's time.

Housemasters advocate for and assist their students when other teachers have concerns about them (either academically or social-emotionally). They are other teachers' first point of contact when they perceive that a student is struggling in some way.

House provides a stable and reliable vehicle for students to develop the strength, resolve, determination, and confidence they need to grow into healthy and productive young adults. In House, students have a built-in support system of 11 or 12 peers who are there every day to encourage them, support them and "pick them up" when they falter.

Students also have their Housemaster who refuses to let them give up. HMs are trained to be good, reflective listeners who know their limits. They are _not_ expected to be formal counselors or therapists. They can help students to resolve some issues and identify other more serious problems that need to be referred to the school counselor or mental health professionals. The bottom line is that the HM is a constant in her students' lives for two full years, a caring adult connection who is always in their corner as coach, cheerleader, advocate, and counselor. Remember, 321 contact hours over two years!

The additions of House and the roles of Housemaster and House Steward take us closer to the kind of schools we all want, **_schools where all students grow, develop, and succeed, in school and in life._** House builds on the fundamental truths that relate to students that I described in Chapter 3. In House students are provided with stability. They experience firsthand the value of team and teamwork. Students set goals, develop a sense of higher purpose, and experience the positive influence of their peers. In House there are adults present who truly care about them and their future. House provides a nurturing and safe environment in which students can learn and grow, one that is devoid of shaming and humiliation. It is there that students experience the initial success that builds their confidence. And in House, students know that if they ever feel like giving up there are caring adults and peers who will provide support and encouragement while refusing to let them fail.

The House System takes 100 individual, independently functioning students and eight teachers and shapes them into eight tightly knit family groups whose members take full responsibility for the success of everyone in the group. It would never occur to members of a House to leave a fellow member "out in the cold."

Major points to take away from *Chapter 9, House*

1. Students in a Learning Community are grouped into Houses, each with 12 to 13 students.
2. Each House is led by a teacher (the Housemaster) who is *totally responsible* for the academic success and social development of every student in her House for *two years.*
3. Each House meets every morning for about 45 minutes and each afternoon for about 10 minutes.
4. In House, students develop a strong sense of belonging through shared experiences, both academic and social.
5. The presence of community members serving as House Stewards helps build bridges between students and the community.
6. House grades and House honor roll recognition give students a shared, higher purpose to work toward.
7. Students provide vital support for other members of their House.

CHAPTER 10

The Resource of Time

"Czarniak is out of his mind. He is completely detached from reality. There is no way that I could do everything he describes in the role of the Housemaster while also effectively performing my duties as a classroom teacher. The things he describes sound great for kids, and I would love to do them, but they just won't happen because my job is already overwhelmingly difficult to do in the time I have to do it."

Anonymous make-believe teacher

THE QUOTE ABOVE is make-believe. But it is what I imagine every dedicated, hard-working teacher would say after reading the previous chapter about House. And rightly so. House and the CP culture cannot survive and thrive in traditional school settings where the critical resource of teacher time is sorely lacking. Time is the whole enchilada.

None of what I described in the last chapter, and none of what I describe in succeeding chapters, will ever come to pass unless we change the environment where we ask teachers to work their magic. We must provide them with more of the all-important resource of time. Where do we find that time?

First, extend the school day by about 45 minutes in CP schools.

We cannot add House periods to students' and teachers' schedules without adding some time to the school day. Failing to extend the school day would necessitate shortening academic periods to an unacceptable length to accommodate House. House is such a critical part of the CP that it warrants the expense of extending the school day.

And second, teaching loads are reduced, and teacher schedules are changed in the CP to give teachers more professional time.

The core instructional unit in a CP school is the *Learning Community*. A *Learning Community* is comprised of approximately 100 students at one grade level and nine teachers (five full-time, one part-time, and three shared). The teachers in the Learning Community constitute a *CP Teaching Unit*. A CP Teaching Unit (CPTU) is comprised of 5 ½ core academic teachers and 3 special area teachers (Art, Music, PE, etc.) who are shared with another Learning Community.

The table below shows how a 7 ½ hour long school day would be structured for the 5 ½ core academic teachers in a CPTU. Please don't be intimidated by this table if you are not an educator. It simply shows the daily teaching loads for each of the core academic teachers in a 7th grade CP Teaching Unit.

Period	Time	Math (Master T)	Math T (Part-time)	Science T	Social Studies T	ELA T	LOTE T
House	7:45-8:26	House	**Student Support**	House	House	House	House
1	8:29-9:10						
2	9:13-9:54			Teach	Teach	Teach	Teach
3	9:57-10:38			Teach		Teach	Teach
4	10:41-11:22		Teach		Teach		
5	11:25-12:06		Teach	Teach		Teach	
6	12:09-12:50	**Lunch**	X	**Lunch**	**Lunch**	**Lunch**	**Lunch**
7	12:53-1:34	Teach	X				Teach
8	1:37-2:18		X		Teach	Teach	Teach
9	2:21-3:02	Teach	X	Teach	Teach		
House	3:05-3:15	House	X	House	House	House	House

ELA = English/Language Arts   LOTE = Languages other than English (e.g. Spanish, French)

Notice that in this CPTU four of the five full-time core academic teachers teach four classes per day (24 or 25 students per class) in addition to their House assignments. This is a significant change from what teachers encounter in traditional school settings where a typical teaching load is six teaching periods of up to 30 (or more) students.

The fifth full-time core academic teacher in the table above (the Math Teacher in this example) teaches only two classes of students. This teacher serves as the Master Teacher, the leader of the CPTU. He or she has many new responsibilities in the CP. Much more about the role of the Master Teacher later.

The part-time core academic teacher teaches the other two classes of students in the discipline taught by the Master Teacher. This part-time teacher must be certified to teach the same discipline as the Master Teacher. In the table above the Math teacher serves as the Master Teacher. However, the Master Teacher and part-time teacher complementing her can be from any discipline, with the other half of the Master Teacher's teaching load picked up by the part-time teacher.

What you likely find shocking when you look carefully at this table is the apparently exorbitant amount of "free time" in each teacher's schedule; six open "free periods" in the Master Teacher's schedule and four open "free periods" in other full-time core academic teachers' schedules. Only one of these non-instructional periods is formally structured to any degree. This period, Unit Planning Time, is used by the entire CPTU for a variety of purposes, all directed toward increasing teacher effectiveness and student success (more on Unit Planning Time coming soon).

If you think the amount of "free time" is excessive you will be even more shocked when you learn that . . .

CPTU teachers are not assigned any additional duties such as study hall, lunch duty, hall monitor, bus duty, etc. during these open "free periods."

When teachers, highly trained and skilled educators, are required to perform these duties their valuable professional time is wasted. This practice is also a tremendous waste of taxpayer dollars since teachers are more highly paid than others who could assume these tasks.

At this point I may be on the verge of losing some of my readers who are principals, superintendents, board of education members, even parents. While teachers among my readers may be cheering in the aisles, other school constituencies are likely outraged, thinking that I am looking to make teachers' jobs "cushy." Nothing could be further from the truth.

CP teachers are provided with more unscheduled _professional time_ (not _"free time"_) because so much _more_ is expected of them in the CP (e.g., serving as Housemasters). Simply put, if we want great teachers in every classroom, we need to provide them with more time to live up to new sets of expectations. Expectations which, you will soon see, extend teacher responsibilities far beyond what is expected in the traditional educational paradigm.

A final note on the resource of time.

Because few people really understand the duties and responsibilities of teachers there is a tendency for members of the public to not feel comfortable unless teachers' daily work schedules are filled to the brim. Taxpayers tend to look askance at teacher "planning periods," considering them to be "free time" and a waste of taxpayer dollars. Even the powers that be in a school district are loathe to insert any more "free time" into a teacher's schedule than the bare minimum to meet contractual obligations. But the real waste of taxpayer dollars is having "busy" teachers with packed schedules who cannot get all their students to achieve at high levels and succeed. When additional professional time is afforded to teachers in the CP, and when their students achieve and succeed at levels previously considered impossible, taxpayer dollars will be seen as well spent.

Major points to take away from _Chapter 10, The Resource of Time_

1. House, the CP culture, and other innovations unique to the CP that positively impact students and teachers will never become a reality unless teachers are provided with additional professional time in their schedules.
2. The school day in CP schools is 45 minutes longer than the school day in schools operating in the traditional educational paradigm.
3. In the CP, teaching loads are reduced, and teacher schedules are modified to provide teachers with additional unencumbered professional time.

CHAPTER 11

Commitment Expectations

NO ONE IS ever required or compelled to work in a CP school. As you read the next several chapters you will come to understand why educational professionals will freely and enthusiastically seek employment in CP schools, knowing full well that such employment requires making serious, formal commitments to their work. Teachers will choose to make commitments to their students, their Master Teacher, and their fellow teachers, because by doing so they will reap all the professional benefits of working in a CP school.

When a teacher enters a CP school, she is not hired to simply teach, for example, 7th grade Mathematics, or 8th grade English. When a teacher is hired or transfers into a CP school, _she commits to working as a contributing member of a collaborative and professional educational team_, the CP Teaching Unit, or CPTU.

The CPTU is charged with teaching and guiding 100 students for two years. Each CPTU is fully responsible for getting _all_ students in the Learning Community to meet the academic standards for their grade

levels at the end of those two years, _regardless of the grade level performance of the students when they begin the two-year cycle_.

A math teacher in a CP middle school will teach all his students 7th
grade math concepts. The next year this teacher will move on with his
students and teach them 8th grade math concepts. From day one of the
7th grade the teacher has two full years (730 days including weekends,
holidays, and summer vacation) to assess his students' skills and then
work with them to bring them all up to grade level. If necessary, the
teacher can recommend remedial work during the summer. The bottom
line is that the teacher, in committing to working as part of a CPTU,
takes on the responsibility for ensuring that all his students succeed
in math. The same is true for teachers at all grade levels in all other
disciplines.

Additionally, and unique to the CP, each teacher in a CPTU is also
responsible for the success of _every_ student in _every_ discipline taught
by members of her teaching unit. Each teacher is, of course, responsible
for her own success, but also for the success of every other teacher in
her teaching unit. To reach these ends, the actions and behaviors of all
CP teachers are governed by specific expectations.

Commitment Expectations

In the CP, expectations are statements of commitment. These "commitment expectations" are traditional expectations turned upside down.
Customarily, expectation statements that you and I might encounter in
our jobs take the form of "I expect that you will . . . [do something]." For
example, in traditional schools a typical statement of expectation from
a principal to a teacher might sound something like this. "I expect that
you will always be on time and prepared for class."

In a CP school, the _teacher_ makes the commitment expectation
statement to his Master Teacher (the direct supervisor of teachers in the
CP). "You can expect that I will always be on time and prepared for
class to get the most out of my instructional time with students."

All the behaviors and actions of a teacher in a CP school are governed by three sets of commitment expectations. One set of commitment expectation statements is made by the teacher to her Master

Teacher. Another set is made by the teacher to her teaching colleagues (Appendix E-2). And a third set is made by each teacher to her students. (Appendix E-1)

On the surface the differences between traditional expectation statements and commitment expectations may seem trivial or inconsequential, simple semantics. They are anything but. Commitment expectations convey informal accountability on teachers. When a teacher makes a commitment expectation statement to his Master Teacher, he then feels a personal obligation to follow through and meet that expectation.

The degree of personal obligation that a teacher feels is even greater when that teacher tells her teaching colleagues what they can expect of her. If a teacher says to her colleagues, "You can expect that I will spend time in a fellow teacher's classroom at least three times a week either team teaching, serving as a teaching assistant, or observing and providing feedback," it is unconscionable that she will fail to follow through. It is one thing to not meet an expectation and disappoint your "boss." It is quite another to drop the ball and let your peers down when they are counting on you.

But the most important and highest level of personal obligation that teachers feel comes when they make commitments to their students. All teachers are asked to make the same general commitment expectation statements to their students (individual teachers can add additional ones if they choose). When a teacher says to her students, "You can expect that I will be available to provide extra help to you whenever you need it," or "You can expect that I will always be fair and consistent in my interactions with you and your classmates," she is saying so much more than the actual words convey. She is also saying that they (the students) and their success is important to her. She is saying that she cares enough about them to put herself on the line. And most of all, she is saying that her students can trust her to be there for them, to do whatever it takes to help them succeed. When a teacher makes commitments to students, she experiences a profound sense of personal obligation to follow through and meet those commitments.

Over the years I learned the power of telling my students exactly what they could expect from me as their teacher. I did this on the first day of school. I also gave my students a written list of these expectations _and_ I asked them to hold me accountable. In other words, I made a commitment to my students. The sense of obligation that I felt to live up to these expectations was a tremendous motivator for me.

In addition to the three sets of commitment expectation statements made by teachers to students, colleagues, and the Master Teacher, there are five other sets of similar statements that govern behavior and actions in the CP. They are as follows:

1. Student commitment expectation statements made to teachers.
2. Student commitment expectation statements made to other students in their House and Learning Community
3. Master Teacher commitment expectation statements made to teachers.
4. Master Teacher commitment expectation statements made to the principal.
5. Principal commitment expectation statements made to the Master Teacher.

This is as good a time as any to explain how teachers and others in the CP are held accountable for meeting their commitment expectations. On scheduled dates, individuals on the receiving end of commitment expectation statements are asked to provide formal written feedback on how well someone is living up to their commitments.

The beauty of all commitment expectations is that they can easily be modified into simple statements. For example, the following commitment expectations come from _Appendix E-1, Teacher Commitment Expectation Statements to Students._

1. You can expect that I will always treat you and all other members of our Learning Community with dignity and respect.
2. You can expect that I will emphasize teamwork in our Learning Community by providing you with regular opportunities to work together with your fellow students.

Modified into simple statements these expectations become the following.

1. ____ Mr. Czarniak always treats me and all other members of our Learning Community with dignity and respect.
2. ____ Mr. Czarniak emphasizes teamwork in our Learning Community by providing me with regular opportunities to work together with other students.

Twice a year, students are asked in a formal survey to anonymously evaluate each statement and indicate their level of agreement or disagreement using the following Likert scale.

1 – Strongly agree
2 – Agree
3 – Neither agree nor disagree (neutral)
4 – Disagree
5 – Strongly disagree

When students' ratings are tabulated (done almost instantaneously with the right technology) teachers get accurate, valuable feedback. With 100 students in a Learning Community attending each teacher's class every day for half a school year (90 days) the results from this type of survey are essentially based upon 9000 student "observations" of the teacher. And you almost never have to question the accuracy/validity of the results because students in grades 7-12, as I previously stated, tend to be brutally honest when given the opportunity to rate their teachers.

Teachers, the Master Teacher, and the principal, also provide feedback to those who made commitments to them by filling out similar feedback surveys. More about these surveys later when I discuss the evaluation models used in the CP.

Major points to take away from *Chapter 11, Commitment Expectations*

1. Teachers are never required or compelled to work in a CP school.
2. When a teacher is hired or transfers into a CP school, _she commits to working as a contributing member of a collaborative and professional educational team_, the CP Teaching Unit, or CPTU.
3. In a CP school individuals provide commitment expectation statements to the people they work closely with, telling them exactly what they can expect during their professional interactions.
4. All individuals in a Learning Community are given the opportunity to provide formal feedback on how well others are meeting their commitment expectations.

CHAPTER 12

The Master Teacher

"To lead people, walk beside them. As for the best leaders, the people do not notice their existence . . . when the best leader's work is done, the people say, 'We did it ourselves.'"

Lao Tsu, Chinese philosopher

"The giant, two-headed, wicked problem that remains unsolved is this. How do we populate all our classrooms with outstanding teachers who will get all their students to achieve and succeed?"

From *Bringing Henry Home*, Chapter 2

I ADMIT THAT I left you hanging at the end of Chapter 2. But now it is time to address the above question and solve this wicked problem that has bedeviled educators for decades.

Recall that a solution to this problem eluded educators and reformers for decades before the Federal government's decision to step in, first in 2001 with No Child Left Behind, and again in 2009 with Race to the Top. Sadly, the authors of <u>No Child Left Behind</u>, feeling frustrated after witnessing years of failed efforts to solve this wicked problem, reverted to the use of a threatening "stick" to try to get what they wanted. The law threatened school districts with negative consequences if they did not demonstrate "annual yearly progress" on student test scores.

The authors of Race to the Top, doubly frustrated after seeing the failure of NCLB, doubled down on the use of "the stick." This time around, however, _teachers_ were identified as the source of the problem. It was teachers who were threatened with dismissal if their rating scores in the new teacher evaluation systems (based in part on student test scores) were considered unsatisfactory. The government essentially said to teachers, "Figure out on your own how to get your students to score better on state tests or you will be fired." This threatening "stick" proved to be no more effective than NCLB's "stick." Now, twenty years after NCLB, and a dozen years and billions of dollars after RttT, the problem remains unsolved.

I do not know what it is about human nature that draws people back to using a threatening "stick" when they get frustrated and cannot get what they want from people, even educational professionals. Seems like there should be better ways to solve our wicked problems, and there are.

Imagine that you have the following problem. You have a large driveway that needs to be cleared with a snowblower. You have someone willing to do the job, but they do not know how to operate your equipment. So, you are stuck. You cannot get your driveway cleared of snow. What do you do? Do you threaten the person willing to do the job with negative consequences and try to coerce them into doing the job well?

I apologize if my questions seem patronizing to you because the answers are so obvious. Of course you do not threaten them. If you want the individual to do the job, and do it well, you "walk with them." You show them how to start the machine, then demonstrate how to operate the machine safely. You let your novice helper try running the machine themselves while you walk along with them, giving them feedback. You may need to occasionally step back in and show them again how to adjust the controls to get the job done well and safely. You continue to provide feedback and walk along with them until you are comfortable that they can do the job on their own. Done!

Now let's break down our educational wicked problem (*How do we populate all our classrooms with outstanding teachers who will get all their students to achieve and succeed?*) in a similar manner.

1. We have a job that needs to be done; getting all students to succeed in school.
2. We have people that we want and need to do the job for us, our teachers.
3. Some of our teachers do not know how, or for some reason are not able, to get the job done and done well (since not all their students are succeeding).
4. Recognizing that, how can we get *all* our teachers to get *all* their students to succeed in school?

The solution to this problem is essentially the same as that of getting your driveway cleared of snow. If teachers do not know how to get all their students to succeed, or if they think they know how but still cannot get their students to succeed for some reason, *then show them how*. Have a highly skilled and successful educator "walk with them." Show teachers what to do. Then let teachers operate on their own and provide feedback to them. And then "walk with them" some more. The solutions are the same, *but to very different degrees.*

Operating a snowblower and teaching are very different tasks. Operating a snowblower is a relatively simple undertaking, but one which still requires some knowledge and practice. Learning the task might require a few trips with a skilled driver walking alongside the novice showing him the ropes and providing feedback to get the new driver to be proficient.

Teaching, on the other hand, is an infinitely more complex task. Getting teachers to master the voluminous skills and strategies of successful teaching is going to require that we "walk with them" (our teachers) a lot longer and a lot farther. One does not master the art and craft of teaching in a year or two while receiving a few bits of coaching from a principal who "walks with them" for two or three teaching periods each year. That is what we do now in the existing educational paradigm.

Having a skilled educator "walk with teachers" for two or three class periods over the course of a school year will not cut it. Nor will two class periods each _month_ be enough. What might work is having a highly skilled and successful educator spend 70 or 80 class periods a year (two per week) in every teacher's classroom, working with the teachers in some capacity, either co-teaching, helping as a teaching assistant, learning with the students, or observing and providing feedback. That amount of "walking with" teachers, over time, would solve the wicked problem of finding an outstanding, highly skilled teacher for every classroom. A teacher who gets _all_ her students to achieve and succeed.

Surely at this point you are convinced that I have lost my mind. The thoughts swirling in the back of your head as it prepares to explode probably sound something like this. "Even if we wanted to have a skilled educator spend 70 or 80 class periods each year with teachers it will just never happen. It is impossible. Principals can barely manage to get into each of their teachers' classrooms two or three times each year, much less 80. No way. Totally bonkers. Nuts. Not worth even thinking about."

But I am here to tell you that it can be done, and it does not need to cost a fortune. We simply need to think about education _differently_. We need to think beyond the traditional educational paradigm where the principal is the sole individual deemed worthy and capable of "walking with" her teachers. We need a new paradigm. And in this new educational paradigm, the "wicked problem" of how to populate all our classrooms with outstanding, highly effective teachers who will get all their students to achieve and succeed can be solved. Enter a new entity in our schools, that of the Master Teacher (MT).

The Master Teacher

Master Teachers are highly skilled and successful classroom teachers who possess strong sets of both educational and interpersonal skills and attributes. The Master Teacher (MT) serves as the leader of a Learning Community (LC) composed of eight teachers (three shared and one part time) and about 100 students. In her role the MT leads more from within than from above. She teaches two periods each day, daily meets with the entire CP Teaching Unit (CPTU) during a unit planning period, and spends two periods each day in another teacher's classroom serving in some capacity.

The MT is responsible for the overall success of all the teachers and students in her LC over a period of two years. She must grow and develop all the teachers in her charge into outstanding, highly effective classroom instructors who work collaboratively to get all students to succeed.

The MT is also the conductor, the master of ceremonies, the overall coordinator of all activities taking place within the LC. At every juncture she reminds her colleagues that in their roles as teachers and Housemasters everything they do, everything they say, and every decision they make, must always be linked to doing what is best for kids. Their collective responsibility, along with the MT, is the success of every child.

Specific responsibilities of the MT include the following.

1. The CP philosophy and culture are key elements contributing to both teacher and student success in the CP. As such, the MT must regularly remind everyone (teachers and students) in her community that they will succeed when everyone around them also succeeds. In addition, she must constantly encourage and nurture, through both words and actions, the culture of Belong, Believe, Work Hard, Succeed.

2. The MT must maintain a constant focus on her primary objective, that of helping all her teachers develop into outstanding, highly skilled, and effective educational professionals who can work together to get all students in the Learning Community to

achieve and succeed at high levels (See Chapter 13, Growing Highly Effective Teachers).

3. Many important decisions in the LC are made via consensus. The MT facilitates this process with her teachers.

4. The MT serves as both a cheerleader and motivator for her teaching staff and students.

5. The MT is responsible for organizing and compiling data and information. For example, she reviews grade printouts to determine which Houses will be recognized on House Honor Rolls, compiles and distributes data from commitment expectation surveys, and tracks teacher progress on promotion criteria.

6. Special events, such as student and House awards assemblies, House competitions, and Learning Community-wide service opportunities, are coordinated by the MT.

7. The MT coordinates activities common to all Houses, including arranging for and/or conducting peer tutoring and other skill trainings for students.

8. The MT serves as a trusted sounding board for teachers in her LC who may be feeling overwhelmed. She is responsible for guiding and counseling her teachers when she becomes aware that they are dealing with issues that can impact their performance in the classroom.

9. The MT arranges for and/or conducts staff development activities, working closely with her teachers to grow and develop them as professional educators. (See Chapter 13)

10. As stated earlier in Chapter 3, much of the great work that a teacher does with students never escapes the four walls of that teacher's classroom. Since the MT is regularly in her teachers' classrooms, she can identify her teachers' best practices and inventory them. Then, when appropriate, she can ask her teachers to share them with other members of the CPTU, as well as teachers in other Learning Communities. In addition, teachers who are notoriously reticent about sharing the great things they and their colleagues do in the classroom are encouraged by the MT to "tattle" on themselves and their peers whenever they observe a best practice.

11. The MT is responsible for supervising and evaluating the teachers in her LC in a manner unique to the CP (see Chapter 14).

12. In Chapter 15 you will learn about a career ladder proposed for CP schools as well as a new form of teacher tenure. Since the MT is the person most in touch with the work of the teachers in her charge, she is the one given the responsibility for making recommendations for teacher promotion up the career ladder, and for submitting tenure recommendations to the principal.

13. Step one in creating a new CP Learning Community in a school is to identify who will be serving as the MT for that LC. The MT then participates with the principal and others in the selection and hiring of teachers for the new LC.

14. Once teachers are selected and hired for a new Learning Community the MT takes responsibility for conducting CP orientation and training of the new hires.

15. The MT coordinates the acquisition of resources for the CPTU through the budget process. She also advocates for her teachers with school administration to get all the resources needed to effectively teach and nurture all students.

16. The MT is responsible for keeping teachers focused on meeting the commitment expectations they make to students, their colleagues, and the MT. Commitment expectations, which reflect the CP philosophy and culture, are not window dressing. Rather, they are valuable tools that all constituent groups can regularly use to focus their efforts.

17. Much like an attending physician doing hospital "rounds" with her interns and residents, the MT works with teachers to identify all struggling students during Unit Planning time. She encourages Housemasters to frequently consult grading data sheets to check on the progress of their students in all classes.

18. The MT then works with teachers to design and implement academic and/or social interventions to help struggling students, i.e., making sure that no students "fall through the cracks" and give up.

19. The MT meets regularly with the school principal to keep him apprised of everything happening within the LC. In addition, the MT serves as a conduit for information coming down from school administration to teachers.

The next three brief chapters focus on some critical parts of the MT's job.

- Growing Outstanding, Highly Effective Teachers
- Teacher Supervision and Evaluation
- Teacher Selection, Motivation, Recognition, and Retention

Hopefully after reading this list and the next three chapters you will better understand the critical role that the MT plays within the CP.

Major points to take away from *Chapter 12, The Master Teacher*

1. The Master Teacher constantly reinforces the philosophy (I succeed when we succeed) and culture of the CP (Belong, Believe, Work Hard, Succeed) within her Learning Community.
2. The Master Teacher coordinates the acquisition of resources for her CP Teaching Unit through the budget process.
3. The Master Teacher works with her teachers to identify struggling students and then helps design and implement academic and/or social interventions to assist them.
4. The Master Teacher is responsible for the overall success of all the teachers and students in her Learning Community over a period of two years.
5. The Master Teacher meets regularly with the school principal, serving as a conduit of information between the Learning Community and administration.

CHAPTER 13

Growing Outstanding, Highly Effective Teachers

THE SINGLE MOST important task the Master Teacher must perform is to grow and develop all the teachers in her charge into outstanding, highly effective classroom instructors. This is a necessary first step toward achieving her primary goal, that of making sure that all 100 students in her Learning Community succeed, academically and otherwise.

In the traditional educational paradigm, the task of improving teacher quality is relegated to two ineffective systems. The first system involves the principal evaluating teachers after two or three "snapshot" observations each year. This system does little if anything to improve teacher quality for reasons previously discussed. Alternative, more effective ways to use teacher evaluation to improve teacher quality are discussed in the next chapter.

The second system is the use of three or four staff development days each year to address topics or issues that impact the quality of instruction. These are usually, but not always, done school-wide, some-times even district wide. This system is ineffective for two reasons.

First, recall the "drive-by-shooting" nature of this form of profes-sional development for teachers that I described earlier. Legitimate and important topics may be addressed on these days, and strategies for improvement can be presented. But rarely is this information internal-ized by teachers and applied in the classroom because the traditional educational paradigm does not provide for any means to follow-up. Valuable information and strategies are allowed to wither on the vine because teachers have neither the time nor opportunity to process and implement them into their classroom regimens.

Second, this system of staff development is ineffective because it is too broad in scope. When a staff development day is planned for an entire faculty, or worse, for an entire district, it is unlikely that the pre-sentations will prove beneficial to all in attendance. The chosen topic may be irrelevant to a large portion of the staff who dutifully attend, but who sit there stewing, wishing they could be back in their classrooms grading papers or otherwise catching up on their work.

In the CP, the growth and development of teachers is ongoing and dynamic. It is not relegated to two or three classroom observations and three or four staff development days. Teachers constantly grow profes-sionally because staff development is intertwined with every aspect of the teaching and learning process. There are four specific ways that teacher growth is achieved.

1. Informal Staff Development I. Master Teacher – Teacher Interactions

As described in the previous chapter, the MT is required to "walk with" her teachers, i.e., be in each of her teacher's classroom, at least twice a week on average. For continuity, the MT may choose to spend four consecutive days in a teacher's classroom one week, to see the flow and progression of the unit being taught, and then not at all the following week.

When in the classroom the MT can act in several different capaci-ties. She may co-teach with the teacher, serve as a teaching assistant, be a "student" learning along with the other students, act as a foil to help spark discussion about a topic, or simply observe the class. Brief planning conversations before (during Unit Planning time) and short debriefs after a class provide great opportunities for informal teacher growth.

MTs are trained in effective techniques to get teachers to reflect on their teaching. Once the important bond of trust is established, the MT becomes a facilitator, providing feedback and opening discussions on all aspects of the teaching/learning experience that she sees during her visits. These interactions slowly increase teachers' repertoire of skills and overall effectiveness in the classroom.

2.   Informal Staff Development II. Teacher – Teacher Interactions

Teachers are required to be in another teacher's class a minimum of three times each week. Much like the MT, the visiting teacher can serve in any number of roles (lead teacher, co-teacher, teaching assistant, observer). Teachers are encouraged to plan so that the guest teacher can be involved in the lesson in some capacity.

Good teachers are notorious for their ability to beg, borrow, and steal strategies and ideas that will make them more effective in the classroom. More than anything else, the requirement that teachers spend time in other teachers' classrooms provides opportunities for teachers to witness (and "borrow") other teachers' great techniques and strategies. You cannot borrow or "steal" that which you have never seen.

The visiting requirement also opens the door for teachers to help colleagues identify and eliminate poor or distracting aspects of their teaching that might otherwise go undetected. In the CP teachers can be comfortable saying to a colleague, "I noticed that Billy was drifting off during class. Here's a strategy I use with him that seems to work when he does the same thing in my class." Or "Did you know that some of the students in your class were tallying how often you said 'OK' during your lesson? I used to do the same thing until a colleague of mine pointed out how distracting it was to students."

More on the all-important Teacher to Teacher relationship coming up in Chapter 16.

Note: This requirement to be in another teacher's classroom three times each week can be waived by the MT if, for example, a teacher explains that she needs to stop into study halls all week to help her students prepare for an upcoming test.

3. Formal Staff Development Days

In the CP, a teaching unit of six teachers (the CPTU) decides via consensus what topics or issues they want to address on the three or four days they are granted for staff development. The MT, in consultation with the principal, is charged with finding and scheduling an appropriate resource to address the desired topics. Teaching units may choose to combine their staff development days with other CPTUs if they share similar needs. Importantly, the topics are _relevant_ to all in attendance.

Just as importantly, the CP provides opportunities for follow-up. During their Unit Planning time teachers can discuss the value of the material that was presented to them on the staff development day. If the CPTU decides that they want to adopt some new strategies or practices, the MT then takes on the role of facilitator, regularly drawing teachers' attention back to the changes that they, _the teachers_, want to make. With regular follow-up provided by the MT, _who is in direct contact with her teachers every day,_ new strategies and practices can successfully be incorporated into teachers' instructional practices. Teachers can grow.

4. Unit Planning Time Staff Development

In Unit Planning time, CPTUs can periodically identify instructional or logistical needs (or wants) that the group wishes to pursue. The MT can bring to the attention of the group some best practice(s) that she observed in one of her teachers' classrooms and ask that teacher to give a brief presentation to the CPTU during Unit Planning time. Or any teacher in the CPTU can suggest an idea for growth and seek a presenter or present the strategy themselves. This process is much less structured than formal staff development days but no less important. If anything, it has greater value because it can be utilized frequently, resulting in the continuous growth of teachers throughout the year.

How might this work in real time? The MT might notice that one of her teachers has developed an effective system for keeping track of assignments that students miss when they are absent. She can then ask the teacher to please take a few minutes during Unit Planning time to share her system with her teaching colleagues. Such mini-staff development presentations require little time to prepare and share. They do not put an additional burden on teachers' time, yet they produce very real teacher growth.

These best practice mini-presentations become part of a school-wide menu that can be tapped by other Learning Communities in the school on future staff development days.

To make all forms of teacher professional development work in the CP it is incumbent upon the MT to regularly bring her teachers back to the goal of every teacher becoming an outstanding, highly effective classroom instructor, and the importance of every teacher taking responsibility for helping her colleagues reach that goal. In so doing she reaffirms the philosophy and culture of the CP within her Learning Community, *I succeed when we succeed*, and **Belong, Believe, Work Hard, Succeed**.

Note: The entire concept of informal staff development will be new and foreign to all teachers. Teachers, as a rule, are not accustomed to having other teachers in their classrooms. Teachers who are perfectly relaxed and comfortable presenting to a room full of middle school or high school students suddenly become stressed out if another adult is in the classroom, especially another educator.

Prior to beginning work in a CP school teachers go through extensive training. One major part of that training focuses on getting teachers accustomed to, and comfortable with, being in other teacher's classrooms and having other teachers in their classrooms. Teachers learn how to give and receive feedback in an unthreatening manner and interact with their colleagues in ways that help both parties grow as professionals. More on teacher training in Chapter 19.

Major points to take away from *Chapter 13, Growing Outstanding, Highly Effective Teachers*

1. The single most important task the Master Teacher must perform is to grow and develop all the teachers in her charge into outstanding, highly effective classroom instructors.

2. Regular, informal staff development takes place weekly through the multiple required interactions between the MT and her teachers.

3. Additional informal staff development takes place weekly through the multiple required interactions between teachers and their colleagues.

4. The teachers in a CPTU identify the strategies/topics/methods they would like to explore on the three or four staff development days allotted by the school district. If the CPTU decides that they want to adopt some new strategies or practices, the MT then takes on the role of facilitator, regularly drawing teachers' attention back to the changes that they, *the teachers*, want to make. With regular follow-up provided by the MT, *who is in direct contact with her teachers every day*, new strategies and practices can successfully be incorporated into teachers' instructional practices. Teachers can grow.

5. In Unit Planning time the MT can periodically bring to the attention of the group a best practice that she observed in one of her teachers' classrooms and ask that teacher to give a brief presentation to the CPTU during Unit Planning time. Alternatively, any teacher in the CPTU can suggest an idea for growth and seek a presenter or present the strategy themselves. These mini staff development presentations are another source of continuous teacher growth.

CHAPTER 14

Teacher Supervision and Evaluation

ONCE AGAIN, PAINFULLY blunt is best.

In the traditional educational paradigm teacher supervision and evaluation do not work effectively. While we have many great teachers in our classrooms, and many students who are successful, we are still very far away from achieving what should be the primary goal of teacher supervision and evaluation, that is, to ensure that there are great teachers in _every_ classroom who successfully get _all_ their students to succeed.

Traditional supervision and evaluation models are static and artificial, with principals sitting down to observe teachers in a single class two or three times each year. These observations are often announced so a teacher can put on "the dog and pony show," that is, a lesson that hits all the points the teacher knows the principal will be looking for. Then, the next day it is back to teaching as usual.

The data obtained in traditional teacher observations have little value. They do not inform the principal of how well teachers perform daily. Nor do they help teachers to grow professionally since data from such observations show what teachers can do when placed in the spotlight on a single day, not what they regularly do to help their students learn.

The principal may make suggestions for improvement to a teacher but there is little chance that these suggestions will become a part of a teacher's repertoire of skills. There is simply no time or opportunity for a principal to follow-up with his teachers (recall the earlier description of the job of principal).

I do not sit on an island alone with this view. The overwhelming majority of teachers, and principals too if they are honest with themselves, will acknowledge that traditional methods of teacher observation and evaluation have little value. Most teachers consider observations by the principal (and their accompanying conferences and written evaluations) a nuisance ritual that must be endured, a box to be checked off the "to do list," so that they can get back to the real business of teaching their students.

Is there a better way to supervise and evaluate teachers? Certainly. But like so many other aspects of schooling, we need to think differently about teacher supervision and evaluation if we want to make them truly effective tools for achieving both teacher growth and student success. Let me start you down that road by telling you a brief supervision story.

Almost 30 years ago I had the pleasure of planning and conducting an after-prom party for a local high school. We converted a local ski lodge into an exclusive, high-end, nightclub/casino for the students. We provided valet parking when couples arrived. Once inside, drinks and hors d'oeuvres were served by waiters and waitresses dressed in formal wear. There were gaming tables run by similarly dressed dealers, and a never-ending buffet with servers meeting our guests' every need. And, of course, there was live entertainment throughout the night.

Parents provided the manpower for the event, serving as valets, dealers, waiters, waitresses, servers, cooks, etc. Prior to the event I met with the entire "staff" of the nightclub/casino to address any of their concerns and to outline their roles as chaperones.

When I briefed the adult volunteers, I made it clear to everyone that no one was to chaperone in the traditional sense. I did not want anyone standing around with their arms crossed just watching the students as they might at a high school dance, making sure the students did not do anything "bad." Instead, I asked the volunteers to play their respective roles fully and just be there with the students as they enjoyed the night at our exclusive nightclub/casino. We (the adult volunteers) and the kids had common goals and expectations for the evening. We wanted the kids to feel special and have a great (and safe) time. The kids wanted to be treated "special" and have a great time.

As they (the chaperones) worked in their roles to achieve our common goals they kept watch for any problems or issues that might arise, that is, they provided supervision. But the supervision was dynamic and participatory. We treated the kids like mature adult guests visiting our "nightclub" and that was how they all behaved. There were zero issues.

In the CP the Master Teacher (MT) is a co-participant with her teachers in all the activities and processes aimed at achieving the Learning Community's (LC) common goal of every student being successful. Supervision flows naturally from everyday interactions between teachers and their MT. Supervision occurs through dynamic participation _with_ teachers, not static observations _of_ teachers. All the interactions between the MT and her teachers that I described in the previous chapter as part of the process of growing teachers are opportunities for "participatory supervision." The MT works together with her teachers to get all students to succeed, while at the same time watching for any problems or issues that might need to be addressed.

The word "supervise" has a couple different definitions.

1. To observe and direct the execution of a task, project, or activity.
2. To keep watch over (someone) in the interest of their or others' security.

At its best, supervision in the CP is closest to the first definition. With the difference being that the MT does not so much _direct_ the execution of a task or activity as _work collaboratively with_ teachers to determine the best course of action to successfully accomplish/complete the task, project, or activity. And as part of that collaboration with her teachers, the MT is in the ideal position to observe them at work.

Unlike what happens in traditional supervision/evaluation models there is nothing artificial or static about supervision in the CP. Teachers cannot put on a "dog and pony show" when the MT is in a classroom because she is seemingly there all the time. Remember, the MT is in the same classroom with each of her teachers at least 70 times per year in some capacity.

In the CP there is no need to "supervise and monitor" teachers in the traditional, factory floor/high school dance manner (sitting there with notebook in hand, ready to record what the teacher is doing, or not doing, correctly). The Master Teacher works alongside the other teachers in her charge, planning with them, teaching with them, observing (and being observed by) them, offering (_and_ receiving) suggestions for improving instruction, growing professionally with them. The MT and the other teachers in the CP Unit have the same goals and expectations for their students and for themselves as teachers.

Evaluation

Throughout the school year the MT provides each teacher in their charge (all five of them) with a bi-weekly feedback narrative. This narrative summarizes each teacher's direct interaction with the MT over a two-week period, both one-on-one in classes and in Unit Planning (UP) time. The narratives may reference all aspects of planning and successfully executing quality lesson plans for instruction, in addition to other classroom characteristics. In the narrative the MT may also discuss specific areas of emphasis which both the teacher and the MT have agreed to focus on. This form of evaluation is effective because the MT can chart progress on these areas of emphasis (and other aspects of a teacher's performance) throughout the school year.

In addition, the MT's narratives may reference activities that are observed during UP time including:

1. teacher planning with other members of the CPTU.
2. teacher involvement in professional development activities.
3. teachers working with colleagues using grading software to identify students in need of extra help.
4. teachers working with colleagues to arrange extra help for struggling students during extra planning time or student study halls.
5. planning and conducting House activities.

The Summative Evaluation

At or near the end of each school year the MT compiles a summative evaluation of every teacher. The bi-weekly feedback narratives provide the MT with a large data set to use when compiling each teacher's summative evaluation.

In addition, the MT can use the results from the feedback surveys filled out by other members of the Learning Community which assess how well a teacher has lived up to the commitment expectations she shared with others at the start of the school year. Recall that a teacher's students, her colleagues, and the MT, all fill out commitment expectation feedback surveys for a teacher twice each year. The results of these surveys are provided to the teacher as soon as they are available so that the teacher can use them to improve her performance. The MT also receives the results of these surveys. Positive changes in how well a teacher is perceived to be meeting her commitment expectations, from mid-year to end of the year and from year to year, are excellent indicators of a teacher's growth and development.

Finally, any applicable state testing results that reflect the efforts of a teacher are also included in the summative evaluation as an addendum added later in the summer.

The data used to compile a teacher's summative evaluation can be summarized as follows:

1. Twenty bi-weekly feedback narratives compiled from a minimum of 70 classroom visits by the MT throughout the year.
2. Commitment expectation feedback surveys filled out by approximately 100 students, five teachers, and the MT.

3. Applicable state testing results.

You may feel that much of what you read in this chapter was redundant, a repeat of the previous chapter. To some degree your observation is correct. Everything that the MT does to foster her teachers' professional growth and development can also be a part of the supervision and evaluation process.

In the traditional education paradigm, it is a myth that supervision and evaluation help teachers to grow professionally. Most teacher supervision and evaluation models that currently exist in our schools do little to assist teachers in honing their craft. The feedback that teachers get is too infrequent and too limited in scope and depth.

In the CP, supervision and evaluation, and by extension teachers' professional growth and development, are participatory and dynamic, occurring naturally throughout the course of the school year. They are so closely intertwined as to be inseparable. While working closely with her teachers the MT can see each teacher's growth, or lack thereof. Her bi-weekly narrative summaries can chart strengths and weaknesses, and progress toward alleviating those weaknesses, throughout the year and from year to year. She does not need an artificial, static, process to evaluate her teachers.

Remember the primary goals of the MT. She must grow her teachers into outstanding educational professionals, ***and*** she needs to work with her teachers to make sure that all students in their Learning Community succeed. Supervision and evaluation in the CP go a long way toward achieving these goals.

A final note: The structure of supervision and evaluation in the CP is in no way meant to diminish the work of people who have constructed intricate models for evaluating teachers. For example, Charlotte Danielson's *Framework for Teaching*[1] is an invaluable resource that can be tapped by teachers and Master Teachers in the CP.

Danielson does an outstanding job breaking down the duties and responsibilities of teaching into 4 major domains. In her evaluation instrument these *domains* are broken down into 22 *components*, then into 76 *elements*, for which there are 104 *indicators*. In traditional evaluation systems principals are expected to accurately determine if an individual teacher is functioning at an *unsatisfactory, basic, proficient, or distinguished level* for each of the 22 components, using data that they glean from between one and three observations of a teacher, each 40 to 45 minutes in length (principals are often required to come up with a numerical rating of teachers based upon this limited data set). I hope you can see how absurd it is to think that a principal can accurately assess 22 components and 76 elements of teaching using such limited data. Sadly, Danielson's great work is often relegated to checklists in traditional forms of teacher evaluation. The principal rates the teacher on each component, hammers out a pro forma evaluation report, meets briefly with the teacher, and then can check that teacher evaluation off his "to do" list.

In the CP, Danielson's Framework for Teaching can be used by both teachers and the MT to regularly identify and address aspects of teaching in need of improvement. The regular contact that the MT has with her teachers gives her more than adequate opportunities to assess and track teachers' progress toward reaching the proficient or distinguished level for each component. Without question, Danielson's Framework for Teaching is of far greater value when used in the CP.

Major points to take away from *Chapter 14, Teacher Supervision and Evaluation*

1. Traditional supervision and evaluation models are static and artificial, providing little data of value to help teachers to grow professionally.
2. In the CP supervision flows naturally from regular interactions between teachers and their MT. Supervision occurs through dynamic participation <u>with</u> teachers, not static observations <u>of</u> teachers (80 in-class visits each year and daily shared work in Unit Planning time).
3. Throughout the school year the Master Teacher provides each teacher in her charge (all five of them) with a bi-weekly feedback narrative. This narrative summarizes each teacher's direct

interaction with the MT over a two-week period, both one-on-one in classes and in Unit Planning (UP) time.

4. At the end of each school year the MT compiles a summative evaluation of each teacher using the bi-weekly feedback narratives, the commitment expectation feedback surveys, and other sources of data such as state testing results.

1. Danielson, Charlotte. Implementing the Framework for Teaching in Enhancing Professional Practice. Alexandria, VA :ASCD, 2009

CHAPTER 15

Teacher Selection, Motivation, Retention, and Recognition

WHILE IT IS always important to have quality teachers as members of a CP Teaching Unit (CPTU), the selection of teachers who will work in the _first_ CPTUs in pilot schools is _extremely_ important. These first CP teachers will be breaking new ground. Their success, or failure, will determine the future of the CP in their school and district. For the CP culture and philosophy to take root in a school, teachers need to be reasonably proficient in all aspects of the art and craft of teaching. But even more importantly, CP schools need teachers who:

1. are passionate about the work they do in the classroom.
2. recognize that they are not finished products as teachers, and who are willing to put forth the effort to grow as educational professionals.

3. are willing to work collaboratively with colleagues and share responsibility for their own success and the success of their colleagues.
4. are willing to share responsibility for the success of _all_ students in their charge and do whatever it takes to help them succeed.
5. are open to new ideas.
6. can acknowledge, to themselves and to their students, that they made a mistake or failed to honor a commitment, and then apologize.
7. demonstrate through their words and actions that they genuinely care about their students.

I will be the first to acknowledge, sadly, that not all teachers possess all the above characteristics. As teachers we are much like the members of other professions, some with more skills than others, some with more desirable attitudes and attributes than others. I also acknowledge that it can be extremely difficult to ascertain that a candidate possesses some of the above characteristics, since almost all are subjective in nature. But the search for quality teaching candidates has always been, to a large degree, a subjective process. We can only do our best.

The Selection Process

The MT, working with her principal, and with the approval of the superintendent and Board of Education, is responsible for selecting the teachers who will work with her in the CP Teaching Unit (CPTU). In a school or district where a CPTU is being formed for the first time it will be necessary to first share information about CP teaching opportunities with the entire teaching staff. A CP consulting group and the MT then spend significant time in the school/district observing all the teachers in the desired starting grade level, looking for teachers who possess the characteristics of CP teachers listed above. Based on these observations a pool of potential candidates will be identified. After these initial steps the application process can be opened.

Candidates for positions will fall into three different categories.

1. Teachers who voluntarily submit applications who are also in the candidate pool identified by the MT and CP consultants.
2. Teachers who do not submit applications but who were identified as strong potential candidates for the CP.
3. Teachers who submit applications but who were not included in the initial pool of potential candidates.

The first group obviously contains strong candidates for positions in the CP. These are teachers who the MT and consultants feel would be a good fit, and who also _want_ to be a part of the CP.

The second group contains teachers who are viewed as strong potential candidates for the CP but who, for some reason, choose not to submit applications. The MT may decide to approach some of these teachers and invite them to apply. The many changes that teachers will encounter in the CP will, without question, leave some teachers feeling apprehensive. If teachers are seen as a great fit for a CP Teaching Unit, it will be time well spent for the MT to meet with these teachers one-on-one to discuss some of their concerns and allay their fears. This will be particularly important if the MT wants to draw in some talented veteran teachers who, understandably, might be more skeptical, having experienced the passing of many educational reform "trains" over the years. But, as was pointed out earlier, veteran teachers are needed in the CP to lend their talents and experience to other, less experienced teachers. Hopefully, some can be convinced to change their mind and apply.

Applications from teachers in the third group should not be dismissed out of hand. Motivation, a positive attitude, and a willingness to embrace a new paradigm, can go a long way toward overcoming other perceived deficits.

Once a CP pilot is underway for a year or two the selection process will change. Information dissemination and classroom observations will continue to be an essential part of the process of recruiting teachers, but the paradigm will begin to sell itself as word of CP teachers' increase in job satisfaction (and other positives) begin to spread in the school community.

The number of positions available at the start of a CP pilot is very small. Only five academic teachers are needed (in addition to the MT) to fill out the first CP Teaching Unit. Each succeeding year the number of teachers needed will increase. For these reasons, after all interviews are conducted and the hiring process is concluded, all applicants should be placed into one of three categories.

1. Teachers who are offered positions for the coming year.
2. First alternates. Teachers who are "next in line" for a CP position, likely the following year. These teachers will also go through training (see Chapter 19, CP Training) the summer before the pilot starts and be ready to step in should a vacancy occur during the school year.
3. The "not yet" pool. Teachers who may be offered a CP position at some point in the future.

Teacher motivation, recognition, and retention.

In this section I describe two new structures designed to increase teacher motivation, recognition, and retention. They are a career ladder and a new form of teacher tenure. But while these two new structures may prove to be important motivators, it is the opportunity to work as a member of a CP Teaching Unit within the CP philosophy and culture that serves as the primary motivator of teachers.

In no traditional school setting will teachers be able to collaborate with colleagues as they can in the CP. In no traditional school setting will teachers be able to develop the strong bonds between teachers and students that are found in House. In no traditional school setting will teachers experience ongoing professional development as they will in the CP. In no traditional school setting will you find teachers treated more professionally. In no traditional school setting will teachers experience the esprit de corps that they will find when working as a member of a CP Teaching Unit. And in no traditional school setting can teachers make as great an impact on the lives of students, academically and otherwise, as they can in the CP. All of these attributes of working in a CP school are tremendously motivating.

A Career Ladder

One of the most disheartening aspects of the job of teacher is that there are few opportunities for promotion within the teaching profession. An individual who graduates from college and takes his first teaching job in a district will, thirty years later, still be "just a teacher" in that district, albeit a very experienced one working at a higher salary.

Teachers who feel like they "want to do more" in education to help kids grow and succeed have few options. Most commonly, teachers who feel this way move into educational administration and become principals, assistant principals, directors of special education, or serve in other district jobs that take them out of the classroom.

Our very best teachers do not want to leave the classroom because teaching, working with students directly, is their passion. In the traditional educational paradigm great teachers who want to do more to help kids, but who do not want to leave the classroom, are stuck. And that feeling of being stuck in place, with no opportunity to advance professionally as a teacher, does nothing to increase teachers' motivation to grow. The failure to tap into the vast reservoir of teachers who want to do more _as classroom teachers_ ultimately hurts our schools and our kids.

Not so in the CP.

In the CP teachers can work their way up a career ladder that contains the following steps.

Teacher I: When a teacher is offered a position as a member of a CP Teaching Unit (CPTU) she must complete an intensive six-week summer training program. Upon the successful completion of this training a teacher reaches Teacher I (T-1) status and can begin teaching in a CP school.

CP Certification: When T-1 teachers successfully complete a two-year cycle teaching as members of a CPTU they can apply for CP certification. Teachers must show mastery of CP concepts on a written assessment and demonstrate mastery of the same concepts in the field as determined by the MT. Teachers must also demonstrate that they have consistently met the commitment expectations that they made to their students, their teaching colleagues, and to the MT.

Teacher II: Teachers who successfully complete at least three years of work as a member of a CPTU, who possess CP Certification and a Masters degree, and who meet all other T-2 requirements, may apply for promotion to Teacher II status. Promotion to T-2 status requires that teachers continue to meet the commitment expectations that they make to their students, their teaching colleagues, and to the MT.

Teacher III: Teachers who successfully complete at least five years of work as a member of a CPTU, who possess CP Certification and a Masters degree, and who meet all other T-3 requirements, may apply for promotion to Teacher III status. Consistently meeting commitment expectations is required for promotion to T-3 status.

Master Teacher: Teachers who successfully complete at least six years of work as a member of a CPTU, who possess CP Certification and a Masters degree, and who meet all other Master Teacher requirements including the completion of a six-week summer MT training program, may apply for promotion to Master Teacher status. Teachers who obtain Master Teacher status are eligible to apply for Master Teacher's positions. As with other CP teacher levels, promotion to Master Teacher status requires that teachers consistently meet the commitment expectations that they make to their students, their teaching colleagues, and to the MT.

Master Teacher Certificate: Master Teachers who successfully complete at least one two-year cycle leading a CPTU can apply for Master Teacher certification. Master Teachers must show mastery of MT concepts on a written assessment and demonstrate mastery of the same concepts in the field as determined by the principal.

Each promotion up the career ladder brings a salary increase for teachers. The table below shows how such increases would impact the salaries of teachers in CP schools compared to non-CP schools.

CP Career Ladder Teacher Pay Structure

Year	Base Pay	Teacher I *	Teacher II	Teacher III	Master Teacher
1	x	x + I			
2	x +1	(x +1) + I			
3	x +2	(x +2) + C + I			
4	x +3	(x +3) + C + I	(x +3) + C + II		
5	x +4	(x +4) + C + I	(x +4) + C + II		
6	x +5	(x +5) + C + I	(x +5) + C + II	(x +5) + C + III	
7	x +6	(x +6) + C + I	(x +6) + C + II	(x +6) + C + III	(x +6) + C + MT
8	x + 7	(x +7) + C + I	(x +7) + C + II	(x +7) + C + III	(x +7) + C + MT
9	x + 8	(x +8) + C + I	(x +8) + C + II	(x +8) + C + III	(x +8) + C + MT
10	x + 9	(x +9) + C + I	(x +9) + C + II	(x +9) + C + III	(x +9) + C + MT

In the above table the column with the heading of "base pay" shows the salary that teachers would be paid in non-CP schools. The starting salary of "x" would increase each year per the negotiated agreement. In Year 7, a teacher in a traditional paradigm school would receive his starting base pay plus six years of negotiated longevity increases (x + 6). A teacher in a CP school who started at the same time and who took advantage of all opportunities for promotion would, by Year 7, earn the same base salary (x + 6) _plus_ five additional salary increases. Salary increases would kick in at each step on the career ladder: Teacher I, CP certification (C), Teacher II, Teacher III, and Master Teacher. The CP career ladder provides significant financial incentives for teachers to grow and develop as educational professionals.

But more significantly, movement up the CP career ladder ultimately produces the highly skilled MTs needed to lead future CP Teaching Units. Outstanding classroom teachers who want to have a greater impact on a larger number of kids, but who do not want to leave the classroom behind, will be motivated to move up the career ladder and become Master Teachers. Outstanding classroom teachers <u>do not</u> necessarily make great principals because the skill sets of the two jobs are so different. But great classroom teachers _will_ make outstanding Master Teachers. Who better to coach developing teachers than highly skilled and effective teachers who are still working in the classroom, and loving it!

A final note on the CP career ladder pay structure.

Some individuals might complain that introducing the CP into a school district will create two distinctly different pay scales for teachers. I have two responses to this concern. First, teachers who work in a CP school as members of a CP Teaching Unit work longer hours and have significantly more and different responsibilities than teachers working in a traditional setting. Quite simply, more is expected of teachers in a CP school. It is reasonable to expect that they would be paid more.

Second, there are already multiple pay scales in every school district in this country. All teachers get negotiated pay increases for longevity. But individual teachers also get stipends or salary increases for a variety of other reasons including, but not limited to: having a masters or doctoral degree, possessing certifications in additional subject areas, coaching athletic teams, and serving as a faculty advisor for student activities or clubs (for example, drama director, band director, Model UN advisor, Mock Trial advisor, etc.) Many of these additions to base salaries can be quite significant.

Teacher Tenure

Traditionally, tenure was viewed by teachers and teacher unions as protection against school administration and school boards which might arbitrarily dismiss teachers without cause. Administrators and school boards generally viewed lifetime tenure as an artifact of an antiquated system that prevented a district from getting rid of poor teachers. In CP schools, positive change requires that we think about and view teacher tenure differently.

Earlier I posed two questions regarding teacher tenure. I asked, "Is lifetime tenure for teachers what is best for kids? And "Would eliminating tenure be what is best for kids?" Based upon my experience, my answer to both questions was an emphatic "No!" But if both eliminating tenure and preserving lifetime tenure are not in the best interest of kids, does tenure have any role to play in a reimagined vision of public education? The answer is an equally emphatic "yes."

Tenure can play a very important role in public education if we think differently about it and reimagine its structure and purpose. Tenure, in the CP, is used by the school district to recognize the accomplishments of teachers and to incentivize them to remain within in the district. Remember, within the CP a significant investment of time and resources is made to grow and develop highly effective educational professionals over time. Once teachers reach high levels of performance it behooves school districts to do everything they can to retain them. In the CP, teachers are awarded six-year renewable tenure in recognition of their instructional skills, professional growth and development, and contributions to student success.

During a teacher's fourth year of service the Master Teacher, in consultation with the principal, determines whether that teacher has demonstrated substantial growth as an educational professional and contributed significantly to the success of all students in her Learning Community. If a teacher meets these criteria a tenure recommendation is submitted to the superintendent and Board of Education. If approved, the teacher is offered six-year renewable tenure. Here is how the tenure process works.

A teacher is initially offered six-year renewable tenure after four years of service. Two years later, upon the recommendation of the MT and the principal, the teacher can be rewarded and incentivized by renewing and extending her tenure out to six years again. The MT literally says to the teacher, "We acknowledge your commitment and how hard you have worked to become an outstanding teacher. We also recognize the ongoing positive impact you have on all your students. As such, we want to extend your tenure for another six years. Congratulations!" This process repeats itself every two years, provided that the teacher continues to grow professionally and contributes significantly to the success of all students in the Learning Community.

If, at the end of the first two years of a teacher's six-year tenure period, a teacher is not functioning at a high level and demonstrating professional growth, their tenure will not be extended. At that point the teacher still has four years to demonstrate that they are growing professionally and making a significant contribution to the success of students. At the end of each subsequent year the MT, in consultation with the principal, decides whether to once again offer six-year tenure to the teacher. Used in this manner six-year renewable tenure serves to motivate, recognize, and retain good teachers.

There is still an "elephant in the room" that needs to be addressed. Veteran teachers moving from traditional schools to a CP school must give up lifetime tenure in favor of six-year renewable tenure. What teacher in their right mind would take such a chance on a new educational concept? Good question. Here is the answer.

Any veteran teacher who makes the transition to teaching in a CP school is permitted to keep their lifetime tenure for the first two years. In essence, a veteran teacher is given the opportunity to "test drive" the CP to see if it is all that it is cracked up to be. At the end of two years the teacher must choose between remaining in the CP school and accepting six-year renewable tenure or returning to a traditional teaching setting and retaining lifetime tenure. In my opinion no teacher who has experienced working as part of a CP Teaching Unit in a CP school for two years would ever want to return to a traditional setting. Why do I say that? It all comes down to my final note.

A final note on motivation.

Think back to Chapter 8, CP Philosophy and Culture. Recall that *I* did not create the CP philosophy and culture. The CP philosophy and culture was imagined by teachers working on the front lines of education. These teachers all worked in traditional school settings, settings which they felt left much to be desired.

Remember that I asked faculty and staff members to complete sentences like these.

1. At "Our Town" Jr/Sr HS I would like to see more . . .
2. Students would really look forward to coming to "Our Town" Jr/Sr. HS if . . .
3. I could be more effective in my job if . . .

4. I would like to see relationships between students and staff characterized by . . .
5. As an educator, I feel proud when . . .
6. What bothers me the most about the old "picture" of "Our Town" Jr/Sr HS is . . .
7. I know it will probably never happen, but in my dream school I'd like to see . . .

What teachers described in their responses was a CP school. Look back at the key descriptors that teachers identified. They did not know they were describing a CP school at the time because none then existed, and none still exist today. But their responses form the framework of the CP concept, _because it is the kind of school where teachers desperately want to work_. Which is why I can say with a high degree of confidence that any teacher who experiences working in a CP school will never want to go back, even if it means giving up lifetime tenure.

Major points to take away from _Chapter 15, Teacher Selection, Motivation, Recognition, and Retention_

1. Teachers selected to join a CP Teaching Unit must possess a reasonable level of proficiency in all aspects of the art and craft of teaching as well as certain other key characteristics and attributes.
2. Working as a member of a highly trained, elite, CP Teaching Unit within the CP philosophy and culture serves as both the primary motivator of teachers and the best vehicle for retaining teachers.
3. In the CP, teachers can work their way up a career ladder that contains six steps, from Teacher I through Master Teacher with Certification.
4. In the CP, teachers are awarded six-year renewable tenure in recognition of their instructional skills, professional growth and development, and contributions to student success.

CHAPTER 16

The Teacher – Teacher Relationship

IN THE CP, teacher interaction and collaboration are expected, _and_ teachers are provided with the time and other resources they need to meet this expectation. The professional relationships that develop because of these interactions are at the heart of the CP. These relationships are night and day different from those found in today's schools that operate under the traditional educational paradigm.

Relationships develop between individuals when they interact regularly. We all have relationships with friends, neighbors, and family members who we see often. We may also develop relationships with our barber (or hairdresser), our mechanic, our mail carrier, and others with whom we interact frequently.

Professional relationships are different. They develop when a substantial amount of _professional_ interaction takes place between individuals. In education, "professional interaction" between teachers can best be described as _any communication that directly, and positively, impacts teacher performance in the classroom and increases levels of student success._

I must again be blunt about today's educational realities. In today's schools little or no communication occurs between teachers that focuses on improving teacher performance. And little or no communication occurs between teachers that is aimed specifically at getting their students to achieve and succeed. The result, sadly, is that professional relationships between teachers are sorely lacking, or nonexistent, in our schools today. And this lack of professional relationships between teachers hurts our students, their teachers, and the community at large.

Professional relationships between teachers are missing in our schools for two reasons. First, teachers simply do not have the time or opportunity to interact professionally with their colleagues on a regular basis, even if they wanted to. Recall that teacher isolation is one of the fundamental truths in education that I cited in Chapter 3 (See FT #15).

And second, teachers are given no reason to interact with other teachers. Professional interaction is not expected or required by school administrators. Teachers are expected to do the very best job they can in _their_ isolated classes with _their_ students. What goes on in other teachers' classrooms, how successful other teachers are in teaching students, is simply not any one teacher's concern.

By contrast, in the CP, teachers no longer operate as islands, responsible only for the success of the students in their classes. In the CP, teachers share responsibility for each other's success, and for the success of all students in every teacher's class within the Learning Community (I succeed when we succeed). This shared responsibility requires, it demands, more professional interaction. Indeed, the establishment and very existence of the CP culture in schools depends, in large part, upon teachers' ability to interact with colleagues and develop strong professional relationships. To meet this expectation/requirement, time, and opportunities to interact professionally are built into teachers' schedules.

Remember all that teacher "free time" (aka professional time) that I told you some people were going to get all crazy about back in the chapter on The Resource of Time? This is where that "free time" is used. It is the resource that is needed to ensure that professional interactions take place between teachers so that both teachers and students can grow and succeed.

What time do teachers have at their disposal in the CP and how do they use it?

A teacher in a CPTU serves as a Housemaster during House periods and is scheduled to teach four classes each day. That leaves four periods of the day where teachers are not scheduled to be in front of students. One of those periods is Unit Planning Time (UP Time), a period when all the teachers in the CPTU meet together and interact. During one of the remaining three "free periods," each teacher spends at least three class periods a week in the classroom of a fellow teacher, again, interacting professionally. And the Master Teacher is in each of her teacher's class-rooms interacting professionally at least twice each week.

To begin to grasp how teachers in the CP use this "free time" take a few moments to read *Appendix E-2, Teacher Commitment Expectation Statements to Colleagues* in the back of this book. Pay special attention to all the commitment expectations that are written in italics. When you finish, please come back.

Starting to get a better feel for the teacher – teacher relationship in the CP? To get a fuller understanding of the kinds of professional interactions that teachers share in the CP please "listen in" below as a Master Teacher speaks to her teachers at the start of their very first year working together as a CP Teaching Unit.

We, the six of us sitting here in this room, have been given the col-lective responsibility for ensuring the academic success and personal growth of 100 students over a two-year period of time. We are respon-sible for making sure that every student in our Learning Community meets grade level standards in each subject area when they leave us in two years, regardless of where they are when they begin with us.

And here is how we are going to do that.

We are going to spend three class periods each week in a colleague's class to help grow our instructional skills. We will debrief our time together with an eye toward improving our lessons, making them more focused and engaging for our students. We are going to become comfortable both giving and receiving feedback so that we can all grow as educators.

We will all spend one period each day together in Unit Planning Time (UP Time) during which we will do many of the following.

We will discuss our strengths, weaknesses, and needs as an educational team and identify areas where we could benefit from professional development training.

We will share our "best practices" with each other so that we can all become more effective in the classroom.

We will make sure that no student in our LC ever falls through the cracks. We will communicate with each other, both as classroom teachers and as Housemasters, about our students' grades, upcoming tests, and major assignments, and identify any students who are struggling.

We will then work together to develop mitigation strategies to help our struggling students get up to speed. We will identify when, where, and how those mitigation strategies are put into practice.

As Housemasters we will serve as liaisons between the students in our House and all their teachers, advocating for them when necessary.

And we will all be openly supportive of any colleague who is experiencing professional difficulties.

Keeping teachers working in isolation where they cannot collaborate with one another is <u>not</u> doing what is best for kids. On the other hand, providing teachers with the opportunity to interact and collaborate regularly with their colleagues so that they can collectively improve their skills as teachers and ensure the success of all their students is, most definitely, doing what is best for kids!

Major points to take away from *Chapter 16, The Teacher – Teacher Relationship*

1. Since teachers do not share common responsibilities in today's schools, teacher professional interaction is not expected or

required by school administrators. Teachers are expected to do the very best job they can in _their_ isolated classes with _their_ students.

2. In the CP, teachers make a commitment to interact and collaborate with each other in order to meet their collective responsibilities for teacher growth and student success.

3. Teachers are provided with the time and other resources they need to honor this commitment.

4. Teacher interaction and collaboration leads to the development of strong professional relationships which are at the heart of the CP.

5. These professional relationships ensure that teachers will grow as educational professionals and that students will achieve and succeed.

CHAPTER 17

The Master Teacher – Principal Relationship

THERE IS A reason why principals' job descriptions, like the one that I shared with you earlier, appear so overwhelming. School principals are ultimately responsible for everything that happens in their schools. Responsible for the instructional success of teachers. Responsible for the success of students. Responsible for the supervision and evaluation of teachers. Responsible for maintaining good communication with parents and the community. Responsible for the professional growth and development of teachers. Responsible for maintaining proper student conduct while administering consistent discipline. And responsible for a boatload of other things that most people would never even think about. Everything.

In the CP that does _not_ change. In a 600-student CP middle school, high school, or junior/senior high school, the principal remains _ultimately_ responsible for the success of all the teachers and students in her building. But the Master Teachers in this school (six of them) each shoulder *direct* individual responsibility for the growth, development, and success of 1/6 of the students and 1/6 of the academic teaching staff. The principal becomes an upper-level manager, overseeing the work of her MTs as they each lead their respective Learning Communities.

The principal becomes responsible for ensuring that her MTs are meeting their commitment expectation statements to their teachers and to the principal. The principal can monitor her MTs in several different ways. She can meet regularly with them to assess their views of the status of the six LCs in the school. The principal can attend Unit Planning times (where the MT meets with all her teachers) to see how well the CPTU is functioning under the guidance of the MT. She can also review the biweekly feedback narratives that the MT provides to each of the teachers in her CPTU. If the principal has a concern about any teacher, she can review the narratives of that teacher at any time and discuss her concerns with the MT. And, of course, the principal can, at any time, visit classes or Houses.

The Master Teacher works with her teachers to achieve common goals, leading from within the Learning Community, not from above or outside. Similarly, the principal and her MTs work together to ensure that all teachers are on the road to becoming outstanding, highly effective teachers who get all their students to achieve and succeed. They work together more as partners than as boss and employee. The same philosophy governs the relationship between the principal and her MTs that also governs the relationships between and among students and teachers. *I succeed when we succeed.* Each MT succeeds when all her teachers succeed. The principal succeeds when all her MTs succeed.

Regular, clear communication in both directions is also a hallmark of a good MT – principal relationship. Yes, it is critical that the principal learn from the MT all that is happening within her LC. It is equally important that the MT serve as a conduit for information from administration to teachers.

At certain times of year, the relationship between MTs and the principal will take on greater significance. As you saw in Chapters 14 and 15, the MTs are responsible for the supervision and evaluation of teachers, as well as for making recommendations for promotion up the CP career ladder. Near the end of the school year the principal and MTs meet to discuss the summative evaluations of each teacher and any recommendations for promotion put forth by the MT. Recommendations must be approved by the principal, superintendent, and BOE.

In addition, the MTs and principal must meet to discuss any possible tenure recommendations, whether for initially conferring tenure or for renewal. As with recommendations for promotion, tenure recommendations must also be approved by the principal, superintendent, and BOE.

Perhaps most important, it is the combined responsibility of the MTs and the principal to promote and foster the CP culture of belong, believe, work hard, succeed, with all individuals in all areas of the school.

Major points to take away from *Chapter 17, The Master Teacher – Principal Relationship.*

1. Each Master Teacher shoulders direct individual responsibility for the growth, development, and success of a segment of the students and academic teaching staff in the school.
2. The principal becomes an upper-level manager, overseeing the work of her MTs as they each lead their respective Learning Communities.
3. The principal and her MTs work together to ensure that all teachers in the school are on the road to becoming outstanding, highly effective teachers who get all their students to achieve and succeed. The principal and MTs work together more as partners than as boss and employee.

CHAPTER 18

Accountability in the CP

ACCOUNTABILITY IS WOVEN into every aspect of CP culture, and not in the heavy-handed "carrot and stick" manner of outcome-based accountability found in many schools today. In the CP a teacher is accountable to his fellow teachers, his Master Teacher, his principal, and his students. Students are accountable to their teachers, Housemaster, and fellow students. Master Teachers are accountable to the principal and the teachers in their charge. The principal is accountable both to the superintendent _and_ his teachers. Housemasters are accountable to their students and their MT. *The CP's culture of shared responsibility (I succeed when we succeed) is maintained through mutual accountability.*

Now, after reading that Master Teachers (who are still teaching) are responsible for observing and evaluating other teachers, you may have your doubts. You might think, "There is no way that teachers can objectively observe and evaluate other teachers. That is the fox guarding the chickens. We must have high stakes testing that principals can use to hold teachers accountable. Teachers cannot and will not hold other teachers accountable. We must have accountability!"

Such thinking clings to a dangerously narrow view of accountability in education. Outcome-based teacher accountability, where students' scores on high stakes tests are linked to teacher evaluations, is **not** the only way to hold people accountable for their performance in schools.

Let me tell you about my teaching experience with Susan.

Susan was an incredibly talented and gifted Earth Science teacher, highly respected by both students and her peers. She was passionate about what she taught, and her enthusiasm for the subject was contagious with her students. That translated into her students always performing well on the NYS Regents Exam in Earth Science.

One summer, when teaching assignments for the fall came out, Susan was shocked to see that she was assigned to teach one section of high school biology. She was certified in both Earth Science and Biology but had only ever taught high school Earth Science. The prospect of teaching Biology terrified her.

We compared our schedules and discovered that she was scheduled to teach Biology the same period that I taught a Biology class. A kernel of an idea began to form, the possibility of team teaching both Biology lecture sections together. We obtained permission from our principal to team teach and secured the use of the large group instruction room at the high school for that period. We were a go.

The result was one of the most memorable teaching experiences of my career. We shared the responsibilities of planning lessons, often meeting to bounce ideas off each other. Susan would ask me why I planned to present something in a particular order or manner, and I would share why. She would do the same. We took turns being the primary instructor during class while the person who was not "on point" that day could circulate and assist students or serve in a point/counterpoint role when the opportunity presented itself.

What I remember most vividly about the experience, which I could not put a name on at the time, was the incredible feeling of responsibility I felt to not let Susan down. Working so closely with Susan I felt accountable to her, not because she was my boss, but because she was a colleague and coworker and we had both committed ourselves to doing our part. I later learned that what we discovered together was professional accountability at its best.

Accountability can take many forms. Lerner and Tetlock[1] identify four ways that people can be made to feel accountable for their performance.

1. *Working with or in the presence of another person* makes you feel accountable either because someone is watching you perform or because you feel obligated to do a good job for your colleague who is counting on you.
2. *Identifiability* – the knowledge that some action or outcome will be directly attributable to you makes you feel accountable.
3. *Reason giving* – Having to explain to a coworker your actions, decisions, and choices makes you feel accountable for those same actions, decisions, and choices.
4. *Evaluation* – The formal assessment of your performance based on set criteria linked to consequences brings accountability.

You may not realize it, but you have already read about most of the elements of the CP that produce accountability. Let me summarize how all parties are held accountable in the CP.

Teacher accountability

1. Teachers work together with and in the presence of the Master Teacher and fellow teachers in the CP Teaching Unit. This is a constant source of *working in the presence of others* accountability.
2. During team meetings, lesson planning discussions with colleagues, and post-lesson debriefs teachers explain why they chose certain teaching strategies, methods, or practices. *Reason giving* accountability!
3. Formal evaluations of teachers are conducted by the Master Teacher after a minimum of 70 direct classroom interactions per teacher per year (lots of *working in the presence of others*

accountability). This evaluation is in the form of a comprehensive summative evaluation at the end of each school year.

    a. Teachers are evaluated based on how well they meet the commitment expectations they make to teacher colleagues and their Master Teacher at the start of the school year.

    b. Teachers are also accountable to their students for meeting student expectations of them as a teacher. Feedback data from student surveys is provided directly to the teacher and is also incorporated into the teacher's summative evaluation.

    c. Students' end-of-the-year test scores (*outcome-based evaluation accountability*) are incorporated into the teacher's summative evaluation.

4. Teachers are required to become CP certified prior to permanent assignment to a CP Teaching Unit. Whether or not a teacher becomes CP certified is directly attributable to the teacher's actions. This provides *identification accountability.*

5. At the end of each two-year teaching cycle the comprehensive summative evaluation is used to help determine teachers' eligibility for promotion up the CP career ladder. When a teacher moves from Teacher I to Teacher II, or Teacher II to Teacher III, they are identified once again as having met certain criteria for advancement (*identification accountability*).

Student Accountability

1. Student collaboration with other students in classes and in House is a constant source of student accountability (*working in the presence of other persons* and *reason giving*).

2. Students are evaluated based on how well they meet the commitment expectations they make to their teachers at the start of the school year. *Evaluation accountability*

3. Students receive individual report cards with grades which serve as a form of *evaluation accountability.*

4. Student also receive a House report card. *Identification accountability*

5. Students may receive recognition as an individual or member of a House (honor roll or House honor roll) which provides *identification accountability.*

Principals, Housemasters, and House Stewards are held accountable in a similar fashion. Each makes a commitment to meeting a set of clear professional expectations and is evaluated based on how well they meet those expectations. Each also provides the people they serve with expectation lists. For example, at the start of the school year the principal provides her teachers and Master Teachers with a list of expectations titled, "What you can expect from me as your principal." Later in the year teachers and MT's provide anonymous feedback surveys to the principal on how well she is meeting those expectations. Principals can adjust their practice based on this feedback. This feedback data is also included as part of the principal's formal summative evaluation done by the superintendent.

The beauty of the CP's embrace of a more professional form of accountability is that it motivates teachers to focus every day on becoming better teachers and providing better instruction, not because they are fearful of losing their jobs, but because they feel a professional responsibility to achieve and succeed as teachers. Best of all, the professionalism associated with these forms of accountability will keep great teachers in our public schools, while at the same time attracting the best and brightest teaching candidates to the profession.

Major points to take away from *Chapter 18, Accountability in the CP*

1. Accountability is woven into every aspect of CP culture, and not in the heavy-handed "carrot and stick" manner of outcome-based accountability found in schools today. CP accountability takes many forms including:
   a. Working with or in the presence of others
   b. Identifiability – the knowledge that some action or outcome will be directly attributable to you

    c. Reason giving – having to explain to another person your actions, decisions, and choices

    d. Evaluation – A formal assessment of performance

2. In the CP a teacher is accountable to his fellow teachers, his Master Teacher, his principal, and his students.

3. Students are accountable to their teachers, Housemaster, and fellow students.

4. Master Teachers are accountable to the principal and the teachers in their charge.

5. The principal is accountable both to the superintendent _and_ his teachers.

1. Lerner, J. S., & Tetlock, P. E. (1999). *Accounting for the Effects of Accountability.* Psychological Bulletin, 125, 255-275

CHAPTER 19

CP Training

AFTER READING THE last ten chapters you should have a pretty good sense of how differently schools operate within the CP philosophy and culture compared to the traditional educational paradigm. The changes are many, and they are dramatic.

So dramatic are the changes that we cannot pull teachers out of traditional classroom settings and plop them into CP schools and expect them to succeed. If we want teachers to make a smooth transition to working in a CP school, we must provide them with extensive, in-depth training. And, unlike most of the trainings that teachers encounter in their teaching careers, CP training must be experiential. _You cannot successfully train CP Unit teachers to work effectively with students and their Master Teacher by sitting them down in a classroom and lecturing them on how to work together._ As any good teacher knows, you learn more effectively by <u>doing.</u> _I cannot overemphasize the importance of extensive and intense "live" training to the success of CP pilots and eventual adoption of the CP in a school district._

There are many adjustments that teachers will need to make when moving to a CP school, none perhaps greater than getting used to being in the same classroom with other teachers, collaborating with them, and giving and receiving feedback from those same teachers.

Imagine teachers moving from a school where they work in total isolation and the emphasis is on individual accomplishment, to a CP school where a philosophy of "I succeed when we succeed" permeates an atmosphere of belonging and collaboration. The change would be more than a little unsettling.

We teachers are accustomed to, and generally comfortable with, working in isolation. It is the way we have always been asked to function in schools. We get assigned to a classroom and it is within those four walls that we work our magic with children, without the involvement of other adults (with a few exceptions, such as special education teachers or teacher aides). We simply do not know any differently. That changes dramatically in the CP, and we need to prepare teachers for that change.

Training format

CP teacher training cannot be done using a "one size fits all" template. The CP is not prescriptive. It permits, and demands, that each CP Teaching Unit be trained to meet the demands of the student and teacher populations in a particular district or at a particular school. Certain aspects of CP training can be shaped to meet students' specific cultural needs, all within the CP framework.

With that said, here are some general guidelines for CP teacher training.

- Plan on six weeks of full-time training in the summer (yes, teachers will need to be paid for this, which will be part of the district business administrators' budget impact projection).
- All teachers (and alternates) who are selected to participate in an upcoming pilot must go through training together, along with the individual who will serve as their Master Teacher in the pilot.
- In weeks 1 and 6 teachers work closely with the MT and become familiarized with all aspects of teaching in a CP school. In

weeks 2 through 5 teachers conduct classes with students who will also be experiencing the CP for the first time in the upcoming school year.

- Training days with students are split into two sessions.
- In the morning sessions teachers teach classes while other teachers observe or function in the same capacities they will in a CP pilot (team teacher, teaching assistant, evaluator/feedback provider).
- These summer classes should be designed as "preparing to succeed" classes and sold to students and parents as an opportunity to work closely with teachers to lay the foundation for higher levels of success in the upcoming school year. For example, a math class taught to 8th graders can lay the foundation for the algebra concepts students will be introduced to during the regular school year.
- In the afternoon sessions teachers will debrief lessons taught in the morning, team plan, and work on the skills they will need to help their students succeed in the CP. This will include training on how to serve in the role of Housemaster.
- These summer classes must be free to students.
- Training should, as much as possible, simulate the conditions that teachers will face during the regular school year while working in a CP school.
- Training must be sequential, i.e., the CP principal and MT need to be trained first, since the MT, and to a lesser degree the CP principal, will participate in the training of the CP teachers.
- Two candidates for each teaching position should go through CP training – the candidate who accepted the position and an alternate – in case the person who accepted the position inexplicably drops out. The alternate would also be next in line for a CP position the following year.

Training in the importance of language

In the CP, language is extremely important, and not in the sense of providing teachers scripts for specific lessons as some advocates of the common core curricula promote. What you say and how you say it is critically important in any work relationship (or any relationship for that matter). In my teacher training in college and during my teaching career I never encountered any formal instruction on language to use with students until the very end of my career when I spent a year and a half working in a juvenile detention center. It was there, during Therapeutic Crisis Intervention training, that someone finally provided me with some formal guidance on how to properly use language to avoid and/or deescalate problems in a classroom by staying away from any language that can serve as an emotional trigger to students (or colleagues for that matter). By that time, thirty years into working with adolescents, I had intuitively figured out how to use language to my advantage in a classroom, but only after lots of missteps along the way.

The language we choose when working with students can make the difference between successfully motivating individuals to press on and work hard and alienating students and turning them off to learning forever. A teacher can have in-depth knowledge of the subject matter he teaches and know everything there is to know about teaching methodology, but if he fails to use the right language when addressing his students, he can crash and burn in the classroom. And, unfortunately, when the teacher crashes and burns so also do his students.

Guidance and practice in using critical language needs to be an essential part of CP training. Teachers should work through scenarios they might encounter in class. What should teachers say to a group of 7th graders who come into their classrooms for the first time, who have never known anything other than the "every man for himself, sink or swim as an individual" paradigm of education? How do teachers begin to sell students on "I succeed when we succeed" and "belong, believe, work hard, succeed?" Language will be important.

What does a teacher say when a student says things like, "You don't really care about me. All you care about is getting good test scores so that you can keep your job?" What does a teacher say (or not say) when a student shares something about a tragic event in their life? Language will be important.

Language is equally important in the communications that take place between teachers in the CP. Teachers are not accustomed to giving or receiving lots of feedback from their professional peers. And yet high levels of collaboration, where ideas and feedback are constantly being exchanged, are at the heart of the CP philosophy.

Educators, as a group, are sensitive individuals who tend to lack a thick skin when it comes to "constructive suggestion." I know, I am one, and am married to another. During training we must provide guidance on the effective use of professional language <u>and</u> provide real-world opportunities to practice using such language to give and receive feedback. Language is important!

Major points to take away from *Chapter 19, CP Training.*

1. The number and kinds of changes found in the CP compared to the traditional educational paradigm will require that teachers undergo extensive training (six weeks in the summer).
2. Unlike most teacher trainings, CP training must be experiential to get teachers comfortable with working closely with colleagues, often in the same classroom.
3. Special emphasis in training will be placed on the importance of language as teachers (and students) become familiar and comfortable with giving and receiving feedback.

CHAPTER 20

Additional Beneficial Outcomes

Any practices that harm kids, ultimately harm society as well. Any practices that benefit kids, ultimately benefit society as well.

THE OVERARCHING GOAL of the CP is to develop outstanding teachers who, working in a highly professional and supportive school culture, can get all their students to be successful, in school and in life. This goal is of paramount importance. But there is a great deal more to be gained from using the CP in schools than the attainment of this overarching goal.

I originally titled this chapter "Peripheral Benefits." Later I changed it to "Secondary Beneficial Outcomes." As I continued to examine the benefits of using the CP it became clear to me that there was nothing "peripheral" or "secondary" about what students, teachers, and communities stood to gain. The beneficial outcomes described in this chapter are, in many ways, just as important as developing great teachers who can get all our students to succeed academically. They are "*additional* beneficial outcomes."

A few months ago I had dinner with a teacher who bemoaned the problems she had with disrespectful students in the hallways of her school and while on lunch duty, students she did not have in class. But that same teacher (an incredibly effective teacher, widely loved and respected by her students) had absolutely no behavior problems with the students *in her classes*. How odd you might think.

I know another outstanding, highly effective teacher who, to the best of his recollection, wrote one discipline referral in his entire career as a teacher – required by administration because the student had skipped class. Imagine how cocky and arrogant this teacher would sound in a job interview when asked how he handles student behavior issues in his classroom. "Uh, I don't *handle* student behavior issues in my classroom because I don't have any."

When teachers make their classrooms "off the charts" exceptionally great places to learn, places where students feel respected and safe, where students are constantly engaged in learning activities with each other, not only do students achieve and succeed academically, but other unexpected benefits surface as well. Great teachers do not stay up late at night trying to figure out how to maintain classroom control. Great teachers focus their energy on creating engaging lessons and a learning environment/classroom culture that draws students in. When students are hooked on learning in a classroom, good student behavior and classroom control emerge as welcome byproducts, additional beneficial outcomes linked to excellent teaching.

Recall that the CP is designed to solve a decades old wicked problem in education. *How do we populate all our classrooms with outstanding teachers who will get all their students to achieve and succeed?*

When the CP is fully adopted in a district it will, over time, successfully solve this problem. And in doing so it will do more than just increase the test scores of students. It will do more than decrease dropout rates and increase graduation rates. It will change the lives of *all* students for the better, and along the way it will produce a host of other positive side effects for students, teachers, schools, and the community.

The "additional beneficial outcomes" described in the rest of this chapter are realized over time. You will probably read this section with a healthy dose of skepticism, which is fine. I expect that. We can talk later about why I believe such benefits will emerge. For now, just recognize that students who attend CP schools for their entire educational careers will be immersed in the same supportive culture for somewhere between 8 and 13 years (depending upon the grade level where CP adoption takes place). Just as a young child who goes to live in a foreign country for several years absorbs the language and culture of the country, so also will a student who spends his/her entire educational life in CP schools learn to <u>live</u> the values, attitudes, beliefs, and practices of the CP culture.

Additional Benefits for Students
A Reduction in Student Stress Levels

In Chapter 6 I described how difficult adolescence is for all students, even students who seem, on the surface, to be happy and well-adjusted. If you add being desperately poor and failing in school to the base level difficulties all adolescents experience you get a perfect storm of negative emotions, confusion, anxiety, frustration, anger, powerlessness, sadness, depression, worthlessness, insecurity, hopelessness, isolation, and loneliness. Adolescents use strategies (good and bad) to cope with these emotions and the events that bring them out.

Today, operating in the traditional educational paradigm, there is little that our schools do to prevent the onset of these negative emotions in students or to mitigate their impact on student behavior. Yes, schools do have skilled counselors who can help students deal with any of the negative emotions above, but they usually do so remedially, after the emotions have triggered negative behaviors.

The CP, while not an emotional panacea for adolescents, provides a culture that reduces stress by proactively preventing the emergence (or reducing the level) of many negative emotions and their related behaviors. By reframing how students work together and interact in school with peers and caring adults the CP can calm the perfect storm of negative emotions and stress that adolescents experience.

- Clear expectations and consistent accountability reduce confusion and anxiety.
- Working with and helping others achieve group goals eliminates feelings of powerlessness and worthlessness.
- Experiencing regular success puts a major dent in any frustration, hopelessness, sadness, depression, or anger students feel.
- The family atmosphere of House gives students a sense of security while reducing isolation and loneliness.

Discipline issues will be greatly reduced in CP schools

This predicted additional benefit is simply an extrapolation of the experiences of outstanding teachers like those I referenced at the start of this chapter. In a CP school the ongoing collaboration and professional development of teachers results in high quality instruction across the board. This, coupled with the culture of "belong, believe, work hard, succeed," and "I succeed when we succeed," creates an environment where students are generally too busy being good students and supportive peers to get involved in misbehavior.

The CP will greatly reduce the incidence of bullying.

When students no longer doubt their own self-worth, they have no need to elevate themselves by putting somebody else down through bullying. Students who feel empowered in their Houses and Learning Communities will not crave or require the artificial sense of power that comes from crushing someone else down. And students who grow up in a school culture where they are lifted up and supported by their peers, and where they, in turn, lift up and support other students, will view bullying as a foreign concept that is not welcome in their school environment.

A Significant Reduction in Poor Life Decisions

Students sometimes make poor life decisions. Students who are frustrated and angry. Students who feel worthless, isolated, and lonely. Students who have lost hope and are depressed. Students who feel like no one loves them or cares about them. Students who feel like their life is going nowhere, that they have no future to look forward to. These individuals are prime candidates for substance abuse, gang involvement, early sexual activity (often leading to teen pregnancy), juvenile crime, and suicide.

Recall all the attributes in a CP school. In the CP no student is isolated or ostracized. In the CP every student knows that there are adults and other students who actively care about them, support them, and will help them to succeed in school and in life. In the CP there are caring adults and peers who a student can talk to, and who will listen, when that student has problems or concerns. In the CP students know they have worth because they all make important contributions to the greater good. In the CP students do not experience the anger and frustration of repeated failure because in the CP failure is not an option. In House, students experience mutual respect, trust, and the unity/connection of a family. There is group pride. There are rituals and traditions that bind House members together. Students feel safe knowing they have the support of fellow House members. House members know that they are an important contributing part of something larger than themselves. In the CP students feel a sense of pride and connection when they celebrate successes with their House and Learning Community. In the CP students have confidence and hope in a brighter future.

In such an environment how likely is it that students will make poor life decisions? Not very. Students who feel good about the direction their lives are headed and who are hopeful about their future are much less likely to make poor life decisions.

Additional Benefits for Students – The Flip Side

I do not want to leave you with the impression that the only additional benefits for students who grow up in CP schools are the elimination of negatives. In addition to reducing many negatives in students, the CP will also produce these student positives:

- Improved student attendance
- An increase in student involvement in school and community

- An increase in positive student attitudes
- An increase of students' hopefulness in the future, for themselves, their families, and their community
- An increase in students' confidence in their ability to succeed in life
- An increase in positive life choices
- The acceptance and welcoming of others as equals

Today, in 2022, at a time when intolerance, divisiveness, hatred, and fear of people who are in any way "different" seem to permeate the political landscape, this last additional benefit is perhaps the most important. Racial and ethnic bigotry are learned behaviors. So, also, is the acceptance and welcoming of others as equals.

In the 1970's people thought that integrating schools would end intolerance and racism. But simple proximity, placing kids of different races and ethnicities in one school, did not guarantee acceptance. In the CP, students in racially and ethnically diverse Houses and Learning Communities, who support one another and who work together to achieve group goals for six, eight, or ten years, are much more likely to internalize the acceptance of others.

Additional Benefits for Teachers

The number and quality of candidates looking to pursue careers in education can spiral up or down depending upon several different factors. As described earlier in Chapter 4, On Teachers and Teaching, low job satisfaction, onerous teacher evaluation systems, low pay, heavy workloads, and the overall difficulty of the job have all contributed to a steady decline in the numbers of individuals entering college programs in education. The number and quality of teacher candidates is spiraling down, as evidenced by teacher shortages now being experienced in various locales around the country.

The CP raises the job of teacher into the ranks of other true professional occupations. In the CP teachers are valued both for their skill and expertise and for their level of commitment to the success of all students. In the CP teachers are always growing. The regular collaboration between peers and with the Master Teacher and ongoing professional development lead to the production of outstanding, accomplished teachers. These teachers, working within the CP culture, can make more of a positive difference with kids than is possible in the traditional educational paradigm. The result is a tremendous increase in teacher job satisfaction. And when teachers feel good about what they are doing in their jobs they are more likely to remain teachers themselves and encourage other quality candidates to enter the profession.

The use of an educational paradigm where teachers experience high levels of success and job satisfaction will lead (once the word gets out) to more quality candidates looking to enter the teaching profession. More candidates wanting to get into teacher preparation programs will result in the programs being more selective, admitting higher quality candidates. When these candidates enter the job market in larger numbers school districts can be more selective in who they hire. The spiral goes up. Schools will not have to worry about teacher shortages that require them to place any warm body in front of students just to fill the position.

And finally, the CP will, once and for all, put an end to the nightmarish first year that all teachers experience when they are starting their careers. Teachers will no longer be "thrown to the wolves," so to speak, expected to make it entirely on their own. The levels of professional interaction between all teachers within the CP will provide new teachers with all the support they need to work through the challenges they encounter during the first year of teaching.

Here is a summary of some of the additional benefits of the CP on teachers and teaching.

- Outstanding, accomplished teachers in every classroom.
- High levels of job satisfaction.
- Lower teacher attrition rates; fewer teachers burning out and leaving the profession in the first five years.
- An increase in the status and prestige associated with teaching leading to higher quality, creative, intelligent, caring, hardworking candidates seeking to enter the teaching profession.

- Increased levels of positive interaction and engagement with parents and community members.
- More widespread public perception of teachers as highly skilled professionals leading to increased community support for education.

Additional Benefits for School Principals

The most obvious benefit to school principals is that the presence of the CP in their schools will allow them to do their jobs and do them well. And I am not trying to be flip in making this statement.

When a school is fully committed to the CP, the impossible job of the principal becomes manageable. Earlier I pointed out how unrealistic it was to expect any principal to meet all the performance responsibilities found in their job descriptions at a quality level. When the CP is fully in place, the principal of a 600 student school has 6 middle managers (the Master Teachers) who are each responsible for the success of all the students and teachers in their respective Learning Communities. This takes a tremendous load off the shoulders of a principal.

The principal can now _oversee_ the work of the Master Teachers, but no longer must do it all herself. No longer saddled with the unrealistic expectations of supervising, evaluating, and growing professionally a staff of 50 teachers by herself, the principal can focus on and successfully complete the other 45 or 50 performance responsibilities in her job description.

When their teachers become better teachers and when all their students succeed, principals also experience a tremendous increase in job satisfaction. And the associated reduction in stress for principals is an obvious additional benefit.

Additional Benefits for Cities/Communities

There is an association between healthy communities and healthy schools. Healthy communities tend to have healthy schools. Healthy, high functioning schools are usually found in healthy, high functioning communities. Similarly, dysfunctional schools are often located in dysfunctional communities, and dysfunctional communities tend to have dysfunctional schools. These associations beg a question. Which came first, the quality of the schools or the quality of the neighborhood/community? This is a "chicken or the egg" question that may not have a good answer. The more important question is this. If we have dysfunctional schools in a dysfunctional community, how do we turn them both around? Where do we start?

Today many urban communities deal with a laundry list of problems: high rates of poverty and unemployment, gangs, high crime rates, poor schools, drug abuse, blighted neighborhoods. Year after year many of the schools in these struggling urban communities pump out large numbers of dropouts, students who fail to graduate, and graduates not fully prepared for college or the workplace. Many of these students reenter their communities as unskilled adults who contribute little to solving the community's problems. In fact, they are likely to add to the problems and be a drain on community resources. Lacking education and having little hope for the future, these students may be destined to repeat the cycles of poverty and unemployment, crime, and substance abuse.

But what would happen if poor urban schools graduated virtually _all_ the students who attended? What if year after year schools in Syracuse, Chicago, Baltimore, St. Louis, New York, Boston, and Eugene, Oregon pumped out thousands of graduates who had internalized, in addition to their academics, all the values, attitudes, beliefs, and practices of the CP? How might they impact their communities and cities over time?

Consider further what might happen if all these graduates went on to two- or four-year colleges or vocational training programs? What if many continued to become professionals in medicine, law, education, engineering, business, or finance while others became skilled tradesmen and technicians? And then, having grown up in an educational environment (the CP) that fostered teamwork, collaboration, family, a sense of the greater good, _and a connection to and pride in community_, what if these graduates then returned to their home communities to live, work, start businesses, buy homes, raise their families, and pay taxes? What impact might these individuals have on their home communities?

I think the answer is obvious. Over time these individuals would have a profound positive influence on their communities. And unlike gentrification, which relies heavily upon an influx of more affluent people from outside the community, the positive changes would be home grown, produced by people who were born and raised in the community. Revitalization of our cities is potentially one of the greatest additional benefits of the CP.

But do not kid yourself. Such changes will not happen overnight. Nor will they happen in one year, in five years, or even ten years from now. CP implementation slowly works its way through schools. It will be six to eight years before the first CP students graduate from high schools. It could be another four to eight years before you start to see former students returning to their communities and giving back.

Unfortunately, politicians (and I include school superintendents in this category) want and need quick fixes. Their job security depends upon seeing rapid returns on any new initiative they champion. They are loath to take the long view and invest the time and money needed to reverse problems that were decades in the making because they too often fall prey to a classic "unless" statement like those I described at the start of this book. *I will always do what is best for kids and my community **unless** it takes so long to see the positive effects that I will not be around to get credit for what I started.*

Making a commitment to the CP and pursuing this additional benefit will require both great foresight and tremendous fortitude on the part of our civic and educational leaders . . . *or* tremendous pressure exerted from their constituents.

Earlier in this chapter I said that I expected readers to be skeptical about the additional benefits I described. I also promised that I would later explain why I believe these additional benefits will emerge. Here is why.

Not long ago my wife and I visited our daughter and her husband in Manhattan. We went out to breakfast one Saturday morning to a little diner on the upper west side. While we were eating breakfast, I could not help but notice the family sitting two tables over. There was a mother and father and three children, ages 6, 8, and 10, I would guess. What was remarkable about this little family group was how incredibly polite and well-mannered the children were. There wasn't a "please" or "thank you" missed when interacting with the waitress. They carried on polite conversations with their parents and each other. They listened when someone else spoke, did not interrupt, and generally behaved extremely well. On our way out at the end of our meal I could not resist the temptation to compliment the parents on the behavior of their children.

My questions to you are these. "During what six-month period did these parents teach their children a class on manners and appropriate restaurant behavior?" What course did these children take in school to learn to be so polite? Who wrote the character education curriculum which, when taught, produced such well-behaved children? Pretty stupid questions, right? Stupid because anyone who has every parented a child knows that it does not work this way.

Parents know that children learn manners and politeness and appropriate behavior when they (the parents) consistently *model* and reinforce these behaviors year after year after year. Parents know that they must constantly remind their children what is expected of them in their day-to-day interactions with other people. Successful parents produce and maintain a family culture in which children can informally absorb desirable attributes which may never be formally taught at any point in their lives.

At the end of a scholastic achievement dinner at our local school my then 6th grade daughter asked me why it was that we always had to stay late after school events were over to help clean up when most other parents just left. I paused a moment, looked at her and said, "I suppose because it's the right thing to do." There was no need for a lecture or long explanation. She knew that it was part of our family culture to help. Over time she internalized this and other aspects of our family culture.

Schools are no different. In schools, if you want something to "stick" with students, if you want students to internalize a certain set of values, attitudes, beliefs, and practices, they must see them modeled and <u>live</u> them, not just for one year with one exceptional teacher in one class, but for six, seven, or eight years in every class and with every teacher they encounter. The additional benefits of the CP will emerge simply because in the CP the internalization of these values, attitudes, beliefs, and practices that lead to student achievement and overall success *is not left to random chance.* Luck never enters the equation ("We were so fortunate that Johnny had a good teacher this year."). Every student reaps the benefit of high quality, caring, and supportive instruction (and instructors) every period of every day of every school year, for their entire school career.

Major points to take away from *Chapter 20, Additional Beneficial Outcomes.*

1. In addition to solving the decades long problem of populating our classrooms with outstanding, highly skilled teachers who get all their students to achieve and succeed, the presence of the CP in schools also produces a host of other benefits.
2. Students, teachers, administrators, and the community at-large all experience additional beneficial outcomes when the CP is fully implemented in a school.
3. Many additional beneficial outcomes can be realized quickly (within the first year or two), while others, such as those experienced by cities and communities, can take years to realize.
4. Many additional beneficial outcomes emerge because students are immersed in a school culture that includes high quality, caring, and supportive instruction every period of every day of every school year for their entire school careers.

PART III
MAKING IT HAPPEN

CHAPTER 21

Deciding "To Go" – Implementing the CP

"All great and honorable actions are accompanied with great difficulties, and both must be enterprised and overcome with answerable courage."

William Bradford

IN THE MOVIE *Apollo 13* Jim Lovell (played by Tom Hanks), the command pilot of Apollo 13, says to his wife, "From now on, we live in a world where man has walked on the moon. And it's not a miracle, we just decided to go." After the decision was made to go to the moon every obstacle became a challenge, not a barrier to successfully reaching the goal. They decided "to go" and then started the process of making it happen. Moving a school district from the traditional educational paradigm that has been in place for the better part of a century to the CP may not be equivalent to going to the moon, but there are similarities.

For starters, somebody needs to feel the urgency to act. Someone in the district must decide "to go" (as President Kennedy did on May 25, 1961), to start the ball rolling toward the adoption of the CP. Someone must start the process. And that someone could be you. Do not be shocked. I am quite serious.

You, as a teacher or parent or community member, can make the initial decision "to go" for the adoption of the CP in your home district. Regardless of who initiates the discussion about the possibility of moving a school or district toward the adoption of the CP, the implementation process is essentially the same. The discussion can start at the top and work its way down, or more likely, start at or near the bottom of the decision-making chain and work its way back up. At the most rudimentary level, the steps of the implementation process look something like this:

1. Gather information
2. Garner support, lots of support
3. Plan
4. Acquire resources
5. Conduct training
6. Execute the plan – begin the CP pilot

Gathering Information and Garnering Support – Lots of Support

Before a school district can start a CP pilot a great deal of information gathering, planning, resource acquisition, and training must take place. But moving the CP beyond being just a curiosity for discussion by a few people over coffee will ultimately require that the superintendent and/or the board of education make the decision to move to the informational phase. That decision will not be made unless those with decision-making power see a great deal of support for the CP already present within the district. It is imperative that early proponents garner lots of support *prior* to petitioning the superintendent or board of education. That support should include teachers, support staff, parents, community members and, ideally, a principal or two.

Supporters need to "do their homework" on the CP and how it can bring about higher levels of student achievement and success. They need to bring on board people willing to stand up and vocally express their support for CP adoption.

Recognize that at this initial stage you and other proponents are not asking the superintendent or board of education to adopt the CP. You are only asking that they investigate the CP, share information about the CP with various school constituencies, and gather feedback from each constituency prior to deciding on adoption.

While gathering support I cannot emphasize enough how important it is to always take the high road. There is never anything to be gained by denigrating the efforts of others who are trying to help kids, even if their efforts have not been very successful.

Every effort to garner support for the CP should be done openly and honestly. Remember, you are not asking people to support a random idea based solely on someone's belief. You are seeking support for a paradigm that sits firmly on a solid foundation of fundamental educational truths. Maintaining the high ground means citing those fundamental truths when voicing your support for the adoption of the CP in your school or district. There is no need to trash talk the paradigm that is currently in place, or the people who are functioning within that paradigm. "Maintaining the high ground" sounds something like this (spoken by a group of teachers to an assemblage of fellow teachers, parents, and community members).

"We have all worked very hard to try to get our kids to be successful, and we have seen some great individual successes. But we believe that everyone in this room would like to see more of our kids achieve at higher levels, graduate, and be more ready for college or a good job. We recently learned about a different way of doing things in schools, a new "paradigm," that we think could make a significant positive impact on our kids in many ways, academically, socially, and emotionally. We want to share that new paradigm with you tonight and explain why we believe it will be better for our students, our teachers, our parents, and our community."

Starting Small . . .

Let me carry the earlier moon landing analogy a little further. When President Kennedy announced to Congress, the country, and the world, the goal of putting a man on the moon before the end of the decade, the United States had not yet put a human into orbit. Technologies needed to achieve this goal did not even exist at the time.

Similarly, it is important to recognize that the CP as described in the previous chapters does not currently exist in any school anywhere in this country. Small pieces may exist, parts of the philosophy may be found in some schools, but the complete CP package is nowhere to be found. Nor has the CP ever been field tested in any school, and it needs to be.

The CP is a significant departure from traditional school paradigms. The fact that the CP is built upon a solid foundation of educational truths does not reduce or eliminate the need to perform field tests to firmly establish the CP's worth. Starting small translates into starting a few very small CP pilots in schools in diverse locations nationwide, with each pilot linked to a research university that will conduct a longitudinal study of the effectiveness of the CP. Data from these studies will eventually pave the way for the expansion of the CP into more schools.

Starting small means that the first year of a CP pilot, even in a very large school district, will only involve about 100 students (Cohort 1 in the graphic below), nine teachers in CP Teaching Unit A (7 FTEs - some teachers are shared, and one teacher is part time), and associated support staff. In the second year of the pilot 100 more students (Cohort 2) and nine more teachers (7 FTEs) in CP Teaching Unit B come on board. After spending two years with Cohort 1 in 7th and 8th grade, CP Teaching Unit A rotates back to 7th grade and welcomes Cohort 3 in year 3. Student Cohort 1 is then picked up by a new CP Teaching Unit as it enters 9th grade (CP Teaching Unit C). Each CP Teaching Unit spends two years with a cohort of students.

Another new cohort of about 100 students is added each year. In the example below, showing a pilot in a 7-12 junior/senior high school, the pilot "grows" to full capacity by the beginning of the sixth year. At the end of the sixth year, Cohort 1 is ready to graduate.

CP Pilot – Years 1-8

	Year 1	Year 2	Year 3	Year 4	Year 5	Year 6	Year 7	Year 8
12th Grade						Cohort 1 CPTU E	Cohort 2 CPTU F	Cohort 3 CPTU E
11th Grade						Cohort 1 CPTU E	Cohort 2 CPTU F	Cohort 3 CPTU E	Cohort 4 CPTU F
10th Grade					Cohort 1 CPTU C	Cohort 2 CPTU D	Cohort 3 CPTU C	Cohort 4 CPTU D	Cohort 5 CPTU C
9th Grade				Cohort 1 CPTU C	Cohort 2 CPTU D	Cohort 3 CPTU C	Cohort 4 CPTU D	Cohort 5 CPTU C	Cohort 6 CPTU D
8th Grade			Cohort 1 CPTU A	Cohort 2 CPTU B	Cohort 3 CPTU A	Cohort 4 CPTU B	Cohort 5 CPTU A	Cohort 6 CPTU B	Cohort 7 CPTU A
7th Grade	Cohort 1 CPTU A	Cohort 2 CPTU B	Cohort 3 CPTU A	Cohort 4 CPTU B	Cohort 5 CPTU A	Cohort 6 CPTU B	Cohort 7 CPTU A	Cohort 8 CPTU B

How many CP pilot schools should there be initially? Nationwide, starting small could mean as few as four pilot schools and as many as a dozen. The number of pilot schools is limited only by districts' ability to link up with a research university partner (Chapter 22, The University Connection), assemble the necessary staff and resources, and navigate through the implementation process successfully. The quantity of CP pilots is far less important than the quality of the pilots.

Starting Slowly – Walk, don't run.

I believe that the paradigm I described in the preceding chapters is a far better way to reach and teach kids than what we do in our traditional educational paradigms. If you share my belief that the CP will do great things for our kids and our educational system you need to be wary (as I must also) of evangelical fervor, the human tendency to want to spread your belief in this new paradigm quickly, to push untested reforms onto schools everywhere. Recall the error of previous educational reformers, believing in something so strongly that they became convinced that it must it true, even in the absence of objective data to support their beliefs.

Nothing would be more damaging to the long-term success of the CP than for energetic, well-intentioned, and overly enthusiastic super-intendents, boards of education, or legislative bodies, to advocate for the rapid, wholesale adoption of the CP in schools, school districts, states, or the entire nation. Attempting to implement the CP in this manner would doom it to failure.

Why start small and move forward slowly? There are several benefits.

1. The first, and most important, benefit of going slowly is student success. It is necessary to go slowly because students must literally grow into the CP, starting in 5th or 7th grade. From personal experience I can tell you that you cannot thrust high school upperclassmen into a CP setting and expect them to succeed. They will resist the changes in the CP.
2. The initial impact of a limited CP pilot on a district's budget is minimal. As a district's commitment to the CP grows with the addition of new CP grades each year, the budgetary impact also grows, but the growth is slow and incremental.
3. Going slowly gives everyone involved plenty of time to internalize and digest the changes associated with CP adoption so that they can make the conscious decision to "buy in." Nobody,

especially those individuals who are initially resistant to the changes, wants to have something new rammed down their professional throats.

4. As positive data slowly begins to emerge from the pilots, overall support for the CP will grow, which in turn will increase the support within the community for additional funding and resources.

5. When school districts slowly grow into the CP there is adequate time to recruit and train teachers, Master Teachers, principals, Housemasters, and House Stewards in the principles and practices of the CP. All the knowledge and experience gained by the first CP Teaching Unit (CPTU) during the first year of the pilot can be passed on to the next CPTU that will enter the pilot the second year. Accumulated knowledge and experience can be passed on to each new CPTU that comes on board, easing the transition.

6. Individuals who are positively impacted in the early years of a CP pilot become the best ambassadors for recruiting others to come on board with subsequent pilots or the more widespread adoption of the CP in a district.

7. Starting slowly with small CP pilots gives districts the opportunity to maintain a high level of quality control.
   a. Moving too fast results in more mistakes being made; insufficient training, design flaws not seen, toes stepped on, haphazard staff selection.
   b. As feedback and data come in, modifications and adjustments can be made to better meet the needs of students, teachers, principals, parents, and involved community members, before the CP is more widely adopted in the district.

8. Most importantly, starting small and moving slowly gives school districts and their affiliated research universities (Chapter 22) time to gather, document, and disseminate information to the educational community at large about the efficacy of the CP. This information can then be used to make informed decisions

on whether to expand the adoption of the CP, make modifications, or scrap the concept entirely.

School reformers feel pressure from all quarters to make broad, sweeping changes in education rapidly. Politicians and educational philanthropists clamor for rapid, bold action to improve our schools. Getting positive results five or ten years down the road is not acceptable since it will not help a politician win votes in the next election, or help a superintendent negotiate his next contract. It is understandable that people with new, bold ideas for improving the education of our children want to see their ideas put in place quickly. But for many reasons, brash, hasty, sweeping reform efforts in education have a way of burning out quickly and vanishing into educational history like a supernova. Starting small and moving forward slowly may seem tentative or weak to some, but it is the smart way to go.

Please do not get me wrong. If you share my belief that the CP can transform the schools in your district for the better, please channel your enthusiasm and go for it, just be wary and smart about how you proceed. Walk, do not run, into a new educational paradigm. And know that there will be . . .

Obstacles

Last June I had the pleasure of attending a high school graduation party for the daughter of a friend of mine. At the party I struck up a conversation with a woman who had recently become a member of her local school board on Long Island. The conversation turned to schools, making schools better for kids, and eventually to the CP. I shared an abbreviated version of the CP with Beth (not her real name) including some of my rationale for developing it. She was interested and intrigued, wondering if a paradigm like the CP could help the students and teachers in her district. But she quickly pointed out what she viewed as insurmountable obstacles to adopting the CP including budget concerns, contracts, teachers' unions, and the governor's recent cap on property tax increases.

Beth's initial reaction was similar to what I get from many people when they first hear about the CP. "I like what I am hearing, but that could never happen in my district or school because of _____ (fill in your obstacle of choice)." The road to CP implementation is most definitely littered with the educational equivalent of potholes, rocks, and other road debris. Depending upon your state and district, obstacles may include (but are certainly not limited to):

- State education laws and regulations (regarding tenure and other issues)
- Mandated teacher evaluation systems
- State and federal laws regarding those new teacher evaluation systems
- Labor law issues impacting the Master Teacher position (half teacher, half administrator)
- Local budgetary obstacles
- Student scheduling concerns
- State funding issues
- Busing schedule issues (for the extended day)
- Union contract issues
- Grade reporting software issues

I could depress you and continue but the list is already rather intimidating. You might even say insurmountable. There is no question that these obstacles are, at the very least, challenging. I confess that at one point even I questioned whether they could be overcome. But then I had an epiphany of sorts while hiking in Mt. Rainier National Park.

The wilderness can throw some formidable obstacles in your path; tree blow-downs, beaver impoundments covering the trail, washed out bridges over raging streams, slopes of loose rock (talus) that can break away and take you for a dangerous ride, late season snow fields that hide landmarks and get you hopelessly lost, and icy steep cliffs where a false step ends your hiking days forever. Some of the obstacles found in the wilderness are easily circumvented. Others are truly insurmountable.

As I was hiking and thinking about the obstacles in our path it occurred to me that every obstacle in the path of CP implementation (yes,

I think about the CP all the time), unlike those we encountered on the trail, is man-made, created and put in place by human beings. My "ah-hah!" moment came when I realized that if the obstacles were created by people, then they could be removed or set aside by people. Or they could be modified by people so that they were no longer an impediment to CP implementation. Human beings are a resourceful bunch. We figured out how to run a train under the English Channel from England to France. We overcame gravity to master air travel and space flight. Surely we can renegotiate a contract that we drew up in the first place. Surely we can modify schedules and budgets that we constructed. And surely we can get state education laws amended or specific regulations waived. If a document as profound and enduring as the US Constitution can be modified through amendment, I think it is fair to say that any state or federal law governing education can be modified if there are compelling reasons to do so. And what more compelling reason is there than to do what is best for _all_ our children?

. . . and Resistance

Obstacles are *things*, resistance involves *people*. Whether you are a superintendent trying to initiate a CP pilot in your district, or a group of teachers trying to convince the superintendent and board of education to move forward with a pilot, you can expect plenty of resistance, and for good reasons.

A lot of things change in a school when the CP is adopted. Change, we know, makes people feel uncomfortable. If we take people out of their comfort zone, it is reasonable to expect that they will resist the CP, at least initially. Additionally, members of various school constituencies will have legitimate concerns, even fears, about how some aspects of the CP will impact them and their jobs. Superintendents will have legitimate concerns regarding Master Teachers' ability to perform their teacher supervision and evaluation functions in an objective and unbiased manner. Principals will have legitimate concerns about surrendering responsibility for many tasks to Master Teachers, tasks which are performed exclusively by the principal in the traditional educational paradigm. Teachers will have legitimate concerns about giving up lifetime tenure and about their new role as Housemasters. Parents will have a legitimate concern that the emphasis on "I succeed when we succeed" will detract from their child's individual accomplishments. All these concerns, and many others, will lead to resistance.

With resistance coming from every quarter, how can you get a CP pilot off the ground? Simple answer, you cannot. The CP is about people and relationships. You cannot move forward with a CP pilot unless and until you develop relationships with some key school constituencies and reduce and/or overcome their resistance. The goal is to get people to "buy in."

You will find that many people agree with all the fundamental truths in education that form the foundation of the CP (Chapter 3), but still cannot bring themselves to support the CP because of some personal agenda ("We always do what is best for kids unless . . .").

As an early supporter of the CP and perhaps the person (or persons) who made the initial decision "to go," it will be your job to allay the legitimate fears and concerns of individuals in every constituent group (overcome any resistance) and enlist their support. To do that you need to know each group's fears and concerns, why those fears/concerns are real, and how to respond to them. You need to be prepared to list reasons why each group should support the CP (what each group gains from the CP). While making the case for a group's support you should be prepared to cite aspects of the CP's cultural, structural, and operational paradigms as well as the fundamental truths of education delineated in Chapter 3. (See Appendix F for a shorthand version of the Fundamental Truths) In short, you had best do your homework before you head off to garner support for a CP pilot.

Never one to leave his students high and dry with a difficult homework assignment, in **Appendix R** you will find the information you need to confront any resistance head on. I list reasons why various school constituencies might resist the CP, and counter with the reasons why each school constituency should support the CP. The school constituencies include students, teachers, parents, principals, superintendents, school counselors, teachers' union leadership, and community members. The key to overcoming resistance is to get each school constituency to recognize that they have a great deal to gain from participating in the CP and very little, if anything, to lose.

If the task I just described seems daunting, there is good news. The good news is that after attaining the support and participation of the superintendent and board of education you will not need to garner the support of every member of other school constituencies. Even in a large district with 1000 or more teachers, to get a pilot underway you only need to allay the fears and concerns of about a dozen teachers, gain their support, and enlist their participation. The same is true of community members. While numbering in the thousands you will only need to enlist the support and participation of less than 20 over two years (to serve as House Stewards) to get a pilot started. Remember, the pilot is a small experiment designed to determine if the CP can do what it is designed to do and produce positive results. Initially, every teacher in the district does not have to be on board with the experiment, only those who are going to participate. Additional support for the expanded use of the CP in a district's schools will come slowly as the effectiveness of the CP is demonstrated.

Designing the Process

The task of designing and putting together a CP pilot can seem overwhelming. Viewing the number and complexity of tasks that must be accomplished probably explains why such an educational paradigm does not yet exist. Who wants to go through all that hassle and work when we can muddle through the way we have for the last hundred years? Hopefully you do.

It will take a district approximately two full years to move from the earliest discussions of a CP pilot to the start of a CP pilot in September. Any district looking to be one of the first to conduct a CP pilot will literally be "inventing the wheel" (not reinventing it). Every task will have to be identified, clearly defined, and then completed for the very first time. After several pilots have been conducted and a basic template for the initiation of a pilot is established the timeline can likely be trimmed to about 15 months, especially if research universities partner with school districts along the way.

It is not within the scope of this book to lay out every detailed step of the implementation process. Nor would it prove to be of value since every district will have to deal with its own unique set of issues and concerns as an implementation plan is developed. But hopefully the list below will give you a feel for the magnitude and scope of the undertaking.

After someone has made the decision "to go" and presuming that the superintendent and board of education have approved moving forward with the CP pilot, the following tasks will have to be completed in the two years prior to the start of the pilot.

1. The district convenes a CP Pilot Implementation Task Force charged with:
   a. Developing the implementation sequence for the district with an accompanying timeline.
   b. Designating the person or persons responsible for completing each task in the sequence.
   c. Coordinating efforts to complete all tasks in the sequence in a timely manner.
2. Multiple formal informational meetings regarding the district's plan to develop a CP pilot are held with various constituencies. At each meeting a presentation about the CP is delivered, written information summarizing the impact of the CP on each constituency is distributed, and a question-and-answer session is held. These meetings should be held with:
   a. Teacher groups
   b. Teachers' union leadership and representatives.
   c. District administrators
   d. Parents
   e. Community groups
3. Contact is made with a research university that is a part of the CP Consortium (See Chapter 22, The University Connection) and an agreement is reached to conduct a longitudinal research study on the effectiveness of the CP pilot. This agreement addresses:
   a. Types of data to be gathered and the instruments used to gather data.

    b. How, when, and by whom data will be gathered.

    c. How, when, and with whom this data will be shared.

    d. School and district responsibilities

    e. University responsibilities

    f. Costs associated with data gathering, tabulation, interpretation, and distribution and what percentage of these costs will be borne by each entity.

4. General staffing requirement recommendations for each year of a 6-year pilot are developed.

5. A career ladder with accompanying pay scale for CP teachers is developed.

6. The school district business administrator conducts an analysis of the impact of a 6-year CP pilot on the district budget.

7. The superintendent and the district business administrator make budget adjustment recommendations and/or locate grant money to fund the CP pilot initiative.

8. Addenda to the teachers' contract are negotiated with the teachers' union that address the following:

    a. Changing tenure for CP teachers to 6-year renewable tenure.

    b. The process to be used for tenure recommendation and renewal under the new form of tenure for CP teachers.

    c. Approval of a career ladder and accompanying pay scales for CP teachers.

    d. Revisions of teacher evaluation procedures for CP teachers.

    e. Safeguards for teachers participating in the CP pilot should the district opt out of the CP at any point in the future.

    f. The establishment of the Master Teacher position outside the teachers' union negotiating unit (Masters Teachers to be represented by a separate entity).

9. State Department of Education is petitioned for waivers for any of the negotiated items above that are governed by state law.

10. Grading software is acquired/developed that will permit the calculation and reporting of student, House, and Learning Community grades from teacher entries for individual students.

11. Commitment expectation lists are developed for each constituency actively participating in the CP pilot. These are, in essence, revised job descriptions in expectation form. See Appendices E-1 and E-2 for examples.

12. A process is established for identifying potential candidates for the CP School principal, CP Unit teachers, and Master Teachers.

13. Information is distributed to all teachers and school district administrators regarding this process in writing and via informational meetings.

14. Candidates (and alternates) are selected for the CP principal and Master Teacher roles in the CP pilot.

15. CP principal and Master Teacher training is conducted.

16. The school master schedule is constructed to include essential aspects of the CP pilot (House periods, CP Unit meetings, the Master Teacher and his/her complement, length of school day).

17. A teacher training program is designed and set up.

18. Candidates (and alternates) are selected from a pool of applicants for all teacher roles in the CP Unit.

19. CP Unit teacher training is conducted with direct involvement of the previously trained Master Teachers and alternates.

20. Potential House Stewards are identified in the community and invited to informational meetings and/or contacted directly and recruited to participate.

21. Formal invitations to participate are extended to House Steward candidates.

22. House Steward training is conducted.

23. A process is developed for the random selection of students who will become the first cohort in the CP pilot.

24. Information is disseminated to parents of students participating in the CP pilot via informational meetings at school and direct one-on-one meetings with Housemasters.

25. School Opens

As much as possible I tried to place these tasks in chronological order. Some of the tasks can be carried out simultaneously by different individuals or groups. Other tasks must take place in a certain order. For example, the CP pilot's principal and Master Teacher candidates must be selected and trained first, before the CP Unit teachers. This is essential because the Master Teacher serves as the primary trainer during CP Unit teacher training.

The "All or None" Caution

As members of the implementation task force work through the process of building a CP pilot it is important that they be aware of one major pitfall. CP pilot schools (and all future CP schools) are defined by the presence of all elements of the CP as described in earlier chapters. The CP is _not_ an a la carte menu from which a district can pick and choose the tasty morsels it wants while discarding the parts it finds less palatable.

If you try to insert a single piece of the CP into a traditionally structured and operated school you will see little if any positive effect, and certainly no lasting positive effects. If you try to start a CP pilot and selectively eliminate one or two elements of the CP, you are asking for failure.

Each individual aspect of the CP works well for students and teachers _only_ when it exists within the larger framework of the entire CP. For example, the value of the Master Teacher is completely lost if he/she is expected to carry a full teaching load. The House System is nothing more than a glorified study hall absent the philosophical underpinning of _Belong, Believe, Work Hard, Succeed_ and _"I succeed when we succeed"_ and teachers having the time to serve as Housemasters. Without the presence of a career ladder and ongoing opportunities for collaboration and professional growth it is doubtful that any teachers would volunteer to participate in a CP pilot. If the grade reporting system does not generate both individual and House grades on student report cards, and if there is no House Honor Roll, what is the incentive for students to work together in House? If feedback forms are not filled out by each constituency, how will teachers, students, Master Teachers, and principals know if they are meeting their commitment expectations, and how can they be expected to improve? The CP works as an educational paradigm when _all_ aspects of the CP are present. The bottom line is that the CP is an "all or none" proposition. To have an effective, high functioning CP school 100% of the elements of the CP need to be present. Anything less and you do not have a CP school.

This is of particular importance when you consider that each CP pilot school will be part of a research protocol. If three pilots contain 7 of 10 elements of a CP school, another three pilots contain 6 elements (not all the same), and still another three pilots contain 8 elements, it becomes very difficult, if not impossible, to draw any valid conclusions about the impact of the CP on student achievement, drop-out rates, graduation rates, and a host of qualitative measures. If all the elements of the CP are present in nine pilot schools, and if those schools fail to produce significant increases in student achievement and graduation rates, then the research will show that the CP was not effective. But, if each of the nine schools was missing different elements of the CP, it would be impossible to know if the failure to improve student achievement levels was attributable to the CP as a whole or to the absence of the missing elements.

Who would be responsible for ensuring that any proposed CP pilot is fully in compliance with all the requirements of the CP? My suggestion is that the associated research university be responsible for certifying that each CP pilot contains all the elements of the CP.

The "all or nothing" nature of the CP at the outset of pilots is important to establish baseline data. We must know how well the CP is working for students and teachers before we start making changes. This does not mean that the CP cannot be flexible going forward. Modifications can and should be made later and any changes should be carefully tracked to determine their impact on student and teacher success.

Another manifestation of the "all or none" concern is post-success erosion. This is a phenomenon that I have seen happen too many times in my career. It works something like this. A new program which requires staffing and funding (like the CP) is initiated in a district and proves effective in helping students succeed. After a time, a new, higher level of functioning becomes the accepted norm. When future budget concerns (sometimes only a few years down the road) lead to a search for places to cut, the person or persons controlling the district purse strings forget what was required (in terms of staffing and funding) to reach this new higher level of functioning. To save money the district starts to "trim" away some of the program's staffing and funding. The presumption is made that the new higher level of functioning is somehow now a "given" that will not be affected if staff or funding are cut. But the reality is that when cuts are made the program no longer produces the intended outcomes it was put in place to produce. Predictably, the program ultimately implodes.

This post-success erosion of support for a successful program obviously hurts kids. But it also can have a serious impact on staff, especially in the case of the CP. When teachers sign on to become members of a CP Teaching Unit in a CP school their participation is *voluntary*. They choose to take on new roles and responsibilities and willingly give up access to lifetime tenure. In return, they expect to work within a new educational paradigm where they will be treated as true educational professionals and afforded opportunities for professional growth and advancement.

School districts have the right to cut programs, eliminate staff, and reduce funding whenever they choose. However, when a school district adopts the CP, it must agree to certain constraints on altering support for the CP in the future. To retain certification as a CP school, the district will be required to demonstrate that the integrity of the CP is being maintained. All the crucial elements of CP culture, structure, and operational procedures must be present in the school.

A district can certainly decide at any point to eliminate the CP wholesale. If that happens contractually agreed upon protections for teachers, Master Teachers, and principals would kick in regarding working conditions, salary, and tenure status. But the district must be constrained from making changes that will nibble away at the CP and negatively impact students or teachers and their ability to function within the CP.

The "Vindictive Resistance" Caution

The quote of the start of this chapter speaks of the courage needed to overcome the great difficulties associated with "all great and honorable actions." If you choose to pursue getting a CP pilot up and running in your home district you will, without doubt, run into difficulties. You will encounter many obstacles to surmount or circumvent and much resistance to overcome. Yes, you will need courage, but also patience, perseverance, boldness, grit and determination, and an unwavering commitment to doing what you believe is best for kids. You need to be courageous, but you must avoid being foolish or naïve regarding what you may be up against in terms of resistance.

You may encounter three types of resistance on the road to a CP pilot. The first is passive resistance. Passive resistance occurs when people simply choose to <u>not</u> participate in the CP. They may not like the concept, or they may think it is "OK," but just not for them. Either way, a passively resisting individual does not try to keep others from pursuing the CP.

Active resistance occurs when individuals choose to <u>not</u> participate in the CP and then actively work to prevent the CP from being adopted. These are the individuals who you must work to convince that the CP has value. You must work doggedly to bring them on board. Otherwise, they can and will undermine your efforts to get a CP pilot started in your district.

The final kind of resistance – vindictive resistance – is the most dangerous. Vindictively resistant individuals do not want to participate in the CP themselves, will actively work to prevent CP adoption, <u>and</u> will act to professionally harm or discredit those individuals who are working to get the CP adopted.

This last category of resistance is not a figment of my imagination. I experienced it first-hand. When you take a stance to do what you believe is right and best for kids, and if that stance runs counter to what the superintendent or other persons in positions of power believe, you run the risk of encountering vindictive resistance. It works something like this.

Two teachers propose some change in their district (such as the CP) that they and others believe will be better for kids. The district superintendent makes it clear to these two teachers that he does not support the change they are promoting, and he "suggests" they not pursue it anymore. When they continue to promote their idea and garner additional support from parents, teacher colleagues, and community members to take to the Board of Education they may be putting themselves in professional jeopardy, even if they are open and honest about their efforts and "take the high road" at all times. If their superintendent does not like having his "suggestions" rebuffed, if he has power and control issues ("my way or the highway"), he can make the professional lives of these two teachers miserable in any number of ways. They could end up with the teaching schedules from hell. They can be assigned extra duties. They can have their teaching load increased. And worst, if either or both teachers are not yet tenured, they may not be recommended for tenure, regardless of the quality of their work in the classroom. You are naïve if you think that this form of resistance does not exist in schools. It does. Any employee who considers pursuing the implementation of the CP against the wishes of a person or persons in positions of authority over schools should make sure that they have the protection of tenure before doing so.

Major points to take away from *Chapter 21, Deciding "To Go" – Implementing the CP*

1. Anyone in a school district (parent, teacher, principal, superintendent, community member) can initiate the process leading to CP adoption.
2. Successful adoption of the CP means starting slowly with a small number of pilots which will field test the CP as data is recorded.
3. Obstacles to CP adoption are manmade, which means they can be broken down or removed by men (and women).
4. Resistance to the CP is often based on legitimate concerns and fears which must be fully addressed and allayed to gain the support and active participation of important school constituencies.
5. The implementation process is long (~2 years) and involved, requiring a significant commitment of energy and resources.
6. The CP cannot be successfully adopted in part. It is an "all or nothing" proposition.
7. Vindictive resistance occurs when someone acts to professionally harm or discredit others working to get the CP adopted.

CHAPTER 22

The University Connection

MOVING THE CP from the theoretical realm to the real world will require collaboration between school districts and universities. Neither entity has all the resources needed to move the CP properly and effectively into schools. Districts have the schools that will serve as laboratories for testing the CP concept and the experienced teaching staff to tap for new CP Teaching Units. Universities have the expertise in gathering data and conducting longitudinal research studies that can be used to evaluate the effectiveness of the CP. Universities also have the all-important capacity to store and disseminate research data to the educational community at large.

Universities have a vested interest in improving K-12 public education. The products of our middle schools and high schools are the raw materials for colleges and universities. University administrators will tell you that they spend far too much time and money providing remediation for incoming freshmen, students who <u>graduated</u> from high school. Support for an educational paradigm that produces a higher percentage of fully prepared college applicants would be a wise investment for colleges and universities.

Universities can serve five key roles in advancing the CP.

1. Assist school districts in setting up pilot programs to test the effectiveness of the CP.
2. Conduct longitudinal studies on the effectiveness of the CP.
3. Maintain the integrity of the CP in schools where it is implemented.
4. Serve as clearinghouses for information on the CP.
5. Develop and teach undergraduate and graduate courses in the CP and, as much as possible, link what is taught in these courses to field work in public school classrooms, ideally in extended student teaching experiences.

1. Assist school districts in setting up pilot programs.

Any school district looking to pilot the CP faces many challenges. School districts looking to run CP pilots will be starting from scratch, breaking new ground with every step.

There is no denying that the number and variety of tasks that need to be completed to get a CP pilot off the ground is a bit overwhelming (Chapter 21). Some tasks include the selection of personnel, developing a budget and applying for grants, designing and conducting staff training programs, developing expectation lists, and defining the new roles of teachers, Master Teachers, the principal, Housemasters, and House Stewards (new job descriptions). New schedules will need to be created, new grading software must be developed, and teacher contracts will need to be modified in consultation with teachers' unions (to address a new career ladder and changes to teacher tenure).

School districts will need all the help they can get to complete these and many other tasks. It makes no sense to reinvent the wheel at five or six different pilot locations around the country. The most cost effective and efficient way to get pilots up and running will be to create a consortium of regional research universities that can work closely with

representatives of participating school districts to address all the implementation issues and hammer out the details of a comprehensive CP
pilot adoption plan. The final product of the preliminary work of this
consortium will be a template for CP pilots that is true to CP principles
and that can be replicated anywhere in the country.

2. **Conduct longitudinal studies on the effectiveness of the CP.**

One of the most glaring omissions/failures of the educational reform
movement that centered around teacher accountability and high stakes
testing was that no data were gathered from small pilot programs to
evaluate the impact and effectiveness of the new reforms _before_ these
reforms were forced upon schools across the country. Imposing any educational reform agenda on schools that is based more on _beliefs_ than
on empirical evidence is a recipe for disaster. CP Pilot programs will
serve to "test drive" the CP on a small scale. However, the CP pilots are
of value only if they produce hard data that can be used to evaluate the
efficacy of the CP. Enter the consortium of major research universities.

A consortium of Education Departments from five or six research
universities can develop a single research protocol that will be consistently applied at several locations around the country. This will permit
comparative analysis of data from different pilot sites. Plus, having data
from multiple sites around the country will meet the need for replica-
tion of the research study.

An astronomical amount of data could be gathered in a longitudinal
study of the CP. Aside from the obvious effects on student achievement,
drop-out rates and graduation rates, data can also be gathered on student
attendance, achievement gap reduction, student attitudes, teacher collaboration, the role of the MT, teacher attitudes, the impact of House (on bullying, student anxiety, and students' sense of belonging), teacher professional
growth and development, principal attitudes, parent involvement, parental
attitudes toward school and teachers, community perceptions, and so on.

The bottom line is that universities have the resources and expertise
to conduct research on the effectiveness of a new educational paradigm. School districts and state education departments do not.

3. Maintaining the integrity of the CP in schools – Quality Control

The ideas I put forth in this book are not patented. Anyone can use them and try to create better schools for students and teachers. I have no control over what parts of the CP someone may choose to integrate into their classroom or school. After all, that is what we all do as educators. We beg, borrow, and steal ideas that will help us be more effective in the classroom.

I am confident that schools which _fully_ adopt the CP will, over time, see tremendous increases in the levels of achievement, teacher effectiveness, and overall student success. However, I am equally confident, perhaps even more confident, that schools will fail to produce such gains if they cherry pick only a few aspects of the CP and leave others out (see the "all or none" concerns in Chapter 21). Quality control is critical. There needs to be some form of centralized control over how the CP is adopted and sustained in schools. Without this, the dangers of partial implementation described in Chapter 21 will become a reality. Corners will be cut, only some aspects of the CP will be cherry-picked for adoption, and students and teachers will suffer the consequences.

Putting the responsibility for quality control in the hands of the research universities instead of school districts is more important than you might think. School districts are notorious for jumping on board with new innovations and then abandoning them a couple years later because of changes in leadership, budgetary concerns, etc. The working reality of school districts is that quality programs for kids are often eroded or even eliminated for a variety of reasons. I can picture how this will play out in CP schools. "Hey, our students are doing great now. We don't need a full period for House anymore. Ten minutes will be enough." Or, "Our students are doing so much better now. Our teachers can get by without all that 'free time.' If we require teachers to teach an additional class and start covering duties again, we can save a ton of money." The erosion of CP principles in a CP school will result in half-hearted efforts to help kids succeed that will eventually crumble and fail.

If CP pilots begin to demonstrate significant increases in student achievement and other positive student outcomes, would it not be reasonable to protect the integrity of the educational paradigm that produced such remarkable results? I think so. School districts should be required to work with some designated outside entity to both acquire and maintain accreditation as a CP School. Maintaining accreditation would require that schools stay true to all CP attributes. Research universities that are a part of a CP consortium would be ideal vehicles for providing such accreditation.

4. Serve as clearinghouses for information on the CP.

If the initial wave of CP pilots proves to be successful, interest in the CP will increase. Anyone with an interest in improving education for our children – teachers, principals, superintendents, boards of education, parents, community leaders, politicians – will see the possibilities of the CP and want more information. At that point information provided by this book will be far less useful than information gleaned from the actual CP pilots. Again, enter the consortium of research universities.

Information and data collected from schools that have fully adopted the CP need to be gathered, collated, moved to a central location, and made available to the public. How better to do this than to have each member institution of the consortium gather and organize data from their partner schools and then post it on a website accessible to all.

5. Incorporate CP concepts into undergraduate and graduate teacher education programs.

School districts will undoubtedly look to expand the use of the CP into more schools if over a period of several years the CP pilots demonstrate that the CP is working effectively. This expansion will create a demand for more teachers trained in the CP who are ready to make the leap to CP schools. At some point, colleges and universities will hopefully recognize this demand and begin to include some key elements of the CP in their undergraduate teacher education programs.

One final thought for the truly visionary individuals in higher education. How great would it be for the world of public education if universities developed master's degree programs that graduated teachers who were truly "masters" of their craft? What I am talking about is a program that uses the principles of the CP and that requires two full years in residence to become skilled in those principles. Candidates would take coursework (mostly in the summer) and teach full-time in a CP middle school or high school that is run jointly by the university and a local school district. Candidates would teach as members of CP Units and serve as Housemasters under the guidance of practicing Master Teachers. In year two, candidates would have the opportunity to take on the responsibilities of a Master Teacher for a period of time.

The real-world experience gained by teaching for two years in an environment that emphasizes continuous professional development would produce graduates who are head and shoulders above other master's degree recipients who simply complete thirty hours of coursework and write a thesis and/or pass a comprehensive exam. Such a Masters program could be highly selective. Teachers who completed the program would earn a coveted master's degree in Secondary Education. They would be ready to step into a CP school anywhere and function at a high level as a member of a CP Teaching Unit.

Ah, but we can dream!

Major points to take away from *Chapter 22, The University Connection.*
Research universities can serve five key roles in the successful adoption of the CP. They can:

1. Assist school districts in setting up pilot programs to test the effectiveness of the CP.
2. Conduct longitudinal studies on the effectiveness of the CP.
3. Maintaining the integrity of the CP in schools where it is implemented.
4. Serve as clearinghouses for information on the CP.
5. Develop and teach undergraduate and graduate courses in the CP and, as much as possible, link what is taught in these courses to field work in public school classrooms, ideally in extended student teaching experiences.

CHAPTER 23

What Next? Where to Now?

I CANNOT WRITE an ending to this book because the CP story is not finished.

At the risk of sounding a bit corny, you, along with other teachers, parents, counselors, principals, and community members, will write the ending. I can do my best to help, but ultimately you will complete the story when the CP is piloted, and hopefully fully adopted, in school districts around the country.

This annoying lack of an ending begs two questions that we each must answer. "What next?" and "Where to now?"

My answers to these questions are straightforward. Because I want to complete the story of the CP and see the CP piloted and implemented in schools around the country, I plan to talk to people, lots of people. I plan to give away free copies of this book (as many as I can afford on a teacher's retirement pension) and then talk with people about their views of the various aspects of the CP. I plan to visit school districts and university schools of education in the hope of finding people who, with *"answerable courage,"* will step up and do what is best for kids and their teachers.

Your answers to the "What next?" and "Where to now?" questions will undoubtedly be very different. Your response to the "What next?" question may be to do nothing. You may choose to simply return this book to the library or place it up on a bookshelf in your room. End of story. And that is ok. I have no problem with that. But before you do, before you decide on your answers to "What next?" and "Where to now?" please take a few minutes to read (or reread) Appendix R in the back of the book, *Why Groups Might Resist or Support the CP.* When reading it, pay special attention to the group or groups that you belong to. (You may be both a teacher and a parent, or a parent and a board of education member.) When you finish reading Appendix R please come back here and we will talk.

Welcome back. Thanks for humoring me.

I wanted you to read/reread Appendix R because most people do not realize how much they can gain by boldly stepping into a new educational paradigm. It is remarkable that every school and community constituency benefits significantly from the CP. But, if after reading Appendix R you do not feel in your heart that the CP is something worth pursuing, then just walk away. It is also possible that you see some merit in the CP but feel it is best to pilot elsewhere, not in your home district. Again, just walk away.

But you might be intrigued, perhaps even excited, by many of the concepts and practices within the CP and see them as being potentially beneficial to the students, teachers, and others in your school community. You might decide "to go." If that is the case, please do not do anything rash or overly dramatic. Do not charge into your superintendent's office or a school board meeting and demand that they initiate a CP pilot in your district. Rather, loan your copy of this book to a fellow teacher, parent, or community member, ask them to read it, and then just talk about it with them. You have my permission to start the discussion with this provocative question. "Is this Czarniak guy totally nuts or is there something to this CP business?" My hope is that the answers you hear will sound something like this. "Yeah, he might very well be nuts, but he does describe some good stuff that could really help our kids and teachers." If this is what you hear, consider broadening your discussion group to three or four people.

And then have fun with it. Talk with people over a beer or a glass of wine. Run hypotheticals by each other. "If we could do this, would it help our kids? Would it help our teachers help our kids? How do you think our students and teachers would react to the _I succeed when we succeed_ philosophy? The _Belong, Believe, Work Hard, Succeed_ culture? Would this positively impact our community down the road?"

When you are having these initial discussions try to avoid getting stuck on whether it would be "practical" to start a CP pilot in your district. Do not get hung up on potential obstacles or sources of resistance at this early stage. Focus instead on whether each aspect of the CP would be good for the students, teachers, and other constituencies in your school district. There will be plenty of opportunities to address the "practical" concerns later if your district decides to pursue a CP pilot.

If your little group's responses to the above hypotheticals are generally affirmative and positive, you may then want to expand your group still further, including members of other school constituencies. Keep talking and learn everything you can about the CP. Find out if there are other schools in your area or state that have already begun the implementation process and talk to someone there. There is no need to reinvent the wheel. As you proceed, remember the importance of starting small and going slowly.

Whether or not you and your small group decide to move beyond this casual discussion phase to pursue a CP pilot is up to you. I will not guilt you into doing more (although I thought seriously about doing just that). Nobody is going to sit in judgement over your decision. I can only speak to what has driven me to continue with this work, an endeavor that has now spanned more than a decade.

When I started work on this concept and book it was anger and frustration that drove me. Anger and frustration at a system that allowed so many students to fall through the cracks. Anger and frustration at top-down education reforms put in place nationwide that did little or nothing to improve students' chances of succeeding in school and in life, and which at the same time hurt teachers and the teaching profession. And anger and frustration at educational structures, practices, and attitudes that resisted change for decades.

Over the years the anger and frustration subsided and my motivation to write was helped along by some semi-selfish self-interest. I wanted my young grandsons to have a better school experience than what students received in public schools operating under the traditional educational paradigm.

But what sustained and motivated me the last several years was, and still is, the simple desire to do right by our kids, to have our schools do what is best for _all_ our students _all_ the time, without any "unless" statements holding us back.

Looking back, I would give anything for another opportunity to take Henry home on that bitterly cold January night. Similarly, I would give anything for another chance to say "yes" to all the kids I encountered over the years who, metaphorically, just wanted me and my teacher colleagues to bring them in from the cold. "Yes," without any conditional (and selfish) "unless" statements to hold us back.

Yes, kids will always come first.

Yes, we will do whatever it takes to help all kids succeed.

Yes, we will always do what is best for kids.

For me, continuing the work of the CP is about doing what is best for kids and their teachers. Nothing fancier than that.

I hope that you will join me in writing the ongoing story of the CP.

"All great and honorable actions are accompanied with great difficulties, and both must be enterprised and overcome with answerable courage."

William Bradford

Epilogue

MY FINAL MANUSCRIPT was done, submitted to the publisher, and accepted for publication. I was left with a few things to do prior to the presses rolling, including a decision on a cover design.

I selected the above photo that depicts an 8th grade boy, "Jack," standing off to the side of the doors to his high school. He is waiting, uncertain but hopeful, for the adults at his school and in his community to emerge and do what is best for him and his peers.

Then two major news events intervened, the mass murder of ten people in a grocery store in Buffalo, New York, and the slaughter of 19 fourth graders and two teachers ten days later in Uvalde, Texas. Both mass murders were perpetrated by 18-year-old young men.

Parents, school employees, community members, and politicians expressed outrage and demanded that something be done to prevent such tragedies in the future. Other people and politicians, while professing horror and outrage, refused to support any substantive changes that would help ensure the safety and survival of our children and community members. They were all too ready to do "something" _unless_ it conflicted with their personal and/or political agendas. It was this mixed response at the local, state, and national levels that made me rethink both my cover photo and statements I made in my final chapter, necessitating the writing of this epilogue.

I originally selected the photo on the preceding page for the cover of my book because I thought that it best represented the reality in our schools. Kids stand by, wanting us to do what is best for them, but unsure if we will. They are hopeful, but at the same time resigned to watching us (the adults) come out of those doors and walk right past them, too busy navigating our own personal agendas of "unless" statements to acknowledge that they, with all their needs, are even present. They know our history.

In rethinking the photo, I realized that the way Jack stands off to the side seems to visually give license to all adults who emerge from the doors to blow right past him and ignore his very existence. For the final cover I decided to move Jack directly in front of the doors to his school so that anyone who comes out must see him and hear him. No one can simply walk past Jack and ignore him.

Jack is today's Henry, metaphorically seeking our help. He represents every student and teacher in the schools of our country hoping to convince the rest of us to think differently and creatively in our search for solutions to problems so that we can always do what is best for kids, _without any "unless" qualifiers._ He is, by virtue of his stance and position, no longer meekly asking us to please, please, please honor our responsibility to our children. No, he is demanding that we listen to him and not ignore his needs. He is demanding that we live up to our responsibilities to do whatever it takes to help him and all his peers survive and succeed, in school and in life.

Jack is struggling students in need of help:

"Look at me. Sure, I struggle academically. And yeah, I am anxious and depressed like a lot of my friends. But I could be successful in school if you opened your eyes to my needs and the needs of my teachers. There is a lot you could do to help me be more successful. But you don't do it. You are so stuck and set in your ways. I'm just a number to you. A statistic. Do you really care about me as a person? If you did, you *would do whatever it takes to help me succeed. But that would be too much trouble, too inconvenient for you. So instead, you will try to walk by and ignore me, again."*

Jack is teachers:

Please don't try to blow by me and paint my professional needs as inconsequential. Look at me. I desperately want to help all my students to grow and succeed in school and in life. I know you want the same thing, but you need to provide me with the resources I need, and a fair opportunity to use them, if you expect me to be successful in reaching the goals we share. Unfortunately, it seems that all you want to do is point the finger of blame at someone else when our students don't succeed. It is easier to deflect responsibility than it is to own your part and be willing to expend the time, energy, and resources to make things better for our kids."

Jack is students who took their own lives or the lives of other students:

"Look at me! Don't dismiss me as a crazy and evil person. I was a kid, just like all the other kids in my school. But I was isolated, ostracized, and bullied because I was a little "different." Over the years my life in school became a living hell and you did nothing to make it better. I felt no connection to my school or to any of the people in my school. They only brought me pain. I was alone, with no plan for what would come next in my life. And you never noticed. You walked right by me. You did nothing. You didn't care. So I stopped caring too."

Jack is the kids in school who are frightened:

"I do well in school, but I am scared. I go to school every day thinking about the kids who have been shot in schools. I don't want to die in school like them. We do lock down drills and try to prepare for shooters but that just makes me feel even more anxious. So I am standing here, not letting you by, until you do something to help me. But my guess is that you won't. Because I am just a kid. I have no power. I can't vote. And you have your political agenda to worry about. You have your re-election to worry about. You say you care about me to the media, but you really don't. Because if you did, you would do something."

And Jack is me. I am standing in front of those doors as well, doing my best to get you to hear me.

In Chapter 23 I wrote this.

"Your answers to the 'What next?' and 'Where to now?' questions will undoubtedly be very different. Your response to the 'What next?' question may be to do nothing. You may choose to simply return this book to the library or place it up on a bookshelf in your room. End of story. And that is ok. I have no problem with that."

I was very wrong when I wrote that.

It is not OK to do nothing.

Our kids and their teachers need us to act.

Acknowledgements

FIRST, A MILLION thanks to my wife, Jean. Thank you for being the best partner a man could ask for. Thank you for supporting my return to teaching at the beginning of our life together. Thank you for holding down the fort with our girls in the early years while I toiled in my classroom with our "other children," and for then living my teaching and coaching dreams with me. Thanks for being an ever-present helper and sounding board for every teaching idea, from 7th grade Life Science to *Bringing Henry Home*. And most of all, thank you for your love and incredible patience over the years as *Bringing Henry Home* transitioned from a kernel of an idea, to an 11-year seemingly never-ending project, to the finished work it is today. Thanks for sharing this dream, and this life, with me.

Thank you to my daughters, Katarina and Laura, who shared so many of my teaching and coaching moments with me. If you only knew how much my love for you shaped my work with my "other kids."

Thank you to my youngest daughter Sarah for bumping me out of my comfortable existence and putting me on a career path that I never expected. Your brief life, and my students' response to your illness, showed me how important it was for students to have a sense of higher purpose.

Thank you to my mother, Catherine, who long ago made it clear to me that there was purpose to my life. She reminded me to never forget the source of my gifts and the importance of using those gifts for the good of others.

I thank God for His (or Her) patience with me, and for helping me to find the right words when I needed them.

Thank you to Margie Kolinski, Kristen Borrell, Kathy Ianuzzo, Sue Pietropaulo, Joe Pounder, Kathy Taddeo, and all the other teachers at Bishop Ludden High School who helped create the House concept.

Thanks to Carrie Frey, Susan Kublick, Mike Powlin, Jean Ann Zenker, Marcia Cornell, Chris Yonta, Laura Norris, Mike Rogers, Gayle Daley, Mary Anne House, Vince Castellani, and every other outstanding teacher I encountered over my career who always put their students first.

Thank you to my administrative assistants, Sandy Haynes, Julie Steinhoff, Carolyn Ruffos, Erin Voisin, and Kathie Hurn, who supported me and our efforts to create schools that always did what was best for kids.

Special thanks to Kathie Hurn, who collated, recorded, and saved for posterity the hundreds of teacher feedback responses to my "dream school" survey, responses which eventually gave rise to the CP culture and philosophy.

Thank you to Marci Butler/Coppola and Patricia Walter, two amazing school counselors who were always there for the kids and who helped me through some tough days as a principal.

Thank you to Tim Murphy for demonstrating what it means to be a caring and committed House Steward.

Thank you to Sister Josetta Jones and Judy Howard, two great principals who shaped me early in my teaching career.

Thank you to my brother-in-law, Dave Hummel, who read my early drafts of chapters and offered uncluttered, candid feedback.

Thank you to my brother Cliff who, in the Fall of 2019 and at my request, became my taskmaster and designated "nag." You got me writing again with purpose when I felt hopelessly stymied. I only wish you had lived to see the final product.

Thank you to Jeanne Randazzo who, as my book neared completion, read and proofed everything I threw at her. Never a complaint. Always honest feedback.

As strange as it may sound, I want to thank those individuals I encountered in my career who were negative role models, who put power, politics, and their personal agendas ahead of the needs of kids. In showing me the way _not_ to go, you were perversely and unwittingly instrumental in creating the CP.

A very special thank you to every young person I ever had the opportunity to teach, coach, lead as a principal, or simply have fun with at *Sarah's Place*. You gave me purpose in life. You challenged me. You inspired me. More than anything else, my memories of you motivated me to not give up on *Bringing Henry Home*.

And lastly, thank you to Henry. You presented me with an opportunity to be charitable, an opportunity that I failed to respond to, miserably. But you taught me a lesson that I have never forgotten. A lesson that I hope will someday change the lives of millions of children for the better.

Appendix E-1, Teacher Commitment Expectation Statements to Students

IT IS IMPORTANT for you, as a student, to know what to expect of your teachers. As your teachers, our commitment to you is that we will:

1. Always treat you and other members of our Learning Community with dignity and respect.
2. *Work together with our fellow teachers to improve our teaching so we can achieve both individual and group goals.*
3. *Take full responsibility for our success, your success, and for the success of every other student in our Learning Community.*
4. *Celebrate our success and the successes of students in our Houses and Learning Community.*
5. *Make our expectations clear to you on a daily, weekly, and unit basis.*
6. Create an enriched, supportive learning environment where you will feel comfortable taking good educational risks (a la Rule #1).
7. Meaningfully connect what we are studying in class to the "real world" outside the classroom.
8. Use a variety of teaching methods that will actively engage you in learning, keep you interested, and eliminate boredom.
9. Make sure that nothing we do, or that anyone else does, interferes with your learning or anyone else's learning (a la Rule #2).
10. Always be honest in our dealings with you, your classmates, and ourselves.

11. *Emphasize teamwork in our Learning Community by providing you with regular opportunities to work together with your fellow students.*

12. Always be on time and prepared for class to get the most out of our instructional time together.

13. Return tests, quizzes, and other graded assignments in a timely manner (tests and quizzes will be returned, or scores made known, the next day).

14. Always be fair and consistent in our interactions with you and your classmates.

15. Be available to provide extra help when you need it.

16. Acknowledge when we make mistakes and apologize when we fail to live up to these expectations.

17. Regularly communicate with you and your parents regarding your academic progress.

18. *Foster a sense of family and belonging in our classrooms, Houses, and the Learning Community as a whole.*

19. *Demonstrate through our words and actions the strong belief that everyone in our Learning Community can learn and succeed.*

20. *Work hard and do everything we can to help you and your classmates be successful.*

21. Seek informal verbal and formal written feedback from you on how well we are meeting these expectations.

22. Welcome your feedback and utilize it to improve our teaching and the overall functioning of our Learning Community.

23. **<u>As a student in our Learning Community you can expect that we will not give up on you.</u>**

Appendix E-2, Teacher Commitment Expectation Statements to Colleagues

IT IS IMPORTANT for you to know what to expect of me as a teaching colleague. As a fellow teacher in our CPTU my commitment to you is that I will:

1. Always treat you and other members of our Learning Community with dignity and respect.
2. Always be honest in my dealings with you and our other teaching colleagues.
3. *Spend at least three class periods a week in your classroom or the classroom of a fellow teacher either co-teaching, serving as a teaching assistant, learning along with students, or simply observing.*
4. *Work together with you and our fellow teachers to improve our teaching so we can achieve our individual and group goals.*
5. *Share full responsibility for the success of every teacher in our CPTU, and for the success of every student in our Learning Community.*
6. *Provide you with feedback (when you request it) after spending time in your class.*
7. *Welcome thoughts, ideas, and constructive feedback from you on how I can improve my teaching after you visit my class.*
8. *Seek help and support from you and our other teacher colleagues if I experience problems or difficulties in my classroom.*
9. Create an enriched, supportive learning environment where our students feel comfortable taking good educational risks (a la Rule #1).

10. Use a variety of teaching methods that will actively engage our students in learning, keep them interested, and eliminate boredom.

11. Make sure that nothing I do interferes with anyone's learning (a la Rule #2).

12. *Share information with you about the students in your House who may be experiencing difficulties in my class (academically or otherwise).*

13. *Work with you and our teaching colleagues to identify struggling students and get them the help they need.*

14. *Always be on time and prepared when we are scheduled to be in class together.*

15. Grade tests, quizzes, and other assignments in a timely manner and quickly record the grades in our shared grading software (tests and quizzes will be returned to students, or scores made known, the next day).

16. Always be fair and consistent in my interactions with my students.

17. Acknowledge when I make a mistake and apologize when I fail to live up to these expectations.

18. Regularly communicate with our students regarding their academic progress.

19. *Foster a sense of family and belonging in our classrooms, Houses, and Learning Community.*

20. *Demonstrate through my words and actions the strong belief that everyone in our Learning Community can learn and succeed.*

21. *Work hard and do everything I can to help you and our teaching colleagues be successful.*

22. *Seek informal verbal and formal written feedback from you on how well I am meeting these expectations.*

23. *Welcome your feedback and utilize it to improve my teaching and the overall functioning of our Learning Community.*

Appendix F. The Fundamental Truths – a short list

1. Children need a degree of stability in their lives if they are to grow into successful, high functioning adults.
2. Students function best and have the greatest chance of succeeding when they know exactly what is expected of them <u>and what they can expect from their teachers, coaches, and the learning environment that surrounds them.</u>
   a. Corollary: Students rarely achieve at levels higher than what <u>*they*</u> expect to achieve and/or what <u>*others*</u> expect them to achieve.
3. Students inherently understand the concepts and value of team and teamwork, and benefit greatly from working in a team setting.
   a. Corollary: Students are drawn to activities that stress team and teamwork.
4. Students (and people in general) rise to the top and put forth the greatest effort to succeed when they have a goal, a higher purpose, that is outside and beyond that which they want to achieve for themselves.
5. Students need to belong, to be a part of a family, to have a strong affiliation with a group.
6. Students' <u>perceptions</u> of how much the adults in their lives (parents, teachers, coaches, etc.) love and care about them directly influence their behavior, motivation, decision-making, *and their ability to learn.*
7. Kids need a nurturing and safe environment in order to grow, develop, and learn. The environment must be physically, emotionally, and educationally safe.

8. Students exert tremendous influence on their peers, and in return can be strongly influenced by their peers.

9. Shaming and humiliation do NOT motivate people to work harder, not students, not teachers, not principals.

10. Students need to experience some level of success to build confidence in their ability to succeed (believing).

11. For learning to take place students' <u>brains</u> need to be fully and consistently engaged.

12. Students sometimes give up, on a variety of different levels and for a variety of different reasons. They may give up on individual tasks, on a specific learning unit, on a subject, on the entire educational enterprise (dropping out mentally and/or physically), or on life as a whole

13. Teachers are most successful when they use a variety of methods and strategies to fully engage their students. Having a large repertoire of teaching techniques is essential for success.

14. Great teaching comes in many different "shapes and sizes." There is no one best way to reach and teach kids. Unorthodox, or very orthodox; both can be very effective.

15. In most schools teachers work in complete and total isolation.

16. Teachers (and other professionals) work best and are most creative, innovative, and effective when they are afforded opportunities for collaboration with others.

17. Veteran teachers have a wealth of knowledge and experience that usually remains confined within the four walls of their classrooms.

18. Teacher candidates fresh out of undergraduate training are ill-prepared for what they will face as teachers in traditional school settings. Most students exiting Masters Degree programs in education are still inadequately prepared for the challenges of the classroom.

19. Some teachers may also "give up" on a variety of levels for a variety of reasons.

20. Tenure is both a blessing and a curse, both absolutely essential for the protection of good teachers (and principals) and an artifact that can be used to shield poor teachers (and principals).

21. Teachers generally know little about their students' lives other than what they learn about them in the classroom.

22. Principals and assistant principals cannot adequately supervise and evaluate an entire faculty of teachers for professional growth and development, nor can they effectively motivate an entire faculty on their own.

23. Any reform or change in education, regardless of the degree of merit it contains, will meet a great deal of resistance and will ultimately fail or fade away if it is forced upon teachers and principals without first getting all of those same teachers and principals to genuinely buy-in to the changes.

    a. Corollary: Even with teacher and principal "buy-in," reforms fade away if both resources (including time) and support are not provided and then maintained going forward.

24. Teachers make the difference!

Appendix R. Why groups might resist the CP - Why groups should support the CP

SOME INDIVIDUALS IN every constituent group related to education will resist efforts to adopt the CP. The reasons why people will resist vary from group to group. Below I outline for you the reasons why I believe people in each group might resist the CP. I also list specific reasons why I believe people in each group should support the CP.

Students

Why students might resist the CP:

In my opinion, the only time student resistance to the CP would be encountered would be when the adoption of the CP is pushed too quickly, and high school students are thrust into the CP without having the opportunity to grow into it from the 5th, 6th, or 7th grade on. If students are first exposed to the CP as 10th, 11th, or 12th graders they will resist the changes, guaranteed.

Why students should support the CP:

Students who attend a CP school starting in middle school will experience greater academic success, less anxiety and stress, fewer instances of bullying, more positive feelings of connection and belonging, and feel more hopeful that they can achieve their dreams for the future. Quite simply, students will enjoy school more.

Teachers

Why teachers might resist the CP:

▪ Loss of lifetime tenure.

- Being comfortable working independently in isolation after many years and not wanting to change to working in a more collaborative environment.
- Fearful of the expectations that will accompany the new role of Housemaster.
- Not being comfortable working closely with, and being evaluated by, a Master Teacher.
- The expectation that all teachers in a CP Unit take full responsibility for the success of every student in the Learning Community.

Why teachers should support the CP:

- Opportunity to become a part of a highly skilled CP Unit of teachers
- Access to opportunities for promotion up a career ladder with corresponding increases in salary.
- A more balanced, holistic teacher evaluation system where teachers are evaluated by an educational professional who is in frequent, regular contact with them (the Master Teacher).
- Regular opportunities to collaborate with other teachers in the CP Unit to plan lessons, share teaching strategies, team-teach, and observe or be observed.
- Teachers will have the ability to provide input into professional development focused on the specific needs of teachers in the CP Unit.
- Increased planning time.
- No duties that take away from teachers' professional work time.
- The opportunity to work in a more professional and supportive teaching environment.
- Teachers who opt to participate in the CP will receive extensive (paid) training in the model to help them become comfortable with the many new features of the CP.
- The opportunity to make a greater difference in the lives of students.
- The security of 6-year tenure renewable every two years.

Parents

Why parents might resist the CP:

- Concern that the House System's emphasis on belonging and family will in some way usurp the role of a child's biological parents.
- Concern that the CP will not be up and running and available for their children because of the time required to implement the CP.
- Concern that the emphasis on "I succeed when we succeed" will detract from a child's individual accomplishments.

Why parents should support the CP:

- In the CP parents are **more** connected to their child's education through regular communication with the Housemaster and regular classroom teachers.
- The House System does not replace the family, but rather, it provides a second "family unit" to support teens during adolescence, a time when support is most needed.
- The constructive nature of House family units meets the needs of students who might otherwise seek to have their needs met through inappropriate or even illegal means.
- Parents' children will be happier with school, will attend more frequently, and will be less likely to drop out.
- Parents' children will learn to focus on both individual and group goals in a way that does not detract from their individual accomplishments.
- Parents' children will still be recognized for individual accomplishments.
- Parents' children will be more successful academically, behaviorally, and socially.

Principals

Why principals might resist the CP:

- Having to surrender the responsibility for accomplishing some tasks to the Master Teachers, tasks which were performed exclusively by the principal in the traditional educational paradigm.
- Skepticism regarding Master teachers' ability to perform their teacher supervision and evaluation functions in an objective and unbiased manner.
- General sense that they are losing some of their power and control.

Why principals should support the CP:

- Principals maintain full responsibility for the success of all students but now have more tools at their disposal to get the job done.
- In the CP all teachers will grow and develop more quickly into outstanding teachers, resulting in higher levels of achievement and overall student success, any good principal's ultimate goal.
- Principals will be less overwhelmed by their workload.
- Master Teachers and Housemasters assume many of the responsibilities that previously fell on the shoulders of the principal.
- The presence of MTs working closely with the teachers in every CP Unit will result in
  - » a **higher** degree of teacher accountability than currently exists in schools.
  - » Better, more informed decisions regarding recommendations for tenure since the administrative team will have far more data on each teacher's performance.
  - » Ongoing professional development to improve teacher effectiveness.
- The addition of two links in a new chain of command, Teacher → Housemaster → Master Teacher → Principal, will result in many student behavior problems being solved before they reach

the principal's desk, thus freeing the principal to focus on school leadership and other more important aspects of his/her job.
- The addition of MTs to the administrative leadership team will give principals more opportunities to collaborate prior to making decisions.

Superintendents
Why superintendents might resist the CP:

- Superintendents may feel that the increased cost of the CP will require a tax levy increase that the public will not approve.
- General sense that they are losing some of their power and control.
- Skepticism regarding Master teachers' ability to perform their teacher supervision and evaluation functions in an objective and unbiased manner.
- Superintendents may not be willing to accept the length of time required to demonstrate positive results under the CP. Urban superintendent turnover occurs at a high rate. Urban superintendents want fast results to demonstrate their worth before being asked to "move on."

Why superintendents should support the CP:

- The initial costs of a CP pilot can be covered by grants, both public and private. If the CP produces the anticipated positive results after a couple years, the community will likely step forward to support it financially.
- If they remain in the job long enough to see the positive impact of the CP on student achievement, superintendents will be hailed as brilliant and innovative leaders, on the cutting edge of educational reform. This makes the superintendent more marketable.
- The CP provides closer monitoring of teachers and a **higher** degree of teacher accountability than is possible in a paradigm where teacher supervision and evaluation is principal centered.

- A change to 6-year renewable tenure will permit districts to remove any teachers in the CP who "check out" and cease to be effective.

Teachers' Union Leadership

Why teachers' unions might resist the CP:

- Teachers' unions will fear that the change from lifetime tenure to 6-year renewable tenure for CP teachers will result in the arbitrary removal of teachers from their jobs.
- The concern that the CP will create two "classes of teachers" that would be treated "differentially." One class, those teachers working as members of a CP Unit in a CP school, would have access to a career ladder, opportunities for promotion, and accompanying salary increases. The other class would not.
- General sense that they are losing some of their power and control.
- Concerns over the loss of union members since Master Teachers will have their own bargaining unit and will no longer be members of the teachers' union.

Why teachers' unions should support the CP:

- In the CP, the role of the teachers' union is even more critical
- In the CP, teachers' unions finally get a teacher evaluation system that is fair and holistic, one that is not reduced to two metrics – test scores and a performance rating based upon two or three principal observations and that does nothing to help teachers grow professionally.
- In the CP teachers are valued for their expertise and experience and treated more professionally. Teachers have regular opportunities to collaborate with other teachers to plan lessons, share teaching strategies, team-teach, and observe or be observed.
- Teachers working as members of a CP Unit in CP schools get higher salaries and accesses to a career ladder. When an entire school and/or district adopts and implements the CP there

will no longer be any "differential treatment" of two classes of teachers.

Community members/Business owners
Why community members might resist the CP:

- Community members may be concerned that the CP will be more costly, resulting in an increase in their school taxes.
- Truthfully, I cannot think of any other reason why community members would resist.

Why community members should support the CP:

- Individuals from the community serving as House Stewards will have a pivotal role in shaping student attitudes toward the community.
- House Stewards will help foster a strong sense of connection to the community in students.
- Students connected to their community will be more likely to make positive contributions to the community, both during their school years and after graduation.
- Successful graduates who have internalized the culture and philosophy of the CP will make excellent employees after graduation from high school, or later after college.
- Students connected to their community will be less likely to exhibit behaviors that will detract from or harm the community.
- Students who graduate from CP schools will be more likely to return to their communities to work, shop, buy homes, raise their families, and pay taxes.

Guidance Counselors
Why they might resist the CP:

- Counselors may feel that Housemasters will take over their responsibilities with students.

- Counselors may be concerned that Housemasters, who are not certified counselors, will attempt to deal with student issues beyond their capabilities.
- Counselors may feel left behind by the CP, since the new paradigm does not appear to directly involve them as active participants.

Why they should support the CP:

- As described earlier, school counselors have ludicrously large numbers of students to support, with the average student to counselor ratio in the country exceeding 400 to 1. In the CP counselors gain a "staff" of Housemasters who will help them manage their otherwise impossible caseload.
- In the CP school counselors have a critical role in training teachers who serve as Housemasters. Counselors will train Housemasters in basic counseling skills who can then deal with low level student issues. This will decrease the Counselors' workloads, allowing them to focus on more serious student issues.
- Counselors will teach Housemasters which types of students issues they can and cannot attempt to deal with themselves.

School Board Members

Why school board members might resist the CP:

- School board members may fear that initiating a CP pilot will make their jobs more complicated.
- School board members may feel that a dramatic change away from traditional educational practices is "rocking the boat" too much. They might perceive the CP as too radical.
- School board members may be fearful that the CP will fail to show positive gains, thus making them look foolish.
- School board members may not want to risk incurring the wrath of other constituent groups who might vocally resist (at public board meetings) any initiative to begin a CP pilot.

Why school board members should support the CP:

- First and foremost, school board members should support the initiation of a CP pilot because the CP will help all the participating students be more successful, in school and in life.
- Yes, the addition of a CP pilot will make school board members' jobs more complicated. Yes, school board members will have to listen to individuals who oppose the CP for various reasons. But they will also get to listen to all the supporters of the CP who will speak to the value of the CP to the district's children.
- In supporting any proposed school reform school board members incur some risk. However, the CP is a reform proposal that is based upon a strong foundation of educational facts and truths, not beliefs. If properly implemented, the CP's chances of success far exceed the possibility of failure.
- By supporting the CP, school board members will be viewed as visionaries who want to see every student in the district achieve and succeed. Supporting changes that help kids succeed is a good thing.

Take a few minutes to look back at all the reasons why someone might choose to resist the CP. Do you notice the common thread that runs between them all? For the most part they are all about the adults, not the kids. Remember the "unless . . ." caveats that I described at the start of this book. "We always do what's best for kids **_unless_** . . . We will make the hard decisions to help all kids succeed **_unless_** . . . We will do whatever it takes to help kids succeed **_unless_** . . ."

The concerns I list above are all *adult* concerns. *Adult* concerns about cost, *adult* concerns about the loss of power and control, *adult* "turf" battles, making *adults* uncomfortable, *adult* concerns about their jobs, *adult* concerns about how they will be perceived, *adults* fearing loss of job security, *adult* concern about undertaking new responsibilities, and general *adult* fear of change.

I challenge you to offer one good reason to resist the implementation of the CP based solely on what the kids think and feel. What can you say? "I am going to resist the CP because the kids will not like it." I don't think so. Students like working together toward a common goal, helping each other to succeed, having fun, being engaged, feeling like they belong, not being humiliated (or bullied), having some freedom in, and control over, their learning environment, **and succeeding**. I am confident that students will love all this. And they will love working with and developing positive relationships with caring and committed teachers, Housemasters, and House Stewards,

When helping an adult to overcome their own resistance to the CP always come back to the students, what the students will like, what will help all students to grow and succeed, what will be good for the kids.